Nigel Smith is a journalist, playwright and TV comedy producer. He has also co-written the BBC One sitcom *Doctors and Nurses* and the comedy series *Teenage Kicks* broadcast on both radio and TV.

In 2001 he suffered a serious brain illness, which inspired him to write the award-winning BBC Radio 4 comedy series *Vent*, as well as chronicle his life-changing experiences in this highly acclaimed book, that you're just about to buy.

He is married with three children and lives on the south coast with most of them.

More praise for *I Think There's Something Wrong With Me*:

'Richly comic and an incredibly entertaining account of the regenerative power of being monumentally fucked off'
David Mitchell

'Fucking brilliant. I read it in a single sitting. OK two sittings, but a guy's gotta eat'
Robert Webb

I THINK THERE'S SOMETHING WRONG WITH ME

Nigel Smith

BLACK SWAN

TRANSWORLD PUBLISHERS
61–63 Uxbridge Road, London W5 5SA
A Random House Group Company
www.rbooks.co.uk

I THINK THERE'S SOMETHING WRONG WITH ME
A BLACK SWAN BOOK: 9780552774024

First published in Great Britain
in 2007 by Bantam Press
a division of Transworld Publishers
Black Swan edition published 2008

A CIP catalogue record for this book
is available from the British Library.

Addresses for Random House Group Ltd companies outside the UK
can be found at: www.randomhouse.co.uk
The Random House Group Ltd Reg. No. 954009

The Random House Group Limited supports The Forest Stewardship Council
(FSC), the leading international forest certification organisation. All our titles
that are printed on Greenpeace approved FSC certified paper carry the FSC
logo. Our paper procurement policy can be found at
www.rbooks.co.uk/environment

Typeset in 11/14 pt Sabon
by Falcon Oast Graphic Art Ltd.

Printed in the UK by CPI Cox & Wyman, Reading, RG1 8EX.

2 4 6 8 10 9 7 5 3 1

For my family.

BRITISH OFFICER: 'What on earth are you doing *there*, man?'

BOMBARDIER SPIKE MILLIGAN: 'Everyone's gotta be somewhere.'

Acknowledgements

The entire book is a love letter to my incredible wife Michele, my incredible family and the incredible NHS, and credit is given where credit is due as we merrily roll along. However, I would like to thank again my whole neurological team at Charing Cross Hospital, with special wishes and love to Alidz Pambakian and all the staff in ITU, without whom this book would have been written with a Ouija board.

Thanks also to my many physios at Charing Cross and the Wolfson, who got me on my wobbly but grateful feet, and to the many others – friends, neighbours, carers, both paid and unpaid – who supported and continue to support me and my family.

The danger of naming some but not all is high and I apologize now if I have omitted certain people I should not have, but some people do deserve special mention, so at the risk of alienating a whole bunch of kind and considerate folk, special thanks to: Philip Goodhew, Jane and John Connor, Dr Phil Hammond, Dr Patrick Kelly, Wendy and Jim Deasley, Gareth Edwards, Leslie Ash, Chris Larner, Glenn Hugill, Susie Parriss, Dave Mitchell, Robert Webb, Nick Symons, Debbie Arnold, Jackie Jones, Sevim Karahan, Annette Taylor, Barbara from the Wolfson, Ellie from the INS, Mary from Homestart, and the incomparable Gerard from ITU.

And the immovable, the unique, the irreplaceable:

Mum.

I should say *slainte* to the very persuasive Ivan Mulcahy, the hound, for persuading me to write the damn thing in the first place, and Michele for making me go to the meeting with him in the first *first* place.

None of this would be in your lovely, wonderful – are you buying or just browsing? Cos the above doesn't apply if you're not going to pay for this – hands without the unwavering, touching, frankly bonkers support of my editor Francesca Liversidge and the grand fromage of Transworld, Larry Finlay. Special mention to designer Claire Ward for choosing the worst photograph of me ever taken (up to and including MRI scans) and putting it on the cover. And a big thank-you also has to go to the lovely Alison Barrow for her tireless work in promoting this book to any poor sod that sits still for more than five seconds.

I apologize here and now for offending those people I did not mean to offend. My only excuse is that this is an honest account of my emotions and observations in an extreme situation. Those I meant to offend will soon know about it.

Chapter One

Bad Vibrations

Wednesday, 14 November 2001

So I'm in the surgery talking to this locum GP, an urbane old duffer who looks like Colonel Sanders. After thirty seconds I reckon he's got the same dedication to keeping his clients alive as the king of the spicy wing. I tell him why I'm here; I have this numbness thing going on. Left side of tongue is numb, ring and fourth finger of left hand, left half of left foot, oh yeah, and left side of my face is heading that way too. I'm turning into Igor.

'Ramsay Hunt syndrome, old boy,' he chuckles, like I'm his naughty nephew with a grazed knee. He does everything but ruffle my hair as he ushers me out. He's busy, he's got four thousand chickens to batter and stuff into stripy buckets. 'Couple of days and it'll sort itself out.' He was right about that. Two days later and I certainly wouldn't have been back for a second consultation with anyone but God. For whom I'd have a few questions.

I learn later, because I do become something of an expert on this subject – something that annoys doctors –

that my presentation (the posh word for symptoms) indicates a classic neurological problem. 'Indicates' is not strong enough. Imagine I am walking about with a giant sandwich board with 'golf sale' crossed out and 'this man's got a brain problem' written on in neon spray paint, with the arrow pointing straight at my head. That's what I mean by 'indicates'.

Instead of sending me away with a smile and a shrug to die at home, he should have immediately referred me to an NHS consultant for an urgent scan. Though the first available scan date would have been six to eight weeks later, and would have come through just as my headstone was being carved.

After my consultation I don't quite make it home cos I'm feeling a bit poorly. In fact I have a little sit-down in the waiting room. I ring my mate and sometime writing partner Phil Hammond (the guy on *Have I Got News for You* when they can't get a proper comedian). Phil is a clap doctor but in the same way country folk prefer to talk to vets than doctors, I give him a call on the moby. This is verbatim:

ME: Oi, ginger bollocks.
PHIL: Oh not you. Can't talk now, I've got someone's knob in my hand.
ME: You at work then?
PHIL: No.

NOTE FROM DR HAMMOND'S LAWYERS: *The implication that our client is in any way homosexually inclined, or indeed sexually unfaithful to his loving wife, is bad and wrong, etc.*

OK, that last bit's not true, but this is:

ME: I've seen some bloke who's told me I've got this syndrome but I think it's doctors' rhyming slang to get rid of me – you know, that I'm a bit of a Ramsay Hunt.

PHIL: No, that's not in the book. We use acronyms, not rhymes. Like, women who are into alternative medicine are GROLIES – *Guardian* Readers of Limited Intelligence in Ethnic Skirts.

ME: Right. Funny. See, but I've got this numb—

PHIL: [*on a roll*]: Or on the notes we might write C. K. BUNDY.

ME [*sigh*]: Go on then.

PHIL: Completely Knackered But Unfortunately Not Dead Yet.

[*We laugh a bit.*]

ME: Back to me.

[*I tell him my presentation and await the usual knockabout stuff. Pause. No, really. A proper, uncomfortable pause.*]

ME: Phil?

PHIL: You serious, mate?

ME: Yeah. What you reckon?

PHIL: I reckon you're fucked.

He tells me to get a scan. I ignore him and go home. My wife rings him and he tells her to tell me to get a scan. I ignore her and to prove I'm fine, go straight to bed. In the afternoon. Look, tomorrow's another day. And bloody hell, it certainly is.

Thursday, 15 November

Every year on 15 November I have a party. It's always on the fifteenth even if it falls on a useless day, i.e. every day except Friday or Saturday. But as few of my mates have real jobs it doesn't matter much. It's known as the 'Nigel's Not Dead Party'. It's always great. If you like this book you can come. You know when it is.

What follows explains why it's on the fifteenth.

I get up. I fall over. Not a good start to a Thursday, I think, as I proceed to chuck up. The wife would be quite justified in telling me off for not listening to her as she bundles me into the car, but she's being nice. *Now* I'm worried. As we stop again for me to stagger about and throw up in the gutter, she's passing up a gilt-edged opportunity to say she told me so. I put my now insane dizziness and sickness down to my not having had any breakfast and her driving, which is, I perceive, quite fast.

We pull up outside a private doctor's in South Kensington. He took half a look at me and did a brief touch-your-nose-with-your-finger-no-that's-your-eye-try-again-ow-now-that's-my-eye, and pointed us in the direction of the Cromwell Hospital. Go straight to the MRI scanner, do not pass go, do not collect £200 (in fact, hand over a couple of thousand).

Magnetic Resonance Imaging uses a fabulously high-tech piece of equipment that enables neurologists to see parts of your brain that were previously only available to them post-mortem, sliced on a Petri dish. Probably with some fava beans and a nice Chianti. It works because most of the human body, around 75 per cent, is made up of water, and water is made up of ions, which are charged particles. The magnets in the MRI machine make these particles stand up and jiggle about, like iron filings on a magnet. Then a computer works out what's in your brain by the movements of these particles. It's all terribly clever.

But if it's so damn smart, why is it so bloody noisy in there? Given that we can reasonably assume that if you are unfortunate enough to get squeezed into the damn thing, like a sausage in a big metal bun, you have a headache *at least*, and given it's doing all this space-age stuff for forty minutes, why does it have to sound like you're in Bob the Builder's toolbox? It's like shoving your head in the bass bin as a death metal band warms up.

But there it was. Deep in my medulla, the signal junction of my brain, the top end of the spinal cord, the vital link between the thought and the action, the area that controls everything from temperature to erections, from heartbeat to breathing, from eyes to feet, in there, was *something*. And something wrong. What it *was* was another question, and one unanswerable from this type of scan, but what it was *doing* was clear:

It was killing me.

Here's something I only learnt later. When the radiologist was handed the scan, he asked, 'Righto, where's the body?' He was quickly shushed as I was sitting about ten feet away. Shame I missed that cos I could have done with a laugh. The verdict came quickly – unlike paying off the bill for the scan, which I only did about a month ago . . .

The lovely old boy who delivered the news was one of those proper old-fashioned consultants with a bow tie, Rumpole nose, a bootful of golf clubs and a basement chocka with Montrachet. He was adamant about three things: that I needed to go into hospital yesterday, that the thing – now given the scientific name of 'lesion' – discovered in my brain wasn't a tumour, and that we were, however, in for 'a rocky ride'. Good old British understatement. When my number's eventually up I hope I get someone like him to deliver the news. He'll tell me I had a good innings, took a tricky googly on the leg side and it's time for a short walk back to the pavilion.

The wife asked him if he could admit me to the Cromwell. He said he could, but asked if I had private-care insurance. 'No,' she said. 'What do you think it might cost?'

'Your house,' he answered, before getting on the phone to Charing Cross admissions. So, I thought, this is probably not a two aspirins and a Lemsip situation.

Charing Cross Hospital is in Hammersmith. Which is fair enough because Hammersmith Hospital is in Acton. The wards are housed in a sixteen-storey tower of the sort favoured by sixties town planners for poor people. In I go, and you know how sometimes it's nice to jump the queue? This wasn't one of those times. No matter how much you complain – and we all do – about endless waits in A&E, you really don't want to be the poor sod who goes straight to the front. It's not like the platinum flyers at British Airways. No, what's waiting for you through those doors when you hit them at speed is not a lightly chilled glass of bubbly and a compliant hostess with a free weekend coming up, but a world which does have its fair share of excitement and adventure, but in its own distinctly unpleasant fashion.

Hold up, I think, as the admissions process begins, and I'm put into an arseless hospital gown with 'for hospital use only' printed all over it (cos you'd really want to nick it, maybe for an evening at the BAFTAs).

Why the hell did the Charing Cross neuroconsultant say 'we' were in for a rocky ride? Not me, but we. Have I given my wife something? Could he diagnose something in her brain just by looking? He did look at her a lot – but then she has got great tits – and if he means she might suffer like me then he's a fool cos I feel terrible, no, quick, give a smile to the wife so she'll see how brave I am, will someone give me some Stematil to stop me chucking up . . . huuuurgh – too late, you bastards. What now . . . no, I'm doing the touch-your-nose-thing again.

Well, the consultant knew what he was saying. We were in for it, all of us. My lovely Michele had just announced she was pregnant with our first child, a revelation that had been greeted with joy by James, seven, and with a more cautious whoopee by her daughter Tara, thirteen, watching her share of family attention – and inheritance – get sliced up again. They, together with my mum, who was about to take the next train down from Wolverhampton and not go home for eighteen months, were in for a right old battering.

Character descriptions in scripts are pretty telling. They have to be short as everyone hates reading them, and it's hard to write short. It means you have to know what you're talking about for a kick-off. You boil down a complex character to the barest essentials, like:

BASIL FAWLTY:
Frustrated middle-aged snob who runs a hotel but hates his guests. Terrified of wife, too mean to hire competent staff. Desperate to climb the social ladder.

Now that's a pretty complex character in twenty-six words. I'll have a go with Michele.

MICHELE:
Showbiz agent. Thirties. Cross between Sharon Stone (looks) and Arnold Schwarzenegger (everything else). Working class but hides it well. Loving, fiercely loyal. Not to be crossed.

Well, that's twenty-six words and it's a start. It doesn't tell you that in her life she's faced several disasters and losses: her father's bankruptcy, an unsuccessful first marriage, estrangement from her late mother, two near-death experiences including the loss of a kidney, and more besides. I think she's planning a talk-show career once she's been in rehab for an eating disorder, drug dependency or rampant sex addiction.

What all this means is that she's exactly the kind of person you want on your side when the chips are down. And my chips were not down, they were *buried*. Here's an example:

I'm finally in hospital on the ubiquitous trolley and after a while I get my blessed anti-sickness injection. I'm seen by a variety of polite junior doctors who really don't want to get involved with this at such a delicate stage in their career and dash off to find some real doctors. Who do the same thing until eventually someone senior enough not to give a monkey's takes the decision to begin treatment.

Because there's no diagnosis apart from 'holy shit, he's going to die', they decide to give me *everything*. In drips. Don't they love drips in hospital? If they could, they'd give

16

you two paracetamol through a cannula. A tip: the only people you should let near you with a needle are the over-worked middle-aged West Indian nurses with six kids, or the anaesthetists. Everyone else needs at least five botched attempts and leaves your veins as free-flowing as the north London tube line.

I don't know this yet. I get the junior doctors with their Cambridge accents and trembling hands and eventually up go the drips. They block ten minutes later. Then along comes another chinless doctor with a saline syringe to shove in until the veins in my hand start to desiccate. After several goes and some polite shouting by Michele I finally get an overworked middle-aged West Indian nurse with six kids who does it properly.

I'm still on a trolley but as a concession to my condition someone moves me next to a real ward. This is like getting one of those tables at the bar at the Ivy. You're not really ready to sit within bread-roll-chucking distance of Melvyn Bragg, but you're close enough to smell the fishcakes.

The trolley is a rite of passage at a big NHS hospital. It's like a salesman's attempt to cop off with his ambitious secretary at the annual conference in a Potters Bar Holiday Inn before she finds someone cool and trendy and her own age. Like the barman.

I'm babbling about this to Michele. The thing in my head is growing, and the swelling, unless stopped, will eventually force my brains out of my ears. I read somewhere that they usually don't let that happen because they have a man with a little chainsaw who lops off the top of your head to relieve the pressure. I'm not sure I believe this, but not sure I don't . . .

I find I am babbling. *Oi, isn't this what the Celts used*

to do, several thousand years ago? Isn't this trepanning? Do you think I'm possessed by evil spirits? What kind of place is this? Where's your wicker man? Isn't this the twenty-first century? I'm starting to get a reputation for being awkward.

To stop the swelling they injected steroids. Gallons of steroids. I should be able to run the hundred metres in about three seconds. I thought about that a lot much later on as I zimmered along . . . On the plus side I didn't end up with a two-inch knob. [*No, it didn't grow at all – Michele.*] And then, because they must have had a job lot, they dripped in a bathful of antibiotics. Just in case. Then they really went to town. There was nothing much to lose so they bunged in a whole pharmacopoeia of Kwik Save drugs. I stopped feeling sick. Now I just felt weird.

There is a moment at 8 p.m. called 'the handover' when nurses smoothly change shifts. In reality it results in complete inertia from about six thirty to nine thirty. Sometime towards the end of this limbo, this Sargasso Sea of hospital life, I was shifted to a ward! A bed was free at the end of the room because it was next to a broken radiator. Broken in an impressively extreme way – blowing out freezing air at about thirty knots (hurricane force six). Straight on to my left side, which was freezing up of its own accord, thank you very much.

Michele called a nurse. Who already knew about the problem. The radiator was broken, she informed us, and stood there for a bit sympathising. It had been like that for days. Terrible, isn't it? Unfortunately she was not authorised to call the engineers. Michele got another nurse. Same thing. Michele got the staff nurse. She also agreed it was broken and agreed it was terrible. She was not allowed to call the engineers. Michele demanded to see the night administrator. *He* would be allowed to call the engineers. She knew there was a night (or duty) administrator because she used to work in the health service. There are certain code words you have to know in the NHS. This is one of them. It was a good card to play and it threw the trio into action.

By now my core temperature was close to that of a frozen fish finger stuck to the back of the freezer. And it wasn't as if my day had started well. Finally, up minced the deputy night administrator, a man so limp I thought he'd donated his spinal column pre-mortem. He was in a nice suit, which was a worry. In the NHS, *the nicer the clothes, the less the work*. He also agreed the radiator was a problem, but in a more chippy and less appeasing tone. The engineers had gone home. They had been here when I came on to the ward, but after all this hanging about, they'd gone.

Michele's blue touchpaper, which had been nicely fizzing, expired. Ozzy Osbourne would have blushed. Very few people can be as profane as my wife. And so . . . the duty engineer appeared, as if by magic. He took the top of the radiator off, turned a knob from 'blow out freezing air' to 'off', and put the cover on. It took under a minute.

'Why didn't anyone call me before?' he asked, puzzled.

Friday, 16 November

Time to meet the team charged with getting me out of here head rather than feet first. They are led by a splendid old chap, Professor Russell Lane, trim, nearing retirement but with a twinkle that suggests husbands down at the Rotary better watch out. Under him (professionally speaking) is senior registrar Alidz Pambakian, a youngish, motherly Iranian with a heart the size of her hips who is to prove one of the most beautiful people I've ever met. Under these Olympians are senior house officer Matt – possibly the world's most uptight human being – and a ginger junior doctor still clinging on to her wild days as a student, despite a grim workload and grimmer patients.

The thing with choosing neurology as a speciality is you're on a hiding to nothing. It's like choosing to manage the Welsh national football team. Most times you're going to leave the arena on the losing side. There's an occasional ray of hope as Ryan Giggs hurtles down the wing and hits the crossbar but before too long order is restored and it's 12–0 to the Faeroe Islands.

Bear in mind that the brain is *Star Wars* complex, and the treatment is still *one million years* BC crude. Here's a list of the things neurologists have to deal with every day:

Strokes
Motor neurone disease
Multiple sclerosis
Brain haemorrhages
Epilepsy
Cerebral palsy
Brain tumours
Demyelinating lesions of an unknown origin (we'll come back to this one).

Here's a list of things doctors who specialise in orthopaedics come up against:

Dodgy knees
Tennis elbow
Broken metatarsal
Bit of a pain in my lumbars, doctor, can I have a sick
    note?

But they both use the same tools:

Steroids
Antibiotics
Hammers
Chisels
Saws, etc. . . .

Because I've stopped chucking up and my dizziness is more controlled today, I try to gee myself up. I ask Michele not to tell my mother I'm ill but she ignores me. I suppose it would have been a bit tricky to fob Mum off for the next five years with excuses as to why I couldn't come to the phone. So Mum turns up this morning after getting the six-thirty train from Brum. It costs £93.50. She's reminded me of that a lot.

Everyone wants to know what's the matter. And there's only a hundred ways to find out. Procedures. Tests. Another wretched MRI inside the hot, noisy, claustrophobic Polo-mint tube.

Patients talk a lot about the dehumanising effects of hospitals. This upsets the medical profession because, after all, they're trying to help. But the open-arsed hospital gowns, the absence of privacy, the intrusive questions, the lack of time with the people doing the

21

prodding and poking and injecting and extracting all add up. The huge, disorienting corridors and wards, the unfamiliar signs and smells, the sights and sounds of the sick – they are all disturbing. And try as I might, I was being disturbed.

And the 'procedures'. Happily, these will be unfamiliar to you. And therefore, unhappily, will be frightening. The scariest monsters are the ones unseen. Procedures are many, varied and differing in length, safety and unpleasantness. My argument is that they are actually carried out to help the doctors write an interesting paper on you. A post-mortem's easier cos you can't start shouting 'ow' during it. Which always upsets the poor old medics.

To put it another way: two aspirin and a cup of tea is *treatment*; a lumbar puncture is a *procedure*.

It's still spreading through me and starting to knock out bits of me. My left side is failing. My left hand is turning into The Claw. I'm being switched off, room by room, like a man turning the lights off in his house as he prepares to leave. Why me? As I'm wheeled about I see people, old people in gowns chatting away, looking much better than me. Why are they here? Why are they trying to get better, the old fuckers? They've had a life. I'm thirty-six.

They begin my angiogram and now I'm strapped to a table and spinning around very fast. In my disoriented state it was spinning before it began to move but now the vertigo is so great I think I will black out. Then they do something so extraordinary I almost, somewhere, smile.

You are not going to believe where they shove the needle in to inject dye into your brain. (It's a photographic procedure.) In your groin.

That's right. The needle starts off right by your

knackers – sorry, just move that out the way, mate – and passes up some handy, if surprised, vein, through your heart and into your equally unsuspecting grey matter, where the dye is finally squirted in. My wife often said the quickest route to my brain was via my groin. Apparently, she was not just being cheeky.

After this there was little time to recover before it was down to the basement for some more touch-your-nose, hammer-your-knee, walk-in-a-straight-line-whoops-you-OK? And then an EEG, the first thing that looked proper. They put an electronic Ena Sharples hairnet on you, then show you pictures. Nothing very interesting, just shapes and lines and patterns, but better than daytime telly.

Back to the ward and they think it's all over. No, it's time for that lumbar puncture. Two words that go together like 'root' and 'canal'. A lumbar puncture draws off spinal fluid from inside your spinal cord. The only way to get at this very necessarily protected, fragile area is to shove a needle in between two vertebrae in your lower back – the lumbar region. It's worse than it sounds. I had been dreading this ever since my uncle Bryan, a bear-like six-foot copper, told me of his, years ago when he had meningitis. He went white just talking about it. He said even now, when he sits funny, he can still feel it.

So I was not gleefully anticipating the experience as human robot Matt approached with some gubbins and a sodding great needle.

I curl on my side, widening the gap between my vertebrae. Matt inserts the needle. Ow, ow, ow. It's over. He wipes away the blood. That wasn't too bad. No, that was just the anaesthetic. Now he brings out a *really* big needle.

Fuck.

They tested the fluid for something that to this day I can't make out what they're saying. 'Oliver Cromwell bands', I think, or maybe 'Olga Korbut bands'. 'Black Dyke Mills Band' for all I know. Any rate, they were bands and the first lumbar puncture was inconclusive so I had to have a second one. This time the young ginger doctor did it. And this time I knew she'd probably only done this on an orange before so I tried to stretch my vertebrae extra wide, but no. It really hurt. And you know what? When I sit funny, I can still feel it.

And *that* was inconclusive as well.

Saturday, 17 November

Today the flowers start coming in. From my workmates. A nice but disconcerting gesture as I'd convinced myself I was going to be out tomorrow. What have these people been told? And by whom?

Let's think for a minute. I'm not popular enough for my colleagues to put their hands in their pockets for flowers if I've got a bit of a sniffle. How ill must I be?

I'm only being *told* I've got flowers, because I've just been moved to what's known as a 'high dependency ward' and I'm not allowed flowers. They might compromise my immune system.

This is getting silly. How knackered is my immune system if a couple of begonias could see me off? If I'm so fragile why am I in a ward full of sick people coughing and spitting and vomiting and spreading their filth all over the shop? Talking of filth, these walls are grey and streaked with grime. Some nurses don't wash their hands

24

and . . . Shut up, I'm turning into Howard Hughes. Yeah, but anyone would in here. Besides, I am ill. Where's the bog roll? And where are my bloody flowers? No one ever buys me flowers cos I'm a rough tough telly wanker and it's not fair. None of this is fair.

Channel 4 sent a particularly lovely bunch. I saw it being whisked away by a cheerful nurse, likely wondering whether she had a vase big enough in her living room. I thought it was enormous because by now I was seeing double. I was surprised because most people I'd worked for at Channel 4 thought I was an idiot. *Maybe it's guilt. Or one of those bunches that can change into a wreath at the touch of a geranium to save money. That's a good business. Like those cars that turn into robots.* Rambling again.

To be fair, it didn't really matter that I couldn't have my flowers because I couldn't open my eyes without vertigo kicking in. They said it was vertigo but it was more like that feeling you get when you realise you've accidentally downed the best part of a bottle of tequila while on a quiet night out with your mates – say, for want of a better example, during a stag night – and you go outside to find some rope and a lamppost and the night air hits you, followed rapidly by the pavement. *That* kind of vertigo. Eight-pints-of-Guinness-and-Macallan-chasers vertigo.

I went to a stag do once in Southampton that was so dull I introduced a few gentle drinking games. Several fights later the party broke up and someone woke up next day on the Isle of Wight.

I feel like him.

The High Dependency Unit was designed by a Ba'ath

party inquisitor. To make sure I haven't died and messed up their statistical averages, two Filipino nurses come round every two hours, day and night, to take blood pressure, SATs (oxygen levels) and temperature readings. But they also make you hold their hands, squeeze, and answer the same damn questions.

'What is your name?'
'Where are you?'
'Who is the Prime Minister?'

About 2 a.m. I'd had enough. My name was Tony Blair, I was being held prisoner by the security services and the Prime Minister was an impostor from the planet Arse.

They started observing me every hour after that.

Now, for most men, the phrase 'Filipino nurse' does something to the dark, hidden, un-PC part of our brains. I don't care how many copies of the *Guardian* you've read, it still has the same nudge-nudge effect as 'Swedish au pair' or 'full body massage' or 'young lady seeks discreet older solvent man for fun times'.

Sorry, ladies, blame *Carry On* films, blame seventies sitcoms, blame society, blame our Neanderthal genes, *we can't help it*. Until you meet my Filipino nurses. The only people who'll want to fantasise about these two are blocked *Dr Who* scriptwriters.

Who are these people fussing over me, waking me up from my precious, fought-for, near-impossible-to-get sleep? They look to me like pepper pots and, my heavens, their skin! Not to be unkind, but it's like they've had their faces set on fire and then put out with a running shoe.

It's the middle of the night and I've not had more than

two hours' sleep since Wednesday and my head is thick with something that must be cavity wall insulation and they're here again and on goes the blood pressure cuff and on slips the finger clip for the SATs and the thermometer gun clicks in my ear and I'm squeezing hands and I'm answering questions though my words are getting thicker and my squeezings are getting weaker and I know my blood pressure's dropping and I see my SATs have gone down again so they put a nasal oxygen tube in and there's the hiss and the plastic smell and I can't move my head cos it hurts and anyway the tube falls out and I can't put it back because my arms aren't working properly and the fingers on my left hand have a mind of their own, and *that* mind is as sharp as Jade Goody's and will you all please go away and let me sleep before the world starts rocking and spinning and no, too late, I'll just lie still in the dark but the ward is never dark, it is infused with a sickly orange glow from the city, and by a dim slice of moonlight that slipped through the grey blinds I watch the hands of the clock crawl from 2 a.m. to 4 a.m. and sometimes, even now, I am back there in the endless sodium half-light praying for those solid hands of the clock to move and finally it's another round of nurses but they won't talk to me except for their questions but at least time, sticky, solid time, has moved on but there's still hours before the neon strip lights flicker on and the day is decreed to begin and the drug trolley comes round and then breakfast and the slow waking of the sick but for now I'm surrounded by people snoring and muttering and groaning and I am so deeply alone.

That loneliness is not gone. Even now, it waits.

Sunday, 18 November

I lie in wait for Michele this morning. The night horrors are gone and the weak winter daylight has some cheering effect. Who did the decorating in here?

I imagine it went like this:

HOSPITAL MANAGER: *Good Lord, this is a depressing place, with all these ill chappies hanging about. Let's give it a fresh coat of paint. Always cheers the wife when she's late for her HRT injections. She whizzes about the place like a dervish. Last year the Labrador got emulsioned to the sideboard. Still, he's a damn sight easier to keep clean.*

ASSISTANT: *Agreed, sir, I'll get some cheap painters in. There's a nice Irish fella who was asking if he could tarmac my drive yesterday. He'll do. Hang on, was it yesterday? Oh, must have been, cos that was the day my car went missing.*

MANAGER: *He sounds fine. Only choice now is the colour scheme. Very important for morale. Takes the mind off the projectile-vomit stains the cleaners never quite shift, or those big aortic blood spurts when we've let the junior doctors try to put the cannulas in.*

ASSISTANT: *Got just the thing. I went past a skip yesterday and rescued half a dozen cans of Dulux monkey-vomit yellow and a bucket of cadaver grey.*

MANAGER: *That'll be lovely. Oh, best make sure it's the really flaky stuff.*

Weekends in hospital are scary times. No one important is

about, from engineers to consultants. The nurses who have turned up are sulky because their colleagues are all off to the Walkabout trying to catch chlamydia from the new intake of junior doctors.

You do get more visitors at the weekends though. This is a mixed blessing. You realise your visitors would be happier with a plaster cast to sign. This weird shit just frightens them. The drips scare them. The huge, disorienting hospital with its slow, smelly lifts unnerves them. My limping walk, spastic arm, dizziness and talking like Don Corleone after he's been shot in the neck freaks them out.

Watching them being scared scares me. I resent them. Most know this but they can't hide it. They can't stop themselves asking the wrong questions. They can't stay away from their fear and the awful thoughts it brings. Michele puts a stop to all this nonsense; she sits there making sure they behave themselves. She's like Richard Gere's PR at a press conference, warding off awkward questions about rodents.

But I feel the need to do my bit and so now I'm the one trying to reassure them. I think it's time to tell some jokes. My favourite joke used to be this one: Two snowmen in a field. One says to the other: 'Can you smell carrots?'

Good joke, but delivery's important. My version was:

ME: Thwosnorminin feed—
MATE: Sorry mate. Two snoring . . . ?
ME: Thnormen.
MATE: Doormen? Norman?
ME: Lithen, you cnunt . . .
[*Cut to: ten minutes later*]

29

MATE: Carrots!
ME [*knackered*]: Yeff. Now fnuckoff.

Other people's visitors arrive and some take an interest in me. I'm the youngest in the ward by about twelve decades. Suddenly, I'm a kid with a grazed knee again, being clucked over by a bunch of grannies just itching to spit on their hankies and rub my face.

I can't complain. There's booty. My haul after the afternoon session is:

Grapes, bunch of
Melon, half
Samosas, six
Woman's Weekly, one
Crossword puzzle book (half-completed)
Lourdes water, bottle of
Geriatric blow job and a good snort of powdered
    Sanatogen.

Yeah, yeah, but the rest's true. The Lourdes water cheers me up until I look at the state of the poor old bloke in the bed next to me who's spent a week being doused in the stuff. I chuck it away.

Monday, 19 November

I wake up with a fanny in my face. Now I have to confess this is not the first time this has happened, but this fanny is seventy-five fucking years old.

Jesus God, please, will you ever close your legs, woman? Opposite my bed is a fat old dear in a short nightie. She has kicked all the bedclothes off in her sleep and she's obviously hot because she's writhing around the bed and oh, nooo . . .

There are flowers on the bottom of her nightie. It's a kind of broderie anglaise. There are exactly 7,435 stitches in the embroidery. I know this because I am unable to move my head and I'm trying to look at anything but the ratty old flange ten feet away. I try to burn any other image into my memory but I know what will remain. Years later it's still there: Richard Branson's face grinning toothlessly at me, for ever.

I manage to press the call button but then wonder what the hell I'm going to say. Please can you remove that geriatric minge? It's not polite, it's not English but dear God, now she's doing the splits. Help nurse, heeeeelp.

Finally, the nurse appears. It's Monday morning so there's a bit more spit and polish about her. I indicate the horror show and she giggles. She gets a friend over to giggle. Then finally they rearrange the bedclothes over the hellmouth and I thank them. 'Don't worry,' one says. 'She's been watching yours wave about all night.'

Marvellous.

This not-moving-my-head thing: I was so traumatised by the pensionable pudenda that I didn't really have time to analyse it. I try to move it right – oh God, the ward spins round, best not. To the left – I said to the left. Come on, stop messing about, turn to the . . .

Bugger.

There is a moment of utter despair.

And then, something strikes me. It's a notion that, along with my family, rescues me. I realise the real battle in hospital, the one you have to win, is for dignity. You must understand a body is just a shell around the real me, the real you. That shell can, and will, go wrong. It will shit and piss and vomit and collapse and bleed and lose control. It's simply what these shells we are housed in sometimes do. You have to let go, and let go of the fear of letting go.

And when I begin to laugh somewhere at the utter absurdity of a wardful of sick dicks flapping about I know I am holding on to the essential *me*. And as Kipling might have said if faced with a manky muff before his kippers, if you can hold on to the essential you, then you can keep your dignity while all around are losing theirs. And you will need it. This is a journey that, one way or another, we will all make.

Comforted, I take stock and try out other bits of me. The good news is my right side seems to be doing what it's told. The bad news is the left side has gone on strike. Maybe I've been lying funny, I reason. It's just gone to sleep. It's like the randy teenage bedroom trick of lying on your left hand so it goes numb and feels like someone else is giving you a – ahem. Anyway, cos it's Monday, my team will be around soon, and I'll get some more information. Maybe the test results will have come through and they'll give me an injection or some tablets and I'll be on my way, hawking my CV round again.

Oh yes. I forgot to mention I was made redundant shortly before I got ill. I won't say who I was working for but it was in TV and to be honest it was a rubbish job in a rubbish company.

I was thinking about writing a sitcom version of my situation (but dropped the idea – who would want to hear it?), when my medical team entered. They were all scrubbed and shiny, led by the old devil Russell Lane himself. I do more touch-your-nose, follow-my-pen rubbish until I shoo his sodding Mont Blanc away and ask for some answers. And the truth, mind. Don't hold anything back. I'm a big boy, it's my body and I can take it.

So the bastards only go and tell me.

A demyelinating lesion of the brain stem. Of unknown origin. Probably viral. Which sounds impressive but is really modern medicine's version of 'evil spirits'; they don't know where they come from, how they work, or how to get rid of them. You're just as well off with a bloke in a grass skirt doing a dance and chucking chicken blood all over the shop. Oh hang on, with all this avian flu, best stick to goat entrails. At least you'll get a nice curry out of the leftovers.

They stop me at this point to tell me the science. They probably feel a little undermined, especially when I ask for a bloke with a bone through his nose and a goat.

First: demyelination. Myelin is a sticky protein that covers your brain cells like plastic around an electric cable. It is impervious to electricity, so when the brain sends out electrochemical signals they pass smoothly through the brain cell system to the bit of you that needs the information. These signals are both conscious – like moving your hands, arms and legs – or unconscious, like moving your heart, lungs or little fella.

If you take the myelin away, i.e. if you de-myelin the cells, well, remember when aged eleven you tried to fit that plug on the toaster and you let the wires touch and plugged it in? If you were lucky there was just a small pop and a bit of smoke; if you were unlucky your Dualit blew up. In my case I set fire to the house.

So that was the first problem. The second was the positioning of this patch of demyelin, the thing they call a lesion. It was in the brain stem, or medulla. The medulla is the grapefruit-sized ball of nerves hanging below the brain proper. It is the signal box linking the brain to the central nervous system. It is easily possible to have a lesion in this area and feel very few effects – perhaps one of your fingers will become numb, or an eyebrow will twitch, or somesuch. Maybe your lip will curl into an interesting and sexy sneer like Elvis's or James Dean's. No such luck with me. My lesion was in what they called a 'very eloquent' area. Which meant it did everything. And was now stopping doing everything and hurtling rapidly towards doing nothing.

Tests had eliminated bacterial infections which can sometimes cause these symptoms, so my best hope of survival was that it was something incurable – a virus. Treatment, I was told, was simply to tackle the symptoms such as the swelling and hope the virus would go away. Like a cold. There was a further possibility – a tumour, and one which absolutely meant game over. If it was a tumour, it was in an inoperable site. And given this thing's aggressive growth it was time to say some goodbyes. And fast.

Five years later and the cause is still unknown. So the medics are sticking to the virus theory. But oddly, a few years ago, a friend of mine of a spiritual bent climbed the Inca trail in Peru and consulted a shaman for me. It was a bit like phoning NHS Direct cos I wasn't actually there for him to see. The shaman thought for a minute and did his woojie-woojie stuff and then said something extra-ordinary. He said I had caught an evil spell (that wasn't meant for me), at a quarter to three on a Tuesday. Now obviously this is utter cock, except that is pretty much the time I first felt ill.

Obvious nonsense. But . . . hmm . . . Just in case: if you are the son of a bitch who sent the spell – it missed, you arse. And if you'd like to send the cure spell, please feel free.

Tuesday, 20 November

Another one of those nights. How do I feel this morning? Like this:

A long time ago I did a stupid thing. I resigned from my exciting job as a trainee reporter on a famous free paper, the *Stratford and Newham Express*, where I was once the lowest-paid (yet still overpaid) journalist in England – *to go busking*.

That wasn't the stupid thing.

We bought an old Bedford van that would be called retro today but was more accurately described by one French garage owner as 'a block of sheet'. The van left a trail of, well, van, all over most major European roads.

That wasn't the stupid thing.

We set off around Europe in this terrible van to peddle a ropey collection of classic rock tunes without actually learning any of them before we left.

That wasn't the stupid thing.

Many months later, at the end of the trip, with the tourist season and the money drying up, me and the surviving member of our trio (the drummer having succumbed to cabin fever in the south of France) found ourselves titting about on a Spanish mountain in the

Pyrenees. I was feeling great. No, more than great, fantastic. I was young, free, bursting with life and I'd broken away from everything – England, my job, my girl-friend, all of it. In the hot September sun I felt like Ernest Hemingway. It was very spiritual. And I'd just had the greatest poo of my life. All in all I felt like a god and suddenly it came upon me that I was indestructible; that day, nothing could happen to me. I walked to the edge of this jagged cliff and looked down at the tiny sheep sprinkled across the valley hundreds of dizzying feet below and shouted to my friend Mike that I could step off and be OK. He was saying something about how he'd rather I didn't, on balance, and how he'd explain this to the Spanish police, when I stepped off.

That was the stupid thing.

Six feet down there was a ledge I hadn't seen. I landed on it. I knew I would. I knew, for that briefest of moments, with an utter certainty, that I would not die on that day.

Back in hospital, today, I remember that feeling and think: 'That's exactly the opposite of how I feel.'

Today I feel like the fucking van.

I'm struggling to get a couple of paracetamol down. Well, OK, they're quite big and a bit sticky. I struggle to swallow my Weetabix. Maybe it's too dry. I try a grape and the soft flesh slides down and it's wonderful but the skin is stuck. It feels hard and I should be gagging but there's no gag. Calm, calm.

I try to cough it up but I can't cough. I make a mooing noise which is why they will call my cough reflex 'bovine'. My throat is shutting down. I sip water. No, I force water down. Just tired, I tell myself, and try to put myself back on that hot mountain with the sun on my face and shining in me and I want to go back there to die.

The smell of food brings me back around 11 a.m. Charing Cross Hospital stinks. Not like old hospitals, of bleach and antiseptic, but of this food. I'm told it's not cooked on site, it's brought in every day on huge plastic pallets from a factory in Wales. Nothing against the Welsh but this insanity is surely compounded by the fact the Welsh can't cook. Their sole contribution to world cuisine is laver bread – seaweed. I'm told this ludicrous system is to save money. Thanks to the Welsh factory, each patient's meals cost something like 35p a day. To put this in context, prisoners' meals cost over a pound. But I suppose armed robbers and rapists need to keep their strength up.

Michele and my mum humour my ranting, but I can see they're concerned about my swallowing problem. I try to force down lunch but only manage a few bites. The doctor we call is sympathetic but not surprised. I might experience some temporary difficulties swallowing. I should stick to grapes for the time being. Peeled.

Wednesday, 21 November

Michele has been off work for a week. She's a theatrical agent and clients measure agents' time away from the office, i.e. time away from them, in dog years. Give it another week and they'll think of her as a Japanese escapee from the Second World War, hiding out on some remote island. I think this need to stay in touch with work is good for her. She can switch between worries, which takes her mind off me. Naturally I say this to her and for the first time in a week she fails to laugh at my jokes.

Maybe I'm getting better. Or maybe it was just a bad joke.

My swallowing doesn't seem to be any better so it's the grape diet again. But today it's my legs that are on their last, um, legs. I'm desperate for a wee. I refuse a zimmer frame so Michele helps me to the toilet. I say *helps*, in fact she *carries* me to the toilet. I stand there, Michele holding me up. We wait. Nothing. She puts the taps on. No. She looks away in case I'm just feeling a bit shy. The pressure can get to anyone. Nope. She offers to hold it for me. I let her. I ask her to jiggle it about a bit. She looks at me suspiciously. Honestly, I say, it might help. Nothing.

Shit. Never mind the piss, I'm not getting a stiffy.

I believe that some people actually enjoy – really get off on – similar experiences to the one I have next. I was told this recently by a friend of mine of the homosexual persuasion – the kind of man my mother, in a desperate search for political correctness, calls 'a pink person'. Now I like to think of myself as broad-minded and I also admit that over the years, in circumstances I'm not prepared to go into, I've heard of, seen, read about, and even participated in most naughty things that have been thought of by rude people. But I was really taken by surprise at this revelation.

Please take my word that if you are ever offered the opportunity, say, at a drinks party, you should just say no. Being cathetered, as a man, is not very nice.

The little tube down the penis was not as bad as I thought it would be, so I had begun to relax until the male nurse said, 'Right, this might be a bit uncomfortable now.' To get to the bladder the tube has to squeeze through the tight little ring of the prostate gland. Organs don't have pain receptors. Glands do.

However, the pain is soon replaced by the pleasure of unloading six gallons of wee into a plastic bag. I feel happy. Medical science has achieved something. Of course, I've also taken another step downward. And I don't think this cliff has a ledge.

It's night-time and I'm alone but now I have my Discman and some CDs. By now I simply can't open my eyes so at least I haven't got to worry about the porny pensioner opposite. I'm also wearing very dark Oakley glasses just in case. They look very cool on the beach or driving an E-Type. Less trendy when they fall into a cardboard sick bucket while you throw up. I would like to point out, by the way, that my glasses disappear from my locker at some stage in the proceedings. May the particular angel who took them get bits of diced carrot in their eye.

My music choice is iffy. I listen to *White Ladder*, the breakthrough David Gray album. I like plaintive singer-songwriters and this is just up my street. It may be dinner-party music but I like dinner parties. However, the final track on the album is 'Say Hello, Wave Goodbye', a plangent if overlong version of the marvellously sleazy Soft Cell track. I liked the original. I should really have been on a winner here. For the next week, all I have going round in my head is David sodding Gray singing 'say goodbye' at me.

Goodbye, goodbye, goodbye . . .

There is a little merry-go-round at the seafront near the house I've recently moved to in Hastings. My little girl – as yet unborn at this point – is quite obsessed with it. I take her every day. She makes me, to be frank. It plays, continually, a version of Simon and Garfunkel's 'The Sound Of Silence'. It sounds as if it's being bashed out by a special kid who's been bought a Bontempi organ for Christmas to stop him shoving fireworks up the cat's arse.

The woman who runs the ride listens to this for eight hours a day, probably twelve in the summer months. She has the same fixed expression on her face as I imagine I had back then. It's the one you see on prisoners released from Gulags, or possibly on Victoria Beckham's record producer.

Much later that night I try to listen to a different song. But I find that something strange and new (and therefore unpleasant) has happened. Now the music presses in through the earphones, hard, piercing, like hot iron pliers squeezing my head. I can no longer listen to music. But I've still got David Gray to keep me company through the long uncomfortable night ahead.

Goodbye, goodbye, goodbye . . .

Thursday, 22 November

Things start to speed up. The illness has gathered pace and I'm sliding away. My swallow is gone. The last thing I eat – that maybe I'll ever eat – is a piece of sweet green grape. Now even water just swills round my mouth. Or worse, tips into my lungs. I have a 'compromised airway'. I cannot stop liquids, including my saliva, tipping down into my fragile, spongy lungs. That's the eventual verdict of my team of doctors, but this is the NHS, last bastion of demarcation – or jobsworths – and to be absolutely sure they need the expert advice of the speech and language therapist, who by the time everyone's faffed about has gone home. She's not due back until *Tuesday*. At 10 a.m. On the bright side, I've got an appointment at eleven (and she's even late for that).

Unless she officially says I cannot swallow, no one will put in a feeding tube. This is called an NG (naso-gastric) tube. Naso for the nose, where it goes in, gastric for the stomach, where it ends up. Unless some bodger shoves it down your lungs a few times first – of which more later.

It's so patently obvious I cannot swallow, though, that I do get a saline drip. The doctors are rapidly running out of places to shove stuff in. I try not to imagine where they'll think of next. The saline drip will keep me hydrated, but only just. It will not moisten my mouth, and there follows a weekend of thirst that Lawrence of Arabia might have difficulty conveying.

It's only a coincidence, though a cruel one, that the young ginger doctor is off on a weekend trip to Prague. She tells me she's quite excited by the cheap, cold, lovely beer she'll be drinking. I went to Prague a few months after the wall came down. It was alien and mysterious, bohemian (no pun intended) and yes, by God, full of cheap beer. The city's now apparently given over to English stag parties getting lairy on cheap, cold . . . oh look, I'm torturing myself.

The entire weekend, as I suck on tiny squares of scratchy pink sponge on a lolly stick to moisten my mouth, I think of her in Prague, drinking . . .

Imagine your jealousy and anguish if the object of your desire flew off on a dirty weekend with your boss, a suitcase full of fizz and half the Ann Summers catalogue? You know the images you'd torture yourself with? Ha. I spit on them. They are the comfy chair to my rack, the feather duster to my iron maiden. Yes, the main cause of pain is the thought of someone swallowing, but the context is entirely different. But just as X-rated.

I see her with her medic chums. Alive, walking, laughing, chucking snowballs and maybe letting the snowflakes melt deliciously on her tongue. I see her in a bright, fire-lit tavern, tables laden with jugs of Budvar, sparkling with droplets of condensation on the outside of the glass.

Vlad offers the creamy glass up to her mouth. She is aware of other eyes upon her. She closes her lips tight but now its hardness is pushing against them, insistent. Already she feels the first tiny, clear droplets kissing her mouth and she knows, finally, she is powerless to resist.

'Now,' urges Vlad, as the others around her hold their breath. She grips Emily's hand tight, knowing she'll be next. She closes her eyes. Her body is alive like never before as she prepares to give herself up to the temptation. Almost involuntarily, but with a sense of excitement and relief, she parts the bud-red lips and her tongue darts out to taste the first droplets of—

Ow, ow, ow! Never get a stiffy with a catheter in! Ow, ow, help me Lord. I've just invented food porn and I'm being punished for being the sick sinner I undoubtedly am. My Lourdes water will be curdling in its Virgin Mary plastic bottle. Just what is going on in my head?

(Several years later, Marks and Spencer use similar images in adverts for ready meals. I've always been ahead of my time. Though never in any way that could be described as useful.)

Soon nothing takes my mind off the thirst. It becomes the central fact of my life. Until now, I've known discomfort and occasional pain. Now, for the first time, I suffer.

I'm not alone. A scuffle in the night, hushed, urgent voices and skittering of feet, the clank of metal, a scrape, a hushed moan, like the arrival of secret police at midnight. Curtains are drawn around a patient with an oedema, or swelling, in his brain. It is swelling so rapidly there's no time to administer steroids. They need to relieve the pressure urgently. Suddenly, it dawns on me they're going to do that thing . . . that medieval, no, ancient thing that I thought was an urban hospital myth. A trolley full of instruments is wheeled in.

I don't see it, but this is what happens. There's no time even to take him to theatre so the young surgeon cuts off the top of his head like a boiled egg in the bed where he lies, just lifts it off with what I imagine is a soft, sucking pop to let the brain swell. The shocked nurses move in and out of the curtained area, ashen. The surgeon leaves, weary, bloodied. Time passes. The patient dies.

What sick bastard chooses neurology as a speciality?

Friday, 23 November

My mum brings in some bottles of fizzy water. We have to hide them from the nurses as if they were crack pipes. I'm 'Nil by Mouth' and I know they worry about a chest infection, but that's in the future and my present is the thirst. And this helps.

No one is allowed to visit except my wife and my mum. I don't want anyone to see me, especially James and Tara. My lips are cracked and blistering and I'm developing sores. I have to be turned by the nurses because I cannot now move. I keep my eyes constantly closed because of the dizziness and even the dim ward lights burn my retina, but in the dark I am left in a tiny black box with my thoughts and they are despairing ones and I must not despair. My hearing is so acute and painful people have to whisper. I can hardly speak. How the hell did I get here? But all I want is for the speech therapist to come and say yes I can have an NG tube. I know then I can get water, real water in my stomach. I will no longer be thirsty. The saline drip is changed for something with minerals or some such, as I can't eat. But I'm never hungry.

The pain starts to kick in earlier and earlier between the painkillers. My left side is cramped. My neck aches. The back of my head, where the thing is still rampant, throbs and pulses as it grows, and someone's holding a blow-torch to the back of my eyes, waiting for them to pop. I try to do something for my wife, to show her I'm going to be OK, but today I'm worried. So are my team, except for that lucky bitch sucking off beers in Prague.

And tonight I get a new visitor. I'm not dreaming, but I wish I was because I see a door. At first I think it's the one to the ward, but it's different. It's nearer, oddly aligned. It's functional and institutional. It's solid and real. I've seen doors like it in the offices of Belsen. It opens a crack and now I can't make a sound. I know I'm sweating because something wants me. A black-sleeved arm slides around the door frame, as if to get at the handle from the other side and push through. I will it, I demand it to stop.

It stops.

Is that why it stops? I keep concentrating, sure that if I relax for a second I will see this thing and I cannot let this happen. I am fighting now, and conscious of the fight for the first time. Nothing moves for a long time. I will not give in.

The hand withdraws, the door closes, and I am left awake, clammy, knowing that it will not be the last time.

Saturday to Monday

Hallucinations are funny old things. You don't know what's real, so can never enjoy the few nice ones but are still scared witless by all the rest, which are hideous. Here are some things that can cause them:

Stress
Disorientation
Sleep deprivation
Brain damage
Dehydration
The withdrawal of massive doses of steroids too
    quickly, you fuckwits.

The latter is called steroid psychosis. That won't kick in for a few days. So we'll start with the lesser hallucinations first.

I've never been a big drug-taker. If my mum's reading this let me amend that to: 'I've never taken drugs and the anecdote that follows is fictional and for illustrative purposes only.'

Glastonbury, mid-eighties. Yeah, like when it was cool, man. I'm sitting by a psychedelic caravan slightly irritated that I'm missing one-hit-wonder hippy couple All About Eve on the pyramid stage while I wait for the Muppets inside to brew up some magic-mushroom tea. I'm frightened of acid, but I'm too widely read for my own good and I feel it's time for the doors of my perception to be if not kicked open, then at least edged ajar slightly before I hastily slam, double lock and bar them and stay indoors with a nice mug of cocoa.

The fey duo are warbling their one hit far away when tea's up. I didn't really want mushroom tea. I just wanted a couple of mushrooms. Now I've got to drink a whole fucking mug of it and I'll be sick and how cool will that be? I feel like I've ordered steak tartare by mistake and I'm too English to send it back and say, 'If I wanted an uncooked burger I could have gone to my mum's for a barbecue.'

I drink a bit and it's the most revolting thing on earth and will remain so until the invention of the McFlurry. I give the rest to my girlfriend, who's up for most things, and toddle off into some field to get re-consciousised.

I was right about the feeling sick. But after about half an hour that passed and I was left with less money and the sense of having been conned. I was also secretly relieved. When . . . suddenly everything around me became two-dimensional, like a huge film screen. There was that foreshortening effect film-makers overuse when they want to show a character in peril and the background zooms up behind them. It's done first in *Jaws*, with chief Brodie on the beach. Hold on, here it comes, I thought.

Then everything went back to normal. The end.

I know it's a pathetic anecdote, but that was the sum total of my hallucinogenic experiences. Until now. Maybe if I'd had more I could have coped better. I doubt it. In *Fear and Loathing in Las Vegas*, Hunter S. Thompson talks about his various terrifying experiences on drugs, but you can tell he's having a blinding time. So he sees bats everywhere, so what? He's the kind of bloke who'll invite them all for tea with his mum and Puff the Magic Dragon.

The diary bit is all over the place here. My notes don't help me make much sense of it. The real world I remember is always a night one, half-lit, with the nurses squeezing my hands and taking readings and asking me the special questions in broken English. But never 'Are you alright?' or 'Do you need some company?' No, they had better things to do, like compare their pay and work out overtime and complain about their teenagers.

No one who has spent any length of time in hospital has any illusions about 'angelic' nurses. Some are good, some incompetent, a few cruel, a handful brilliant, but almost all are competent but indifferent. Perhaps they have to be. And know what? Whisper it, but their pay is good. Better than mine. Overtime is lucrative, private work more so. They're doing less and less 'hands-on' work and wouldn't pick up a J-cloth if their lives (as opposed to patients') depended on it. They spend much of their time form-filling and scoffing Celebrations, and they possess qualifications that can take them anywhere in the world. Plus they see more action than Colin Farrell's mattress. You'd think they'd be happy. But no – they whinge. I have to listen to it. The land of the damned with my funny head companions is almost preferable.

But not quite.

Because here they come again, led by the black sleeve, trying to open the door. He's pushing through and part of me is curious to see him, part of me is terrified, but there is a cold logical part that is telling me this is a visual construct of death. He's not a mythical figure with a

*scythe and a cloak, and he's not about to play Kerplunk
with me for my soul, but he's death all the same. I think
it's a coded message to say hang on and don't relax, keep
fighting, but another part of my brain – my inner critic,
my Tom Paulin – says now I'm talking bollocks, and that
makes me smile somewhere and the sleeve goes back
behind the door. For tonight.*

At some stage over this weekend a decision is made to
take me off the steroids. I am unsure why. This should be
done slowly. It is not. I am unsure why. They are just
stopped. This is a bad thing. I am sure of this.

Monday Night to Tuesday Morning

I am demented with thirst and tormented by visions. I am
bound with invisible, burning cord. I am Prometheus
chained to a rock, vultures tearing at my liver. I am
shaved, blinded Samson, eyeless in Gaza, at the mill with
slaves. I am Satan falling, blazing, I am Jesus nailed, I am
Job, I am a Mayan sacrifice, face peeled and hanging like
a wet red cloth for crows to eat my open eyes, I am drawn
and quartered and thus die all traitors, I am really far too
well read for my own good.

Again I smile and they subside, but then I am aware of
an absence of something, far worse than these phantasms
that I know are unreal.

I cannot see my children. I try to find their faces in
amongst the horror show and my wife is now by my bed
and despair cloaks me and I try to sob but I can't even do
this, and I look into her face and try to see my children but
there is nothing. Only a plastic doll's face. A face with
teeth. A melting face coming closer and now I am dry

sobbing, heaving in the arms of Alidz my doctor, who has just come on duty and is shocked at the state of me and unable to speak, but she holds me and I am so unspeakably grateful to touch her. Then finally – four days and a bit later – in ponces the fucking speech and language therapist. Still, now, writing this, I want to kill her.

There is a delay, because I have said as much in my demented guttural way so now, of course, she has flounced off. But Alidz and Michele calm me and some drugs are found and the bad things stop. But there are no good things now for a long time but yes the decision is made to give me the NG tube and after an hour of shoving and twisting and pushing this thing down my clamped throat, finally using wire to stiffen the tube which keeps slipping into my lungs, I get water. The steroids are resumed, my visions and my thirst subside and I can see my children. They are not smiling, but I can see them.

Tuesday p.m.

In the sedated afternoon, there's an MRI and a conference where it's established that the lesion has slowed down and I'm out of immediate danger. What damage has been already done, and what the thing is, is still unknown. But for now, I am safe. As long as my heart and lungs keep going.

And then I stop breathing.

Chapter Two

First Cut

I *had* remembered what happened next as just a one-day affair, but after a bit of research it turns out it was more of a three-day event. Now that's irritating because it's bolloxed my neat chapter idea: the plan was to do a gripping, minute-by-minute, blow-by-blow, action-packed account of these twenty-four exciting hours. The urgent call to the wife, the quick decision to do a tracheostomy, the tearful nurses, the slicing open, the fight to suction my collapsed and mucus-infected lungs, the clock ticking down in the fag-stained waiting room, the final, heroic, sweaty triumph as the life support kicks in and the crisis is over . . . all that riveting, neatly tied-up stuff, you know, like the TV series *24*. It would have been great. I fully expected it to be the chapter that got read out at literary festivals, where I'd be wedged in a hot tent between Julian Barnes, Martin Amis, Jordan, some bread rolls and six bottles of warm Sauvignon Blanc.

Anyway it's all to cock now, so this is what actually happened.

There I was, taking such a turn for the worse that even

the night shift noticed. Usually your head has to explode all over the telly or you have to get a visit from Chelsea Football Club for them to get off their arses, but at any rate one of them saw I'd turned an interesting shade of eggshell blue and, after doing a colourmatch to take to Paints R Us cos it was just the right shade for her bathroom suite, she called someone who knew what the fuck they were doing.

This someone was Doris 'The Cutter' Doberenz: a lovely if strange surgeon of a certain age who rarely goes home and who I imagine haunts Charing Cross like a revenant, knives at the ready, always looking for something to practise on. I suspect she has cats. Really fucking nervous cats. She decided I needed a tracheostomy. Fair play, good call and everything, but I have a horrible feeling she thinks most people could do with one, whatever they come in with, as they are her speciality.

It's interesting how proper medicine's become so incredibly specialised, just when 'unconventional' or 'alternative' or shall we say 'useless' medicine's got more and more general, or holistic or useless. I suppose it's because the men in white coats are terrified of how complex we are as working machines, and so will only dare to suggest they know how one teeny bit works, whilst the women with beards and lentil socks have tapped into that same fear – and want to reassure us that we're not that complex, and that a rub down with Ian St John's warts will heal both our corns and our limp wotsit.

Back in the real world – my real Charing Cross world, and unless you're a lentil-munching, crystal-tapping loony, *your* real world – there are specialists for everything. Which is why if there's anything more complicated than a sprained ankle wrong with you, you're stuck on twelve waiting lists to see a dozen 'specialists'. It's enough to drive anyone to Holland and Barrett for the echinacea and make you wonder if you can afford the air fare to Machu Picchu.

Can I just remind people at this juncture that those wonderful, mystic, know-all ancient Mayans all fucking died out? While we, the children of the Findus crispy pancake and two paracetamols, are still here, trampling on their remains and wondering what time the gift shop closes.

Back to me, jumping queues like a German in a cake-and-beach-towel shop. Cos once you're already *in situ*, or in the *shitu*, there are no waiting lists. On the contrary, specialists are lining up to have a go. I think Doris had a cut-throat quota or something, as by the time my neuro team turned up she'd already got the leather strop out and had lathered me up for a far closer shave than you get with a Gillette Mach 3 – turbo or no bloody turbo.

There now followed a truly pointless, drawn-out, ludicrous discussion of the sort you could only have in the NHS. It's one reason why this chapter was never going to be *24*, and why I'm never going to be played by Kiefer Sutherland. It was basically a 'What do we do now?' discussion. But first they had to summon my poor strung-out missus and mum, who'd only just got home and were having enough trouble deciding which ready meal to heat up.

There are still nail marks on the passenger-side door handle of my car where Mum grabbed on as Michele drove to the hospital that night. Alidz my neurologist had had to make the hideous call. This is verbatim:

9 p.m.

ALIDZ: You should come to the hospital. But get a
   taxi.
MICHELE: Is he dead?
ALIDZ: He's very poorly. Get a taxi.
MICHELE: Are you ringing me up to tell me my
   husband is dead?
[*Pause.*]
MICHELE: Please tell me now if he's dead.
ALIDZ: He's not dead, but he's very ill.
MICHELE: Promise me he's not dead.
[*Pause.*]
ALIDZ [*slowly*]: No-oo. But we need to make some
   decisions. And we have to do them quickly.
[*Phone goes down.*]

My mum, hovering in the kitchen with a frozen
shepherd's pie, only heard one side of this conversation.
Sometimes she still hears it in her sleep.

Alidz told me recently, 'By four o' clock that day I
thought you might die. By nine I knew you would.'

Ha. Five A-levels, a medical degree, forty-seven letters
after her name and she still got it wrong, silly cow. Still,
she saves my life in a bit so let's cut her some slack.

There were two options available to me. I say that as if
I was part of the debate. In fact by now I had very little
say in the matter except a kind of gurgling 'uuuurgh'.
There was general acceptance that I needed to be on a
ventilator, which perked Doris up as it meant I might need
a tracheostomy. And therefore I needed to be put in a
coma. The question was – a big coma or a little one?

The choices worked like this. A 'permanent' coma could be induced with drugs – I would have a plastic breathing tube inserted into my lungs through my mouth, clearing the airway and enabling a mechanical ventilator to breathe for me. This is a relatively straightforward and quite common procedure. I think it was the preferred option of most of the physicians. They argued that this would give my body, and in particular the thing in my medulla, time to heal. It would avoid an invasive operation – I can see Doris shuffling unhappily a bit here – which always carries a risk; and it would be less unpleasant for me because I wouldn't know anything about it. They could shove as many drugs into me as they wanted, take blood samples, biopsies, take my head off, anything. I'd be the perfect patient. And when/if I got better, they would wake me up. If you want to be cynical, they preferred this option because it meant that I could shuffle off the old mortal coil without any shouting and bleeding and fuss. I think they genuinely thought this was the most humane thing to do. It was the equivalent of taking faithful old ageing Rover out for one last walkies with his favourite squeaky bone and a loaded 12-bore.

The other option (and no prizes for guessing who advocated this) was that I should be given an immediate tracheostomy – that is, an operation to insert and stitch a tube into my airway, just under my larynx. I would then be put on a ventilator, but be brought round as soon as possible. The argument here is that I would be conscious and perhaps able in some way to 'fight' more.

That's a surprising shift in medical thought. Most doctors have traditionally ignored the effects of the mind on the body – we're all used to feeling as if we're treated as machines. A doctor finds something wrong with your big end, has a look under the hood, does a bit of tinkering, kicks your tyres, wipes his hands and away you both go. (And if he gets the chance to shove his finger up your arse while he's at it, he's even happier.) There's a school of medical thought that refuses to accept the patient's mind can have any effect – or even exist, in some cases. (This in no way appears to contradict the other traditional prevailing thought – that many illnesses are 'all in the mind'. Particularly in the mind of women of a certain age.)

Either way, it was über-scientific, socially constipated Doris, bless her, who believed in the power of a patient's will. Perhaps it was just her German genes. Trouble is, she was assuming I had some fight left in me.

9.15 p.m.

The car now parked/abandoned by the front lobby of Charing Cross Hospital, Michele and my mum are sitting in a small, hot, grim office with a team of experts who are looking mostly at the floor. They remember Alidz, Dr Lane, Matt and the little Prague-loving ginger one, a female staff nurse whose name I forget but who looked to me just like a more masculine Tommy Cooper, a kindly camp male nurse called Gerard, and the ever-hovering Doris. And yes, the clock was ticking. By now I was unconscious, on oxygen, with my O_2 levels hovering somewhere around Apollo 13's, and they are being asked this question.

Do the nice people in white put me in a coma and on a ventilator sort of indefinitely, so my body can pull itself together, springing up all better in a month or two, or do they just knock me out long enough to whack in a tracheostomy tube and hook me up to life support, and bring me round as soon as, to go twelve rounds with the bastard in my brain?

During the nasty pause, Alidz took this opportunity, in a professional, well-meaning and modern-doctor sort of way, to add that things were about as bleak as they could be, and there was a very good chance I might never regain consciousness.

'I think,' she said, 'you should say goodbye to Nigel.'

She meant say it while I was still semi-conscious, and just in case. Whatever the details, I was going to ITU, I was going to be put on a ventilator, unconscious. I might not come round. They might not get another chance. Michele understood why my ashen-faced doctor was telling her this. Mum's never really forgiven Alidz for saying it.

Shell's only just told me that she went to my bedside then. It was the hardest thing she ever did, but as she held my hand and looked down at me – gasping for air, tortured, insensible, dying – she refused, *refused* to say goodbye.

But there was still this question of what to do? I had to go on a ventilator, that much was certain, but big coma, little coma? Big coma, little coma? Red lorry, yellow lorry? They are not stupid people, these two women. However, Michele's a theatrical agent, Mum's a pensioner. If they were being quizzed for their view about the weekly rate for doing panto in Frinton, or the best place for a nice cup of tea and a slice of Battenberg, they were definitely the people to ask. But this decision? They asked for advice. There were advantages and disadvantages on both sides, they were told sagely. Like that helps.

They do this a lot, doctors. Once I had a lump on one of my nadgers. I ignored it for a while for the sensible reason that it might be cancer. Finally I went for tests – again they had to shove a finger up my bum – any bloody excuse. Anyway, after a not entirely unpleasant ultra-sound scan the lump turns out to be a lump of calcium. Or sugar. Or a bit of an Action Man – I can't really recall, but either way I wasn't going anywhere. Sadly, neither was my little lump. The consultant gave me two choices. I could have it cut out . . . or just leave it in.

What's the best option? I asked. He shrugged. On one hand, it's a bit uncomfortable but not doing any harm. On the other – you have to have an operation. He couldn't give a shit. He just had to sign one of two chits – one saying 'Bugger off home', the other 'Slice this man's balls open.' I buggered off home.

A few years and the odd achy-bollock episode later, here's Michele and Mum in the little hot room trying to make a much bigger decision. With much the same information.

Anyway, as Mum recalls, still amazed, the pair of them dutifully trotted off to the dreary fluorescent-lit canteen overlooking the dreary fluorescent-lit Fulham Palace Road, stared at the November drizzle a bit and actually *discussed what to do*. Like this was a sensible, rational chat. About whether to get the BOGOF on mince at Iceland or go mad and have the steak.

9.45 p.m.

They've no fucking idea.

10 p.m.

They decide on something. They decide that the canteen is a shithole, so they go back to the hot little room full of medics to ask for more advice. But now things speed up. I stop breathing. My lungs are overflowing with an infection and the debate is all a bit academic until they can clear them and get me breathing again.

I'm rushed somewhere – I don't know where – to get 'bagged'. Gerard takes over. A mask is shoved over my mouth, urgently. It's attached to a thick green plastic balloon. Gerard's squeezing the balloon and a lovely Australian nurse is telling me to keep breathing. I would but there's not enough air in each squeeze. I cannot move any part of me. I try to breathe from my diaphragm, like when I was a child and scared in the dark and my asthma was bad and the room was filled with my wheezes. Nothing. I try to breathe from my ribs, pushing them out as far as I can. Shit, *nothing*. I've heard hippy yoga teachers tell their middle-aged fat housewife students to breathe through their arse and I'm happy to give that a whirl, but no. I always suspected it was cobblers.

I must concentrate. This is hurting. I'm suffocating for sure now. I don't know it yet, but I've caught MRSA – the superbug – in my left lung. So that's collapsed. My right one hasn't, but it is full of thick green mucus, my body's own defence against infection having gone into overdrive. I'm drowning and I've been chucked a concrete lifebelt.

Now everything is green. My eyes are closed but I know everything is green. The uniforms, the bag, my putrid insides. I'm under a limpid lake, the sun darkening as the duckweed closes over me, filtering green light. Slime surrounds me, seeps into me. I am wet through, going under. The voice is still there and it's strong and sweet and I'll always love a Sydney accent but it's not enough. I'm drowning in my own fluids, filling my lungs. But the voice keeps urging me:

'Breathe, Nigel. That's it. You're doing good. One more. You're doing fine.'

Liar.

Darkness.

3 a.m.

Michele and Mum have over the last two weeks developed that terrible unspoken relatives' pact of *never crying in front of each other*. Hence they take it in turns to 'go to the loo', 'just go and get a paper', 'have a fag break', 'grab a coffee', 'check on the progress of that interesting hole the workmen are digging in the Fulham Palace Road' – any damn excuse for a private five-minute sob. It's not false bravery or putting on a show. They just know that if they both started together, they'd still be sobbing now.

I see them coming back, eyes shining and pink, sniffing like a supermodel at a Colombian coke-testing competition.

'*I have to confess the Rocky Mountain snorter has a decent kick but leaves a terrible bitter finish, whilst the Left Bank speedy, though a trifle more pricey at £75,000 a stuffed condomful, is a real septum-loosener. Two weeks of this and you'll be finding more than a bogey in your hanky.*'

However, tonight is different. They are beyond tears.

But the cavalry is on its way. Not for me – I'm decidedly

lost in Injun territory and the wagons have already circled around my knackered body. This is a rescue mission for Michele, who by now, in the horrible sickly *un-time* between midnight and dawn, the hours when you're at your lowest ebb, is still wired, still waiting for the result of my bagging/suctioning/resurrecting. There's been weeks of this now and she knows it's been leading up to this: me, lost somewhere in a small room, surrounded by doctors working on me. If I'm going to die it'll be tonight and she's still keeping it together.

Philip, Michele and me

Tonight, even at this horrible hour, Michele's rung her best friend. This is that friend you're talking about when you say, 'Oh, of course, my best friend is —. I just know I can call him/her any time of the day or night, and he/she will drop whatever they're doing and be there.' Well, maybe. I hope you're right, just as I hope you never have to make that call. But you'll never *really* be sure until you do make it.

Philip was that friend, that was that call, and what he was doing was getting determinedly pissed at a black-tie party *in his honour*. It sounds a bit grand, but he'd just made a low-budget British film that had three distinct characteristics:

a) There were no gangsters in it
b) It made some money despite not starring Hugh Grant
c) It wasn't utterly shite.

The one thing it does share with the vast majority of British films is this, though:

You've never heard of it.

And yes, he dropped everything – except a bottle of champagne, cos he correctly thought he might need it – and yes, he left his own party and got straight in a cab and yes, he pitched up at Charing Cross Hospital in the wee hours wearing a tuxedo, grimly clutching a bottle of Bolly and unsteadily demanding to be shown up to 'itenanshive care'.

The psychiatric wing was the floor below. They sent him there first. We're all still amazed he wasn't sectioned.

'. . . Yes, of course you're a film director. Absolutely you just won a prize at Cannes. We'll let you draw a picture of it in crayon in a minute. Just sit here. Oh, and you used to be an actor in Crossroads – no, that makes perfect sense. Perhaps you could put that bottle down now and take a couple of these. No, no, this white jacket is so much more stylish than the tuxedo. It does do up at the back. I hear they're all the rage at international film festivals. Why, Bruce Willis was wearing one the other— Come back – Nurse, rugby tackle him, he's getting away. I'm on a bonus scheme, dammit.'

At this time, Philip was far more Michele's friend than mine. I admit I was partly – um, entirely – to blame. We'd got off to a bit of an iffy start a couple of years previously. I'd just started seeing Michele, and was still amazed that this belter let me anywhere near her postcode, let alone her La Perla. But for whatever reason, I'd pulled. Short fat bald broke ugly guys like me rarely get the cover girl. We get the girl in the 'before' pictures. You know, 'Before I lost 18 stone', 'Before my plastic surgery', etc. Fair enough, occasionally we *do* get the girl in the 'after' pics, but those are the after-the-fire/crash/lobotomy/axe-attack/ prison-sentence pics.

I think it was the famous psychologist and thinker Dr Hook who said: 'When you're in love with a beautiful woman . . . watch your back matey, cos all your mates are lining up to pork her' or something equally well observed. Basically, cutting through the poetry, he's talking about insecurity and jealousy. So what happened that night wasn't technically my fault. It was psychology's. I was a puppet to my id, as opposed to my trousers, which was a new and unsettling experience.

So I meet my lovely new girlfriend in some private club she's a member of – and of course I'm not – and she's already there, sitting cosied up to a bloke who's *even prettier than she is*. Oh shit. They're clearly old mates – they're sharing jokes, drinking Pinot Grigio and looking like a beautiful couple from *Fantasy Island*. They were the friends who just needed that little bit of magic to make them realise how beautiful and gorgeous and well-suited they actually were. I was the midget jumping up and down going, 'Da plane boss, da plane.' They were the Martini couple giggling on the yacht in the sunset, I was the homunculus boathand scrubbing the spinnaker and scraping the barnacles off the hull. They were the Cretan demi-gods wandering the vineyards of Bacchus, I was the goatherd covered in lumps of goat shite. They were . . . Oh, you get the idea.

Even in our wedding photos they look like the happy couple and I look like the fucking waiter.

So like all real men, I tried to convince myself he was a poof and got trolleyed. Very very quickly. This undid my only real selling point as a boyfriend. On a good day, I'm not the unfunniest bloke in the world, and I am living proof that making a woman squeal with laughter does sometimes give you the chance to just make her squeal. And thank God, cos if it really was just down to money or looks, I'd still be a virgin. And try having a sense of humour in your thirties then.

A couple of drinks can, it's true, give a certain lustre to one's loquaciousness and help open the floodgates to the reservoir of one's wit. Getting wankered like a sulky teenager at a bus stop who's nicked a two-litre bottle of White Lightning does not. Stupid, stupid, stupid. More so when you're still trying to impress someone. See, I'm a shocking drunk anyway. I go from happy to miserable to irritable to unconscious via persecuted and pompous in less than half a bottle of Shiraz. Thinking about it, each glass of alcohol turns me into another of Snow White's seven dwarfs.

These days I generally lay off the booze full stop, for the effects of my illness, combined with the effects of the drugs to combat the effects of the illness, mean I'm effectively turbo-charged for getting drunk. It's all much quicker. I've hardly blown the froth off my Guinness before I'm telling the entire pub I love them, realising they hate me, picking a fight and falling asleep. I'm not asked out much any more. Besides, even sober I feel half-cut, so why bother with alcohol? I've got the double vision, wobbliness and chippy attitude already, so I've saved the price of six pints of best before I even start.

Back then, though, I was drinking like I was on a mission. To be an arse. As the awful evening wore on I felt more and more left out of the conversation – partly cos I didn't have their shared history, partly cos I was too bolloxed to follow much of it, but mostly cos no one wanted to include this dribbling berk *in* it. After behaving like a sarky, narky knob for several hours I decided it was time for us to leave and perhaps-we-should-arrange-a-date-to-meet-up-soon-been-lovely-meeting-you-honest-blah-blah. I think what I actually said was, 'Come on wench of mine, we're going. Let's grab a kebab before I pleasure you over the bonnet of a Vauxhall Nova.'

I went home alone.

And serve me right, frankly. The bloke who owned my local Interflora bought a villa on the Algarve soon after.

I thought all this – ahem – *misunderstanding* was a sort of family secret. However, when he made a speech at our wedding two years ago, Philip (who to his eternal credit had never mentioned this incident), said, 'Nigel and I have become great friends. *And who would have thought it?*' And a hundred people pissed themselves laughing.

I looked across at my new gobby wife, but she seemed to be very busy with a bit of cake.

God knows how, but by the time I was taken ill, four years after our initial meeting, things had changed between Philip and me. Michele loved him. I loved her. Hence I grudgingly supposed I should love him a bit too. But in a very manly, rugger-playing, vindaloo-eating, bird-pulling kind of way, understand? Good. Glad to get that on the record.

The day before my collapse in high dependency, when I came round after another plunge into the abyss, I saw him there by my bedside, trying to think of something to say. He had that look on his face P. G. Wodehouse once observed 'of an Englishman who's about to attempt to speak French'. I knew things were getting bad, what with the paralysis and blindness and pain and nasal feeding tube and drips and drugs and all, and I said something to him then that I'm still proud of.

I said, 'Please look after Michele.'

He thinks that's amazing. I've never told him what I really meant was, 'Let anyone lay a finger on my bird after I'm dead and I'll come back and haunt the fucking lot of you,' but I didn't have enough breath. Anyway, they would have been terrible last words.

Talking of last words, can you believe what went through my ridiculously overworking and shockingly shallow mind as I was lying there being bagged. I tried to remember what my last words had been. I know, it's all me, me, me, but I'd become terribly introspective of late. I'm not saying the matter held huge importance for me, as another pint of pus was hoovered out of my lungs, but I have to confess I thought about it.

Of course I knew I wasn't important enough to make it into the Oxford Dictionary of Quotations, *but you hope to leave something spiritual or meaningful at your last; something enlightening for your family, something for them to hold on to in the dark days ahead as they mourn. A nugget of comfort mined from a lifetime of experience that also showed you faced death with equanimity and dignity.*

I had a horrible suspicion my last words had been me moaning about not being able to take a piss any more.

I'm lying there thinking about last words and my favourite popped into my head. Forget 'Kiss me Hardy' or 'Bugger Bognor' or 'I die God's servant first,' or even 'Told you I was ill,' it's this. It's the American Civil War and some general is strolling on the ramparts of some fort talking to his nervous troops, who are facing the encamped enemy near by. 'Relax, men,' he says. 'They couldn't hit an elephant at this dist—'

That's it. I refuse to die until I come up with something as good as that. And I think I'm breathing a little easier. Am I? Yes? YES. YES!

But bugger. I'm slipping down again. Into the green water.

Early Morning

Obviously I didn't die. Obviously I came through the crisis, cos this isn't *Sunset Boulevard* or even *The Sixth Sense*. I pulled through and all, so it was time to go on the ventilator. It was Doris who helped Michele decide what to do with me on the 'big coma, little coma' issue. She argued for an immediate tracchy as soon as I was stablised, and that they should then attempt to bring me round as soon as possible, '*zo he kin fight.*' Maybe the idea of fighting appealed to Michele; maybe everyone was too scared to disagree. Either way, Doris got the nod and padded off happily to get her Sabatiers.

This is what Doris does:

She positions me on my back, puts a rolled-up towel under my bare neck to stretch it for her knives and hooks. She's careful not to over-extend my neck in case this narrows my airway too much, or leads her to place the tube too low and too close to a major artery. If she tears this artery, I will either choke or bleed to death within minutes. Her aim is to insert a breathing tube, safely and securely, into my windpipe or trachea. That's where the name of the procedure comes from. Unfortunately, there are a lot of other things in the neck that get in the way. Things I'm going to need.

Delicately but firmly, she massages her 'landmarks', like a navigator setting his bearings around a coral reef. They are the thyroid notch, the sternal notch and the cricoid cartilage. If you put your fingers around your throat you'll feel lumps and bumps and ridges. They are made mainly of cartilage – a substance somewhere between flesh and bone, like the inside of your nose – and they are part of the combined swallowing and talking and breathing mechanism going on hugger-mugger in your throat. All frighteningly, bewilderingly close, like the insides of a flesh watch. They might be mysterious and unknown to you, but to Doris they are as familiar as the rooms in her house. She marks them with an ink pen. She is planning a 3cm vertical incision, starting at the cricoid cartilage.

She injects a local anaesthetic made up of lidocaine (1 per cent) with 1:150,000 parts epinephrine. She makes her first cut – a clean, vertical line.

If she had found too much fat under the skin she could have removed it with an electric wire, the fat spitting and smoking like pork rind thrown on hot coals.

She's cutting my throat deeper now, until she reaches what are known as the strap muscles, which run horizontally. She reaches into the slit she's made to find that dangerous artery and make sure it's not in the way. Smaller blood vessels are cauterised or tied off as they ooze blood. She takes a retractor and inserts it into the strap muscles, spreading them open.

Doris now needs to cut through another structure in my

throat known as the thyroid isthmus. It is hard and she needs to cut sharply, and quickly cauterise or stitch to stem the resultant spurt of blood. My trachea lies open before her. My throat is cut.

The first half of the procedure is now over.

She cleans the wound and prepares the tube. It will go under my voice-box, my larynx. There is an inflatable 'balloon' attached above the tube to close off and protect my upper airway from nasal or mouth secretions while I'm on the ventilator. When it is inflated, I will not be able to speak. I will also breathe through my neck. I will be able to put my fingers over my nose, close my mouth and still breathe. It's a curious feeling and the most fun I'm going to have in intensive care.

The local anaesthetic is utterly crucial now, to stop blood seeping into my trachea and filling up my lungs. When Doris is sure it is safe, she takes a metal hook and lifts the glistening cricoid cartilage wide before cutting into my neck further. There are three ways she can cut now, to get the tube in. Her preferred method – whose slight scars I bear to this day – is an upside-down T-shape.

She makes a 2cm horizontal incision through the membrane between the second and third tracheal rings. She takes a pair of heavy scissors and cuts into the rings to make the T-shape. With silk thread, she stitches the loose flaps of skin to my neck to keep them out of the way, so they don't have to be re-cut if there's a problem with the tube in the near future. I have tiny marks on my neck as evidence this was done.

Doris slides a guide tube into the opening. Secretions are constantly suctioned and retractors used to insert the tracheostomy tube proper. Once she is certain it is in the correct position, she stitches the tube to my skin. She attaches a tracheostomy collar, places a sponge soaked with iodine or petrolatum gauze between the skin and the collar flange, and she is done.

I can now be wheeled away to be hooked up to my iron lung; Doris can breathe more easily, strip off her bloody gloves – and what? She has done her job again, quickly, efficiently and safely. Of all the invasive procedures I had done in that hospital, that was the most successful. There are often problems with discomfort, bleeding, infection or blockage, but my tracchy was perfect, textbook. I thank you for it now, Doris. But please get out more.

I know now how she did it. I have studied every cut, every retraction, every stitch, every decision made. But I don't know how she *felt*. And of all the dozens of medics I met – the surgeons, neurologists, physicians, radiologists, phlebotomists, biologists, nurses, physios, all of them – the one person I want to understand, and the one person I cannot get close to, is Doris.

I can still see her now, sitting in the little café taking tiny, rapid bites of her sandwich, talking to students, bustling along corridors, always leaving, always on her way somewhere else. I would see her out of the corner of my eye, like a cat at the window too timid to come in. Yet what bravery! What decision-making, what clarity, what strength. That night she did not go home, although her shift was long over. The night she cut my throat and let me breathe again, although she knew she had done the perfect job, she stayed, she observed, she hovered. She cared.

I touch the crinkled hollow at the base of my throat and I remember.

So that was how it happened. Swiftly, efficiently, expertly.

Although it didn't. The hospital bolloxed it all up.

Remember Doris had to be sure the tube was in correctly? To do so she needed a delicate glass instrument – some kind of air-pressure manometer thing – to be sure. The hospital had two. Sadly they'd lost one and earlier that day a porter had dropped the other.

As mentioned before, the huge benefit of the tracchy is that you don't have to have a big plastic tube down your gob. But because they couldn't do it that night they shoved a big plastic tube down my gob while they waited for a new glass thingy.

Then, of course, next morning the bastards woke me up as per original instructions so I could 'fight'. Or rather, so I could wake up in some hideous fucking ITU hell with the same old problems plus an enormous plastic tube down my gob. Now this is just taking the piss, I thought.

The delicate glass thingy would take another day to arrive.

I never told anyone but I came round towards the end of the procedure to put that plastic tube in. I was conscious, could hear, could feel – fuck me, I could feel – but couldn't move, couldn't tell them to stop, couldn't say that I could feel a doctor scratch-scratch-scratching around at a broken vein in my left wrist, could feel a tooth break as the retractor opened my mouth, could hear Gerard the nurse ask the anaesthetist if he was sure I was under.

Just another item on my list of nightmares. I think I didn't make a fuss because it just seemed par for the course. There's a fine line between true stoicism and

70

Post-Traumatic Stress Disorder and I've been hopping backwards and forwards over the bloody thing ever since.

ITU, Morning One

When I woke I wasn't in a fit state to be accepting gentlemen callers. I was writhing about in this strange white ward with the tube in. I could at least breathe, but that was about it. I wasn't ungrateful for that, but you know . . . Also, I couldn't help noticing I had grown more 'lines'. By which I mean more tubes dripping more medicines into my arms and feet.

Where are they going to put them next? I thought. My knackers? Oh, if only I knew . . .

I was now hooked up to a ventilator via the mouth tube. I'm amazed they had a ventilator spare – I thought perhaps a porter might have dropped one. But my lungs were temporarily free of fluid, and of course I had a handy 10cm-wide plastic airway to help things along, and a bloody great Dyson pumping that plastic-smelling, metallic, sweet air into me, so it could have been worse.

Michele had by now crashed out on a bench in the smoke-stained relatives' room, and Mum had probably wandered off to the revolting canteen to find some other poor sod with a shocking story (she always found them, even *outside* hospitals).

Against family instructions, a dopey nurse allowed someone in to see me. The poor bloke, a good friend, had been following my progress, but because things had moved so fast he'd basically missed a couple of episodes. It was like those blink-and-miss-it daytime US soaps, where within a week Charlene will have revealed herself to be a man, Darlene will have married her gay brother and Billy-Ray will have become a junkie, been into rehab, become a priest and run off with two choirboys and the church organ fund.

He was a bit startled to find me in intensive care, and even more surprised to find me in what can only be described as 'a fucking state'.

Gareth

Gareth is such a nice bloke that when I first came across him I thought he was being nice as some kind of evil cunning plan. No one could be that nice without a secret agenda, like taking over the office, say, or the Western world. I only went round to his house to see if he'd got a retractable swimming pool with a collection of solar-powered nuclear missiles, or something. But no. Gradually I had to admit that he was just nice. That didn't stop him making me feel slightly uncomfortable. It's only been in the last few years when he's worked with enough knobheads to give himself a few sharp edges that I feel I can relax. Now he's one of us.

There are several versions of this meeting, which lasted about twenty minutes before a horrified Michele showed up and rushed the poor sod out.

Gareth's version
I can't think of anything to say. This is awful. I've suddenly realised I shouldn't be in here, but I can't just leave. I know, I'll blather on about my job and normal things like we used to talk about as if nothing's happened.

My version
The fucker's talking about his lovely TV job despite the
fact that I a) have been made redundant and b) am
probably going to die. What is wrong with him and why
won't he just piss off?

Michele's version
'Gareth was sitting there with tears rolling down his
cheeks, holding your hand and doing his best, you
ungrateful sod.'

Complicated sometimes, this truth business. And I'm a
qualified journalist. I say that. I would have been, but I
only got my shorthand up to 80wpm and I needed 100 to
get my badge. Maybe that's the problem. A few more
hours on my Teeline and the world might have seemed
much clearer.

I'm a trainee on the Dagenham Post, *all fresh-faced and
knowing less than – I'm trying to think of a metaphor for
someone who doesn't know very much but I think 'trainee
on the* Dagenham Post' *pretty much covers it. The fresh-
faced thing means I often get sent to 'death knocks',
where you go to the family house and get the story – and
more importantly the photo – of some Herbert who's just
died, hopefully in gruesome circumstances. In this
instance the unlucky chap had been nicking car radios. He
was only a teenager, but he was ahead of the game, seeing
as he'd decided to pinch the things from cars just out of
the Ford factory and still on the rail transporters.*

*Trouble is, he was doing it under railway power lines
and in the fog, which – and I didn't know this either, to be
fair to the lad – conducts electricity. Tragically, as he put*

his hand on the metal car he acted as an earthing wire for six million volts and was instantaneously connected to a Ford Fiesta and his maker.

One lad, many truths. To his family, a good boy who loved playing for hours with his little sister and riding round the concrete communal yard of their low-rise flats on his bike. To the old bill, a loser who was heading for more and more trouble. To the new owner of that Fiesta, a hood ornament.

I'm awake and Gareth's gone. It's a shame cos I'd just remembered an old story. But I can't speak anyway, and death seems too near and jokes too dark and flat. I try to hold Michele's hand. It hurts even to touch her. My nerve signals are shot, electricity running amok in me. I flinch and she doesn't know what to do. I ache to feel her but I can't speak. She puts her hand out again. The pain's worth it.

Outside there's fog.

I think we both know, here, in this disorientating white place, this place of hush, of machines and efficiency, of science and numbers, this un-space, this otherwhere, that I've fallen as far as I can. We wait quietly for the equipment to arrive for my operation. It will be better, I know. I want the ventilator, want to stop struggling, to let something else do it all for me. Breathing, pissing, shitting, fighting infection, fighting pain, fighting fear. Just fighting. There's nothing left of me, nowhere for me to go, and this thing in my head only has to make one more push, one tiny smiling breath of a push and I'm gone. There are no reserves, there's no fight, no strength. I am ethereal, yet solid in pain. Rooted in pain. There's only the pain to let me know I'm still here. And Michele. Always

Michele. As Doris arrives with her entourage and her knives and hooks and needles and gauze and tubing and yes, the glass manometer, as more lines are prepared, six in my groin, three on each side, as I am readied for the machines that I will in some way become a part of, as I slip away once more, Michele still holding me though the pain has now gone, we know we are at some crossing point. I am no longer me.

What neither of us know is that I have now fallen as far as I'll go.

What neither of us know is that Michele has just begun her fall.

Chapter Three

Happy Birthday

Before we get into this intensive-care malarky remember how I'd been given – very kindly, I'm sure – a little bottle of holy water from the genuine holy Lourdes inside a genuine holy plastic Madonna? Weirdly, for an atheist who thinks Richard Dawkins is something of a Catholic apologist, this gift gave me a bit of comfort. Well, it gave me a bit of a laugh actually, but that's a similar thing. Now, without drawing too many conclusions, I did go downhill quite rapidly after I got it. As gifts go, it was less the peace that passeth all understanding, more a dose of the black death.

This is important, cos if ever anyone needed the power of prayer at this moment, it was me. Except I've just read that in a recent study, 51 per cent of a group of patients being diligently, sincerely prayed for daily, got *worse*. I draw no conclusions.

It's said there are no atheists in foxholes. I sort of thought in a woolly way that was true, but now I'm in a fucking great foxhole with shells going off and mud and blood and shrapnel and shouting everywhere, and not so

*much as a pea-shooter to fight back with, so . . . righto.
I'm ready for God to enter my life and tell me it's going to
be OK. I wait. Nothing. Not even a bit of Vivaldi or Call
Waiting or a message to tell me to hang on a minute cos
the deity will get back to me and my prayer is important
to him. I'm in a bit of a hurry, so is there anyone else up
there? I don't mind what – male, female, three-in-one,
something with the head of a Hindu elephant and the
cock of a randy Roman bull, a sodding great sun-
munching Mexican winged serpent for all I care,
whatever. But no. And there's nothing in me. I can't send
up a prayer. I know there's nothing outside this room that
can help me.*

I'm going to be proved wrong about that. But later . . .

Bear with me in this chapter cos it's a bit gory and it's
best to read some of it with a cushion ready to put over
your face. (That way you'll also get a flavour of my ability
to breathe at this point.) Trust me on this, I know what
happens and it *is* gory. I'll give it an 18 rating. Anyone
under eighteen reading this will not only have nightmares,
but worse, far worse: they won't get the jokes.

But do stick with it through the gore, cos there's a great
climax which you really won't see coming unless some
idiot tips you off and, um, best get on . . .

I need to tell you what ITU looks like and I will, I will,
but I really hate long descriptions. They're only there cos
writers are paid by the word. I remember 'doing' Thomas
Hardy for O-level – see, under-eighteen person, you're lost
already. Now piss off and read *Zoo*. Or *Closer*. I'm not
sexist. I'm assuming you're an under-educated, over-
confident, attention-seeking, attention-deficient fuckwit,
which yes, makes me *something*, but not sexist.

Anger, I'm reminded by Michele, is a good thing. Which is a good thing, cos right now I'm fucking furious. What on earth am I doing here? I've come round, which is a good start, and I don't have a plastic tube shoved in my mouth, which is another tick in the positive-things-that-happened-today smiley box, but I'm connected to so much medical hardware I'm like the Bionic Man's spastic brother. Someone's going to get a good talking to, but hang on, I can't talk. I need to think about this.

I'll get back to ITU in a minute, when my blood pressure goes down, but I was in the middle of something. Oh yes. Old Tozza Hardy spends an entire page in one book describing how some ratty old farmer *smiles*. Now, sorry and all, but I know how people smile. I see them do it every day. Obviously, not directly in front of me, which is perhaps something to address, but I've got a pretty good idea of the general physiognomy of a fucking grin so I don't need five hundred finely honed words about it. Get on with the story, Tom. Where you kill some poor bugger off for no reason whatsoever. Hmmm. Wish I hadn't remembered that last bit.

Actually, what I'm rather cleverly doing here is pointing out in a literary way that there's f— all to do when lying flat on your back strapped half-paralysed to a bunch of beeping machines except let your mind wander about the place. And not *this* place. Any place but this sodding place. You really don't want to be here.

Except, perversely, right at this moment, I do.

I finally feel safe. It's very warm, and there's lots of subdued humming. I'm fed continuously and automatically through a tube and, to complete the baby analogy for those who are a bit slow on the uptake, I'm in a fucking nappy. That's to make the nurses' lives easier. They'd rather change a shitty pair of absorbent wraparound pants at their convenience than, well, bring a convenience to you.

But I quickly come up with another theory of why I feel safe, and it's a damn sight less Freudian. Which makes me feel a bit less uncomfortable, bearing in mind how much time my bloody mother's going to put in by my bedside.

I reckon that most of the worry about being ill is taken up with the fact that you can't get anyone's attention. And you do struggle with that on the NHS. First you can't get seen by a specialist, even though you know that the nasty swelling on your left nostril/bollock/boob is clearly a carcinoma, and once you *are* in hospital, there's the continual nagging worry that you've been forgotten and are being left alone to fester and die quietly in a bed/trolley/car-park/bog.

Not so in intensive care. It's like suicide watch in Strangeways. Big Brother is watching you and praise the Lord. About sodding time.

In the great slabby sixties tower block that is Charing Cross Hospital, there are two ITUs – or, more accurately these days, ICU (standing for Intensive Care Unit, though everyone knows it as ITU – like those other places now known by another name: Myanmar/Burma, Chennai/Madras, Wolverhampton/shithole). Hospitals are very proud of their Intensive Care Units. They're at the sharp end. It's quite glamorous to work there cos it's all a bit more life and death, a bit *ER*. It's glam in the way James Bond is glam – groovy if you're the super secret agent, i.e., super know-all consultant, pretty shitty if you're the lone guard in the black woolly pully with a sudden garrotte around his neck.

Anyway, I'm in the older, twelve-bed ITU. There's a newer, even sexier and groovier six-bedder in another wing, that's probably got more gadgets and vibrating beds and for all I know vibrating nurses, but I never find out. I could make it up, but then where would I be? Oh yes, stuck on a bed unable to move with my attention wandering.

It's very hard to concentrate in here because it's like living inside a new fridge – white, whisper-quiet, but actually full of mysterious electrical noises. I think of myself as the greasy carton of leftover chicken tikka massala you shoved drunkenly at the back of the bottom shelf, having forgotten to a) cover it with cling film and b) turn the bastard fridge on. And then you went travelling. All summer. Basically, this place, with its electronic doors, rubber-gloved staff and cleaners who actually use more than one part per million in their Jif/water mix is a Howard Hughes wet dream. But me? I stink.

I am putrefying so rapidly that I have to have my lungs hoovered on a regular basis. I always thought regular hoovering meant twice a week if the Albanian cleaning lady remembered to turn up. The sucking up of the pus that oozes into my airway is more like every *five minutes*. There is a hole in my tracchy tube and through it a nurse inserts a long, thin, see-through suction tube. It goes right down into my airway. She wiggles it about, there's a noise like a cheap cappuccino-maker with asthma, and great gobbets of green slime streaked with blood are slowly – and visibly – drawn out. To be stored in a big see-through container behind my head. A sort of conversation piece for visitors.

'Oooh, is that your new Pollock? From his greeny-red period? A Tracey Emin bogey installation? No, no, don't tell me, it's a dear Damien Hirst pickled thing gone orff.'

I realise what the container behind me reminds me of. It's A Knockout. Well, most games involved filling a big jar with coloured water, usually blindfold while dressed as a giant Womble. One of those. In green. Which presumably makes me Great Uncle Bulgaria. These hallucinations haven't quite gone, have they?

The pus is due to a combination of pneumonia, pleurisy and the virulent dash of MRSA that I've somehow caught from somewhere. Can't think where there might be bucketloads of MRSA lurking, but bizarrely, against all expectations, I've caught it. The hospital – whoops – superbug. The bastards have also given me nappy rash, but that's the least of my worries.

There's a nasty stinging pain in my stomach and a young doctor has just let slip the chances are the feeding tube has irritated my stomach and given me gastritis. I wonder if there's anything else they're planning to foist on me. A touch of cholera perhaps. Yellow monkey fever? A splash of the Blue Nile virus with a twist of malaria? I know, there hasn't been any smallpox about for a while, and they've got a jar of it in the safe downstairs . . . Go on, you might as fucking well.

The medical staff are starting to pick up on what they refer to as my hostility. They're being nice to me. Which makes me want to kill them. Or cry. I want to go home.

Remember I said you're always monitored? That's not strictly true. There are two nurses always on duty in the ward, and they don't have one of those great big nurses' stations to hide behind like the rest of them, cos these are the border guards, the ever-vigilant front-line troops. Thing is, though, they are only human, which means their attention can wander and then you may overhear far more than you wanted to about their favourite topics, i.e. comparing pay grades, working out their holiday entitlement, moaning about their kids and eating Celebrations. If you want to get the attention of a nurse on an ordinary ward, you press the little red button by your bedside. Then sometime in the near future, depending on other commitments like defibrillating a patient or fighting over the last mini-Twirl, they shimmy over.

Not so here.

Because ITU patients are generally unconscious and because the nurses are supposed to be always watching you, like the Eye of Sauron, you don't get a button. Which means that if you can't move or speak, it can be tricky to get their attention.

I'm in a ward that probably cost twenty million quid to build and a few million a year to run and our solution is to tie a bottle of pills to my cot side. I just rattle the pills with my good hand and over they come. That is, if they've been told the system. Otherwise they spend two hours puzzling over where that funny rattling noise is coming from. And isn't it odd how there's a kind of gurgling going with it?

Beds are called cots because we're as helpless as infants. Each bed is surrounded by banks of machines. I have a blood-pressure cuff permanently ringed about my right arm. It inflates every so often, including in the middle of the night. It's a puffing squeeze that is sometimes disturbing, sometimes oddly comforting. On my index finger is a clip to monitor my oxygen levels. It's on the same side as the cuff, so when the cuff inflates the blood supply is stopped and the alarm goes off. Each time, a nurse runs over, fiddles about a bit, wonders if she should call a doctor, the cuff automatically deflates while she dithers, the alarm stops, the clip is carefully replaced on the same finger.

I should say something, but I quite enjoy the panto. And it makes up for the two-hours-a-day pill-rattling.

Not forgetting the bloody great ventilator – connected via a sharp, hard plastic green box under my chin. I'm also on a heart monitor and there's something strapped to my leg, though for the life of me I can't remember what for. It could be left over from a particularly interesting romp with Michele for all I know, and frankly any more detail about ITU and we're in Thomas Hardy territory. Just a few more: a catheter, naturally, and to complete the cycle, up my nose and into my stomach goes this feeding tube. An NG tube. I feel like a suffragette on hunger strike. Every few seconds a millilitre of thick brown liquid called Jevity is squeezed in. This happens for about fourteen hours a day. Then I get some water, then my stomach is allowed to 'rest'. I watch the bottles drip into me. I watch the drips drip into me. I listen to my ventilator wheezing away. I wait for the pressure cuff to inflate. I count the seconds until my oxygen monitor alarm goes off and watch the nurse rush over. Better than *I'm a Celebrity*, this.

I'm on several drips, obviously. The jury is still out on exactly what this thing in my head might be, so in the meantime they're treating it with everything that can be put through a drip. Up to and including Cillit Bang.

My veins break up – or 'granulate' – regularly as a result of such heavy usage, so there's a daily hunt-the-vein game usually only played by smackheads and members of the cooler rock bands. I soon get to know which staff are good at finding veins – the water diviners, the skilful, firm yet gentle experts who strike gold with their sodding great cannula needles within, say, three attempts – and the others: the bodgers, the ham-fisted, short-sighted, cack-handed buggers who couldn't find a main line at Clapham Junction.

And yet as I recall the needles, it's the smell that comes back and makes me shudder: the aroma of plastic as the blister pack containing the works is popped open; the sickly glue on the sticking plaster that holds the cannula's plastic tubing in place in my vein; the tinniness of both the metal and the blood.

Life is full of coincidences. Some people find God in them. I sympathise with this, having endured one which must have come from the other direction. The first day on ITU, my skin becomes hypersensitive to water. This is a charge my wife has often levelled at me, but be that as it may, this time it's literally true. The smallest droplet seems to pierce like a needle, unlike a real needle, which doesn't hurt until it's really dug in. The very same day – and this'll make you laugh – I begin to sweat. Big, viscous gobbets of cold sweat. Unpleasant enough on its own, but with the added frisson of the whole being-stabbed-with-needles thing as it runs down me. And it pours. I look like a close-up of a Magnum ice cream in an advert.

I'm so wet I have to be changed every few hours. Which means a long process of unhooking me, turning me over a few times to change the sopping sheet underneath me, and hooking me up again. By which time I'm once again covered in sweat. Marvellous.

I can't sleep very well, despite serious sedatives, but I doze a lot and have a recurring nightmare. I am inside a tiny box. It's a first-aid box and I'm sharing the cramped space with the usual gubbins – gauze, bandages, scissors, TCP, syringes, etc. – and I'm waiting for my family to join me. It's utterly real, so much so that even today the memory of it is as fresh as real experiences. Whatever they are. ITU is a hallucinogenic, unreal world at the best of times. Even if you're just visiting it knocks you sideways. But me, I can hardly move, what with the machines, let alone the paralysis. I've got these sweats and this weird skin reaction, and stress and sleep deprivation, so when I wake one day with my head twisted round to find I'm seeing the ward turned 90 degrees so everything is sideways, I'm not frightened but curious. I'm down the rabbit hole and if the Queen of Hearts pops up to chop my head off not only will I not be surprised, I'll sharpen the fucking axe for her.

I try not to pass any of these rather negative thoughts on to my family, particularly James and Tara. Tara's pretty squeamish, bless her, but she makes an effort. As a normal teenager, i.e. stroppy, self-absorbed and gobby, she'd rather do *anything* than be with her parents at the best of times. It's bad enough coming on holiday with us to Tenerife, so this must be torture for her. I try and sympathise. She is genuinely horrified by the state I'm in, and especially by the suctioning. James, a trainee ghoul, on the other hand is fascinated. I let him have a go with the tube and we have a right laugh playing Catch the Bogey until

Michele comes back from the loo and tells me off. Little boys really are made of different stuff.

Poor old Tara. Teenagers are hideous creatures not just because of their hormones but because they're becoming aware that they have to join the adult race. Actually, first they have to rejoin the human race, which they left at the age of twelve. Anyway, Tara's found herself, as sadly many kids do, dropped into the deep end of adult life too soon. We've always tried to protect her, but that bloody word *circumstance*. She's already been through a divorce (not hers, we don't live in Wales), got used to a stepdad who was almost as surprised by the new situation as she was, moved house and school, changed friends, and was just settling down – i.e., perfecting the bedroom-door slam, painting her room black and listening to Nirvana more than was strictly necessary – when *this*.

My memories are one thing; I'm a grown man and I can rationalise them, I can work through them, I can cope. Like an ugly scar or an unfortunate tattoo on your bell-end, memories might be regrettable but you can live with them. But I would give anything to take these memories away from my kids.

I communicate by writing. I write reams of notes – to the doctors, the nurses, my family. I kept them. I have since read them only once, before writing this. There are requests for things: painkillers, a towel, a suction, water. They are often half a conversation, sometimes banal, sometimes not. Sometimes it's easy to work out the response, sometimes one can only marvel at how Michele coped with such conversation-stoppers as:

I'm dying.
I love you.

What saves that page from nauseating mawkishness is that I did a rewrite. I clearly felt a bit better after someone administered – oh, I dunno, a quick rubdown with Vic or something – and under those two sentences I later put:

How fucking melodramatic.

The second or third night here I begin to take more note of the people around me. I don't get much choice, because some poor old git is wheeled in who clearly lost his marbles either before, during, or after major surgery. He's ventilated through his mouth, like most post-operative patients, and spends the whole night moaning and trying to rip out the tube. I don't blame him. It's uncomfortable. The downside to ripping it out is that'll kill him, but after several hours of the noise and the nurses shouting at him to stop it, I'd have gladly yanked the bastard out for him.

It's half-lit night and he's in No Man's Land, hung out on the wire. Pinned. Unrescuable. He's calling for his wife, but she's in another country. He struggles and cries out and I want to sleep. I've slept so little. He goes quiet and I manage to find a position within these hard machines to rest and he starts again and he's pulling his tube and this awful shouty horsey old nurse is telling him off again and again and again but louder, like she's shouting slowly and clearly in plain English at an Indian traffic warden clamping her Volvo. But he's too far away and she's making more noise than him. A murderous rage fills me and I try to move and reach for my rifle, but I'm unarmed and anyway any move could be fatal, and dimly I watch as she ties his hands to his cot sides and now there's a rustle of blue-aproned nurses around him and finally, mercifully, he falls silent.

Next day the old cunt's sitting up chatting to his missus like nothing's happened.

The thing about moving to a new ward is there's a new team – and now *teams* – of people to get to know. And to get the best out of them – as a relative *and* as a patient – you do have to get to know them and get on with them. Sometimes that's easy; occasionally in the health service you come up against people whose teeth you wouldn't piss on if their mouth was on fire. Fortunately for me, in ITU there were far more of the former.

I'm now in the hands of the ITU consultants. I suspect there's some kind of rivalry between my neuro team and the ITU folk. I'm not sure on what basis, but I imagine the ITU bunch have now taken over in the way the FBI step in when the hard-working but resource-strapped local coppers can't quite manage to clear up the mystery of the Tuscaloosa shoelace strangler. It's all a bit, 'We're here now. You've had long enough and look where it's got you. Step aside from the body and get me a bagel with lox over easy, sweetcakes,' or however it is they speak. I dunno. Michele watches these things constantly on Sky, despite me reminding her there's a perfectly good episode of *Top Gear* on Living Motors UK G2+1 or something. At this point she tends either to cop a deaf one or smugly hand me the controls. Which is worse, because I can't work it. Nothing to do with my remaining disability, I've just never figured it out. So it's back to the macho antics of the guys and girls in the sharp suits and the chemistry lab that looks like it's been funded by Roman Abramovich in one of his more generous moments.

They must have one of those über-labs attached to ITU, because tests are done within hours. And do they love a test in intensive care. Results of my daily blood and urine tests are back before lunch, and the same speed is seen with my twice-daily chest X-rays. Twice a day! And they always forget the lead shielding over my meat and two veg. When the lights are turned off my gonads are so radioactive it's a wonder they don't light up like the Regent Street Christmas decorations.

Now when you, as a normal slightly sick patient, wonder why it takes a month to get any info about your scabby leg or cloudy water, it's cos those bloody bed-blockers in intensive care take priority, matey. And don't you forget it.

Throwing a sartorial spanner in this FBI theory is my real consultant, Mark Palazzo. Who looks like a pizza maker. Or an escapee from a Super Mario Brothers game. Short, round, and with thick stubby fingers you really don't want up your bum. Fortunately, he shows no inclination for rectal wanderings, which makes him pretty unique in the medical field. (And in telly, but that's a different and potentially libellous story.) I like Mark. Despite my ill-concealed fury at my situation, I do like him. He's smart, funny, competent, and spends time talking to me. Rather, he talks to me and waits while I write something back. Without interrupting. He can also take a joke. Which is just as well. When he's on call, some of the more dopey nurses seem to be on the ball too. He even puts up with Mum continually getting his name wrong. And ordering a twelve-inch spicy with anchovies.

Lovely, bonkers old Doris does the rounds too. I never know whether she's *actually* an ITU consultant or whether everyone's too scared of her not to let her in. She spends most of her time checking my tracchy and smiling to herself. She always trails edgy young trainee surgeons behind her, hanging back just out of scalpel reach. Tell you what, you'd always let her carve at Christmas. Obviously there's always the risk that what she'd be carving is Auntie Elsie.

The third regular is a woman it's hard to take to. Big, shouty, horsey. She'd probably describe herself, in the village where she no doubt lurks, as 'colourful'. I bet she has a black Range Rover, two golden retrievers, sixteen pairs of green wellies, a rowing blue and a red-nosed husband who's rapidly losing his hearing and who, if he's got any sense, spends most of his time on the putting green. And I'd bet my mortgage no one has ever dared try to pot her brown.

She's the sort of doctor who reads your chart out to her acolytes before shouting good morning at you over your head and might then deign to bend over and bawl, 'How are we today? A bit better? Good, good, keep it up,' before galumphing off, her great fat hooray arse in your face.

I wrote her a note one day. It took a while and I could see her junior staff – most of whom had got to know me a bit by now – watching as I wrote. Some started giggling cos they were ahead of the game. But she went on, declaiming loudly about my SATs, magnesium levels, white cell count, blah blah, until finally she turned to me, by now quietly holding up my pad. On it I had written in great big shouty, council-house, comprehensive-school letters:

I'M DOWN HERE, AND I'M NOT FUCKING DEAF.

There was a pause. A junior doctor stuffed a rubber glove in her mouth, shaking; others were open eyed. All were enjoying the moment and waiting to see what would happen next. Her expression was . . . expressionless. She came over the bed. She loomed down, her big fat face next to mine. She gave out a hoarse whisper. Or in her case a horse whisper. But at any rate she said, 'Feeling better today then?' and she rewarded us all with a huge smile. Which I thought was fair enough. She was less of a cow afterwards. Which goes to show.

Being inside the system for so long gave me an us-and-them mentality I've never managed to shake off. A bit like an old lag in Winson Green. Little victories, that's what you're after. You can't escape unless Ronnie and the boys have organised a chopper to lift you out of the exercise yard, and Ronnie and the boys are, as well you know, larging it up in Marbella drinking a toast to absent friends. But you can win little victories: a gambling game here, some smuggled fags there, a quick half-hour with a copy of *Razzle*, something.

It's also left me with an uncontrollable urge to get one in first. Get the bastards on the back foot, get their attention and force them to recognise you as human. A bolshie annoying human, perhaps, but one they have to pay attention to.

My opening gambit these days when meeting a new GP

or specialist or physio or whatever is to stick the metaphorical boot in right away, just before they start thumbing listlessly through your notes and are preparing to sigh that sigh of: 'Oh, another sickie. I suppose I should see it.' If they are quite young, I might begin with the cheerily offensive opener, 'When's your dad coming?' which usually plays well. There's a great all-purpose 'Oh it's *you*, is it?' delivered after they tell you their name. That always brings out their latent paranoia, medicine being so fiercely competitive. If they answer, 'Why, what have you heard? Who's told you?' you've won. Although, on the minus side, that sets you off wondering just what it is they *have* done – and a patient's paranoia does trump a medic's.

So you can't really win. But like losing out on parole, or getting a bit of solitary, it's sometimes worth it.

In every horrible situation – school, prison, living in Wolverhampton, being held hostage by the PLO, Christmas with the in-laws – there's always someone who makes it bearable. Someone you learn to trust. It might be your English teacher, a kindly warder, a sympathetic terrorist, or just Doris whipping something out of Auntie Elsie after she's nodded off during the Queen's speech. In here, that person was the male charge nurse called Gerard. He was not the butchest of individuals – but when he was on duty he didn't half run things with efficiency, precision, and a genuine, fierce protective care for his patients. He had suctioned my lungs when they collapsed, and I think he felt responsible for me not being dead. The nights I knew he was on duty, I slept easier. As any long-term patient will tell you, there's no higher praise.

He also gave great advice. He told Michele two very

important things. Firstly, that recovery moves like a wavy line going slowly upwards – it might seem some days that things are worse, but the trend is always up.

Thank you for that. Thank you, on the days when things go down.

And secondly, he told her to go back to work. Not just so she wouldn't lose her job, but for her sanity and mine. I needed, he said, to hear normal things every day. To talk about things in the outside world. To know there was more than *this*.

And to know her conversation wouldn't be as fucking boring as my mum's.

Of which more later. It can wait – her conversation never varied much. It was hardly Stephen Fry standard because all she did every day was come in on the Number 33 and sit by my bed. Sometimes I pretended to be asleep just so she'd bugger off for a fag and stop talking about the Number 33 bus route.

A small note here: occasionally you're watching the news and there's a report from a war zone or other interestingly governed regime and the reporter is at pains to tell you that the price of access to the scene of whatever unpleasantness he's about to beam into your sitting room is that 'this report has been compiled within the restrictions of the ruling junta' or some such pusillanimous cant. Then, reporters being the devious little buggers we know them to be, they'll also slip in some clues as to the real story, perhaps showing a grainy film smuggled out up a dissident's bum. Bearing all that in mind, I'd like to point out several things: Mum now lives with us. She managed to get her hands on an early draft of this tome. She often makes me cups of tea, *unsupervised*.

Entirely unconnected to this, I think it is my filial duty to say *my mother is an intelligent, articulate woman who for many years held down a responsible managerial job.*

Admittedly that managerial job was in the NHS but I'm sure the irony is lost on me, as that organisation is in a fine and robust state today. Fortunately Mum has quite a decent sense of humour, but even so I'm not touching any cappuccino she'll be offering for quite a while yet . . .

One of the many reasons Michele's under so much pressure with my illness is that there are hundreds of different ways I can take a turn for the worse. The only constant is that I keep doing it. It's like commuting. You know your train will be late three times a week, but it's never for the same reason. There's a power failure at Stoke Poges, trees on the line at Sevenoaks, a drunk train driver at Ashford International, an escaped nude lunatic running up and down the track at Pitlochry, a misalignment of Gemini in the house of Pisces on the 26th, a fucking comet in the outer horseshoe nebula. The reasons are always different but the result is the same: you get home long after the kids have gone to bed, clutching your P45 for being continually, if imaginatively, late.

Michele realises that the doctors are only firefighting – treating symptoms as they come up and bite me on the bum, not getting to the heart of the problem and finding a cure. She knows that they're doing a great job in tackling each new problem, but also knows their knowledge and resources are finite. And one day they won't have an answer.

The key, of course, is to get a diagnosis. There are by now fourteen neurologists on the case. That's hundreds of years of experience, based on millions of hours of the best medical research from clinical trials all over the world, involving thousands of patients and decades of lab work.

And they're buggered if they know.

Yes, I know we've been told I've got a demyelinating lesion, which sounds grand but in fact is a scientific statement of the bleeding obvious. It's the equivalent of an electrician saying your toaster's exploded when there's a bloody great hole in your Dualit and bits of flaming Kingsmill all over the place setting fire to the dog. It's the 'why' we're after, not the 'what'.

And there's some disagreement about what has caused this lesion. Actually it's a right rumpus, academically. They're an odd bunch, neurologists. Most of their work seems to be carried out post-mortem, which, I suspect, is how they prefer it. Unfortunately for them, I'm refusing to get mortem in the first place. Of the fourteen egg-heads, seven now think I've got a tumour. Because of its position, this will soon make me very mortem indeed. The other seven think this is just a one-off, slightly mysterious event, probably caused by the ubiquitous 'virus'. The seven fancying the tumour option think this is a cop-out and place bets that they are right. The man in the path lab with the thick plastic apron warms up his electric saws, and we wait. Either way, they all reckon, we're soon going to know.

Michele picks up this new tone – i.e., 'He's doomed, don't start reading him any long books' – the very next day. As she's admitted on to the ward, waddling a bit now that our baby is starting to make her presence felt, no one meets her eye. Know that feeling when you're about to be fired cos of one too many broken rails at Newport Pagnell and by the time you arrive at the office everyone else knows and you've already been Tippexed out of the Lottery syndicate? And you walk in and everyone seems ever so interested in the new bit of carpeting by the water cooler? And you get to your desk to find some empty crates and a few bin liners by the door? And there's a Post-it with 'Can you pop in to see me – signed your erstwhile boss' on the phone?

That feeling.

And the boss is of course the urbane Dr Lane, trailing poor old Alidz in his wake. Alidz can't take her puffy eyes off Michele's bump, because here comes my P45.

Except . . . except . . . they have a cunning plan, apparently. It's about as good as Baldrick's but I've already sort of agreed to it the night before. I was lying there, for want of anything better to do, when up pads Dr Lane with his pal, a small, portly Indian chappie in a suit called Tipu Aziz. He's clearly very important because Dr Lane defers to him like Charlie Boorman showing off Ewan McGregor. Professor Aziz has a plan to find out what's in my brain. By taking a bit of it out. While I'm not only alive, but *awake*. This is considered a great honour, because he's the only man in the country who can do this.

Leaving aside the fact that it used to be a great honour to hop into a giant wicker man every year in Orkney, I'm impressed. The procedure will work like this:

I'm propped up in a bed and my head is put in a cage similar to the one at the end of *1984*. But instead of adding a rat, they'll ram a Black & Decker down into the top of my skull. I'll be watching images on a TV screen and hoping they're doing a better job with the drill than I did the last time I put some coat hooks up.

In the resulting hole, using a robotic, computer-controlled wire, old Prof Aziz will root about at the back of my brain until he finds the medulla. He'll dig about in there for a bit until he comes to the damaged area. Then, you know those fairground games where you guide a big grab handle on to a pile of toys and you singularly fail to capture the gonk? Just like that he'll grab a piece of brain and bring it out. I need to watch the screen all the time so that if I go blind he'll know he's arsed it up and phone the hospital's legal team, making sure they do some duplicate statements in Braille. Same if I start asking for my Stretch Armstrong and a packet of Blackjacks. If I ask for the complete works of Jeffrey Archer, I've signed a form saying they can shoot me in the head immediately.

The problem with this technique – wait, I'll rephrase that: one of the many problems with this technique – is that it's insanely dangerous. Everything could be damaged if the wire's fractions of millimetres out. Speech, hearing, sight, touch, movement. And even if the fantastic voyage is successful, the bit of brain he takes out can never grow back. The technique will destroy cells that might otherwise one day repair themselves. If, of course, they're not lying on a Petri dish somewhere.

I'm told the risks: there's a 20 per cent chance of permanent injury of one kind or another, and a 5 per cent fatality rate. That's 20–1. I back 20–1 horses in the Grand National. Sometimes I win.

And as the wire is burrowing its way through the old grey matter, who knows what memories are going to end up on the cutting-room floor? I mean, there's one or two I'd quite happily pay him to chuck out, particularly one involving half a pint of Smirnoff and a girl with a moustache – please God it was a girl – and there's quite a lot about my primary school, Rough Hay County Primary and Community Borstal, I'd be happy to see in slices on a lab bench. But the memories I *could* lose . . .

After the visit, that night, after I've sort of said yes but before they've got my written consent, I make a list. It's ostensibly about memories I don't want to lose but it rapidly becomes an inventory. Have I done enough with my thirty-odd years? Have I trodden that less-travelled road, smelled the flowers, climbed every mountain and forded every stream? Course I fucking haven't. What I have been doing is dicking about and having quite a nice time with as little effort as possible. There are memories I'd *like* to have – generally involving my Oscars getting in the way while I snort cocaine off Angelina Jolie's babylons – but I still want to keep the best I've got.

In no particular order I come up with:

1. The first time I kissed Michele. (Oh be fair, she's going to read this.)
2. The first time I kissed Michele. (Really, really.)
3. Standing with hundreds of thousands on the Berlin wall, midnight, New Year's Eve 1989/90, just in front of the Brandenburg Gate, the world changing around us by the second. A deeply moving, joyous epochal moment only slightly spoiled by David Hasselhoff, in a crane, miming a pop song that he reckons brought about the collapse of the entire communist system. He might have been right; if the CIA promised to jam the airways throughout Russia with it, no wonder they all came out shouting 'Perestroika! We give in. Show us the way to the fast-food joints and titty bars.'

4. Causing a small riot in a French bar during a gig, man.

5. The view on Waterloo Bridge on a clear morning on my way to my bestest ever job. I say morning, I had this great thing going once in telly where my timekeeping wasn't a major priority, so it may have been a clear lunchtime. In fact, I did once show up at 5.45 p.m., to which my lovely hardworking colleague Gareth wryly commented, 'Any later and you'd have been in tomorrow.'

6. Going out with my grandfather to collect some 'carry-out' beer from the Red Lion. He'd always stop for a quick one and I'd stand in the corridor between the bar and the snug with a bag of scratchings. I was just tall enough to peep over the serving hatch and yes, there was sawdust and yes, there were old men in caps, and the light was smoke-yellow and warm and the beer was nut-brown and the smell of the hops was the sour smell of a sweet night. And I still miss that man with an ache and no, I'm not going to see him again and so he only lives in my memory cells and so—

Enough of that. Numbers 7–124 have been edited on the grounds of moral decency, for avoidance of divorce proceedings and the fact that by now my catheter was starting to hurt.

Next morning, Michele and her bump are told of the biopsy plan and she's not convinced. She phones my doctor friend Phil, who says something brilliant, something that should be tattooed on the back of every patient's eyelids. He says, 'Always ask what the benefit will be to Nigel.' (If you are planning on the tattoo, please remember to insert your own name.) Phil's theory being that doctors are simply curious beasts and will always try and find out *stuff*, whether or not it's of any practical value.

So Shell beards Dr Lane in his lair. He tells her the biopsy will determine if my lesion has been caused by a tumour, and hence stop the huge weekly rows between the fourteen warring neurologists. Apparently it got so heated last week a teacup was almost knocked over. Clearly this cannot go on. She must see that.

She doesn't, actually. What will change, she asks, if it's found to be a tumour?

Ah. Well, he admits, nothing. Cos there's nothing they could do. I'd have had it.

So she presses the point. The practical advantage of this dangerous procedure is . . . ?

She called off the biopsy. It had already been pencilled in. She unpencilled it and she and her bump came back to sit by me and told me not to agree to anything without her *ever again*. Which I agreed to. And which reminds me, I should look into that deal again some time.

Things hang in the balance. The medics agree to wait and see, because something's going to happen quite soon anyway. I'll either stop getting worse or be dead in a few days. There's no real third way and it's becoming increasingly clear to Michele which side of the coin most people are betting on. So she decides to do something about it.

And what she does is extraordinary. This is over and above the daily extraordinary things she is doing, the stuff that is taking a mental and physical toll on her, and for which she is going to pay heavily. Not now, but later. She has never given up, she has never cried in front of me, she has kept the closest eye on my care, she has hectored, she has bullied, she has charmed the staff until I am the one getting the best care, the most attention. My left hand is now twisted, clawed and held tight to my chest. She's told it needs regular massaging or it will stay clawed for ever. So every day, for hours, she massages and pulls and manipulates my hand and fingers, willing movement back into them. She's doing all but breathe for me, and in the nights when breath is short I know she's doing that too and I rest a little easier.

And she has another life outside this weird, awful place. She has two children at home, she has a baby growing inside her and we're both silently aware that the stress and the exposure to so much sickness can only be putting at risk our much-wanted unborn baby. She also has a successful career and looks after many actors, some of whom you'd have heard of. Actors like to know they are at the centre of their agent's life. Michele is taking days off work, she's leaving early, she's not seeing her actors give their all at the RSC with a damp towel around their neck. By Christmas, several will already have left. But not the ones you've heard of . . .

I must, in the interests of journalistic fairness, state that many of Michele's clients – some of whom were already mates, others who are just very, very nice people – went on to play a blinder. From the actress who immediately offered a rather enormous loan – I dunno, maybe she thought we could bribe a better second opinion out of someone – to those who thought a charity fundraiser might be more appropriate (and obviously far more cost-effective), from those who turned up at my bedside with terrible books or films to those who just turned up at my bedside with terrible forced smiles, it was all gratefully received. Even if I appeared really pissed off at the time. And I'd name names, only as the acting fraternity is notoriously publicity shy I can't.

They'd *hate* it.

She's being pulled all ways and she hardly sleeps. Mum and our dopey but willing au pair are helping bail out our little sinking ship, but all the responsibility lies with Michele and she knows I am at crisis point. She makes a decision. Right, she says to herself, fourteen of the country's top neurologists have given up on Nigel. I'll find one who won't.

And bugger me she does.

6 a.m., Heathrow airport, a few days later. Michele is standing with my uncle, waiting for the man considered to be the world expert on brain diseases, Dr Patrick Kelly, to arrive from New York. He was flying to Stockholm to pick up some prize from an obscure body called the Nobel Institute, but after one telephone call from Michele he's agreed to see her during his stopover at Heathrow to examine my notes and scans instead of wandering off for a cup of coffee and a bagel. *Two* phone calls from her and he'd probably have agreed to have me legally adopted, but that's by the by.

She tracked him down after Dr Phil put her in touch with a woman whose daughter had been diagnosed with an inoperable brain tumour. Turns out what's inoperable in the UK is an exciting challenge in the US, where they have a rather more muscular health service. Doris would like it there. (And she could do a little moonlighting as a researcher on *Nightmare on Elm Street 8*.) Dr Kelly had helped this woman's daughter, and she gave Michele his email address. She had him in her sights. The poor bloke never stood a chance.

So far, so marvellous and high-tech and groovy. But of course, Michele then came up against good old British jobsworth work-to-rule, we-do-it-our-way-whoops-another-one-for-the-body-bag bureaucracy. Kelly was landing early in the morning. The hospital wouldn't let her have my notes or scans. They weren't her property, they were theirs. So ya boo sucks. Turns out they were worried she might lose them.

She was dumbfounded. *Lose them?* The details on her husband's condition? The stuff they needed to keep him alive? What did they think she was going to do? Leave them in a lap-dancing club while she went for her evening gyrate? Auction them on eBay? Put 'em on *Car Booty*? The hospital bosses held their legally correct, morally disgusting ground. By this point it was 8 p.m. Kelly's plane was due to land in ten hours.

So she nicked them.

You might think that this feat would only be possible with the connivance of a doctor, say a very nice junior doctor whose name escapes me and who put his career on the line by doing this. But no, for any twopenny lickspittle lawyers out there, she did it all on her own, got that?

This non-existent doctor, had he existed, would have reminded her that on no account could she copy them, so it's further proof of his non-existence that at around midnight Michele crashed into the drunken, dying embers of a dinner party at the only friends of ours who had a photocopying machine, to copy them. Our bleary friends were startled, presumably, but bless them, they got the machine to work despite the six bottles of Chablis and a nice '90 Meursault they'd just chugged.

Shell then crashed out at home for a couple of hours before heading off to the airport at around 4 a.m. My uncle drove, partly out of kindness, partly because as an ex-copper he recognised someone on the edge when he saw them and was keen to keep death off the roads.

So there they were, at the gate, watching the New York red-eye disgorge its tired passengers. Kelly wasn't on first class. Shell had made a huge banner, just in case the bloke who'd changed his entire transatlantic schedule wasn't looking out for her. By now the plane was almost empty and Michele had bobbed up in front of a dozen startled men in smart suits, all of whom backed away from this crazed little blonde thing as if she was offering them timeshares in a Baghdad apartment block.

Then there was a tap on her shoulder. A leprechaun in a flat cap was standing before her, barely reaching her chin. His stubby little spud-grubbing hands jabbed at the notes. 'Are they for me?'

So, by the light of the Avis rent-a-car sign – the only light in the vicinity strong enough to see the scans by – this little, slightly railroaded surgical genius made two pronouncements:

1. This is not a tumour.
2. If I'm wrong, and it is, it's not inoperable. I'll prove it by operating.

They shook hands, he said goodbye and he vanished. Not literally. He's not *really* an Irish mythical spirit. I mean he scuttled off to get the next flight to Stockholm and sanity. (And before Michele could talk him into anything else, like, for example, taking UK citizenship so he could do me on the NHS.)

The effect of his diagnosis on me, though, was magical. It was the first good news. And there was a galvanising effect on the medical team at Charing Cross. Blimey, I was worth saving. With the tumour off the table the neurologists began to focus on a new theory: that my white cells are, for some reason, attacking the myelin in my brain. My drugs are changed and Alidz suggests an experimental and hugely expensive treatment – plasma exchange. She's read about it in *Last-Chance-Saloon Digest*. The staff start looking at Michele again.

Everything's going swimmingly, the wheels are being put in motion and it's now my birthday. In a couple of hours my family are coming in. In a few days the plasma-pheresis bloodsucking machine will have been brought down from Castle Dracula or Doris's shed or wherever it's stored and I'll be hooked up to it. I think I'm feeling a little better and the sweats are less severe, but the gastritis is really playing up, so I ask – well, beg – the doctor on call for some stronger painkillers.

The only thing stronger than what I'm on is morphine. So he gives me that. It stops the pain.

And puts me in a coma.

Chapter Four

Merry Christmas

Shit last words are one thing, shit last memories quite another. Now be honest – you, like the rest of us, have thought about how you'd like to go. The last scenario – the closing moments of your final reel. I don't mean brooding on it, like when you're a teenager, listening to Nirvana/Nick Drake/Leonard Cohen/Kylie in a very dark bedroom after your parents have stopped you doing something *all* your friends can do and knowing that they'll be sorry at your funeral ha that'll show 'em the bastards. No. I mean everyone has come up with their ideal way to say Goodbye cruel world. Admit it, go on. No one's looking.

Of course this changes over time. Younger folk may think wrapping a Porsche Spyder round a tree at 100mph is quite cool. Young ladies may well think being shagged to oblivion by Robbie Williams is not the worst way to go. (With Shell it's the young Gene Hackman but the principle's the same.) Public schoolboys probably fancy being Hector or Ajax or Jif, or whoever it is that kills lots of Greeks heroically before embracing the still, cool waters of Lethe. (Older public schoolboys probably have more chance being spanked to death by Miss Whackalot in a Muswell Hill semi whilst sucking on a satsuma, but that's another story entirely.)

Problem is, the live-fast-die-young-leave-a-beautiful-corpse philosophy looks good on a T-shirt, but living fast and dying young sadly means you *won't* leave a beautiful corpse but a mangled or vomit-stained or beer-bloated or otherwise hideously disfigured one. Cos young people are *hard to kill*. They bounce back from pretty much anything, so they have to go some to knock themselves on the head. As you get older and wiser you generally look forward to something more genteel, and more importantly, a long, long way off.

Oh, and I don't mean those take-me-now moments. They're not planned, they land on you like a tractor dropped from a 747, and then almost before you realise you were perfectly, unimprovably happy and wouldn't it be OK to go now – they're gone. The times when life has smiled upon you so heartily that things cannot possibly get better. For some it's the birth of their first child – for blokes it's more likely to be the conception, but anyway. You may only have a handful of these moments, but by Christ they make the rest of the time worth trudging through, don't they? Mondays, tax demands, mortgage application forms, trying to change your bank, call centres, ITV1, *hospitals*. Savour those moments, bottle them, hold them tight to you. In a quiet moment, alone, release them. Smell, taste, feel, *remember*. Good, eh? Now get off your arse and make some more, you lazy bugger.

I had an ideal last-moment scenario. It was holding hands with my lovely missus while we're sprightly nonagenarians, watching the sun go down over our cypress trees as we sip the last of our own-label wine at our hideously expensive, well-appointed and much-loved Tuscan villa – a gift from the Nobel Institute as they didn't think the prize was big enough. I still haven't managed to improve on it. Tell a lie, I have – but the wife won't let me do it.

What I actually got when my time almost came – and, knowing my luck, what I'll end up with when the time *does* come – was hallucinating about appearing in *Celebrity Squares* with Les Fucking Dennis. And this after a morphine overdose. So all you young rockers out there, thinking the needle's pretty cool and groovy, think on. Yes, you might end up giving it loads of 'Smells Like Teen Spirit' with Kurt and Sid, but you may just as easily find yourself on *Blankety Blank* with Terry Wogan trying to shove Ronnie Corbett up your arse.

I could not fucking *believe* it. One minute there's a nice well-meaning medic whacking several cc's of top-grade smack into me – which did, incidentally, kill the pain from the gastritis, so well done old boy – the next thing I know I'm up in a box with Les, Lennie Bennett, Keith Harris and his bastard green budgie and assorted other light-entertainment stars. I swear if I'd seen Jeanette Krankie it would have pushed me over the edge. No Jimi Hendrix to greet me with a bloody great spliff and a bit of 'Voodoo Chile', no Keith Moon asking me to have a jam, no angular New York punks, no French poets, no John Wilmot, Earl of Rochester, no De Quincey or even Sherlock sodding Holmes. No, it's Paul Daniels and me trying to remember the capital of Lithuania while Les is gurning over us. If that doesn't bring you back from the brink pronto I don't know what will.

Actually, that didn't bring me back. It was my thirty-seventh birthday and I was desperate to see my kids. They came. I'd been getting a bit better, remember? I managed to stay awake and compos just long enough to open their presents and say Just what I wanted and Have you kept the receipt? before things started going quite Pete Tong. They were ushered out and driven home by a friend. Michele and Mum were also shown the door, but were ominously told to wait. After an hour or so they were allowed back and my medical team admitted things weren't going according to plan. Viz: they were unable to wake me.

By now Les D. had buggered off and I remember finally being quite at peace. Maybe that old guff about the waters of Lethe isn't such cobblers after all. But let me state now: there was no lead kindly white light, no tunnel, no gates, pearly or otherwise, no gentle voice, no Our Fathers – elephant-headed or many-armed – no nervous virgins in gardens, no beery geezers in mead halls, no giants, dragons or unicorns, no Aslan, no cherubim, seraphim, dominions or thrones, no one waiting to bung my soul into a rat, a dog or, worse, a young conservative for another go round. No nothing. Which, after all the shouting and prodding and pain and fear, was rather a relief.

Back in the land of the living, there was quite a crowd gathering. My entire team, plus a hovering Doris and the ashen-faced doctor who'd given me the morphine, were trying to bring me round. What my smack dealer hadn't known was that my lesion was in absolutely the wrong place for me to be given opiates. The morphine suppressed my breathing, even with the ventilator. The poor bugger wasn't to know, but that didn't make either of us feel any better.

Know what did it? After sternum rubs, drugs, shakings and Doris whipping off a spare arm to see if I flinched (joke), Michele got really pissed off. She took hold of me, shook me like a terrier greeting a small rodent and said, very loudly and angrily, 'Nigel! Wake up. You're scaring everyone.'

I woke up. And asked what all the fuss was about.

I know this reveals quite a lot about our relationship, but there are several ways to interpret it. So I try not to think about it too much, except to say, Thanks, baby.

I kept drifting in and out of consciousness for the next twenty-four hours. I got irritated by all these buggers waking me up until they accepted that the next sleep I was going to go into wasn't the sleep of the just. Doris never went home. She kept popping in and I couldn't help suspecting she had a plan as to how to wake me if I dropped off again, so that helped keep my eyes open. The poor sod who'd given me the morphine never left the ward. I liked him. He'd always been kind. He was a good doctor. He'd made a mistake. It happens. He wasn't careless or negligent, he wasn't dirty, infectious, supercilious, stupid or cruel. Quite the opposite. Just recently he'd recommended a change of antibiotic which my lungs had responded well to. There was less suctioning. Maybe down to every fifteen minutes. Top man.

When I recovered from my coma a couple of days later, he'd resigned from ITU medicine. I think that was a mistake and I wish him well.

ITU's tough on everyone. And my time there was far from over.

'Mistletoe and Wine'

Were sadly lacking over the next few weeks. Instead I was treated to my course of plasma exchange – plasma-pheresis, to be accurate. I think I was only the second person to get this treatment at Charing Cross. The other poor sod had something called Guillain-Barre Syndrome.

Guillain-Barre. I ask you. It makes you long for the days when you were just poorly. These thousands of obscurely named ailments just remind you there's so much weird shit out there waiting to get you. And the doctors name it all. They're not so hot at curing things, but bugger me, give 'em a new disease, a thesaurus and a rhyming dictionary and watch them burn the midnight oil.

They should follow the Australian method of naming stuff. When the Aussies discovered a great big sandy desert in Western Oz they must have thought for seconds before naming it the Great Sandy Desert. And you'll never guess what the Snowy Mountains are famous for – or fuck-me-sideways-Bruce-it's-boiling-here-mate-town. Saves a lot of time. And I may well be running out of it. I mean, what is everyone doing now? They've stopped most of my drugs except the ubiquitous antibiotics and industrial-strength painkillers, so I assume I'm in a shed-load of pain in real life cos I'm in quite a lot even with them, but let's not dwell. Now everyone's just hanging about waiting. There's less fuss. It's like everyone's holding their breath. Is this good? I suspect not. Why don't they do something?

And they do. They do the plasma thing. And guess what? It doesn't half come sharp.

We're entering the realms of experimental medicine

now. So that's me, the mouse with a human ear growing out of its backside, the sixty-a-day beagle and the two-headed baboon. Science fiction, almost. But the machine that's finally wheeled in looks more like a tea trolley. Or science fiction as seen in 1930s *Flash Gordon* films. Forty grand a pop for this? It's rubbish. It looks like the love child of a milk float and an Austin Allegro. They've bought it off Del Boy, surely. They can't really expect me to get hooked up to this piece of—

Oh. They've hooked me up to it. Via ugly, bloody tubes going into my groin. There are only two or three people who have the high level of training and skill required to operate this fantastically complex bit of machinery. Sadly, today appears to be their day off. I've got a muppet and the thing won't work.

The lines are getting blocked with my sticky blood. There's fiddling, swearing, and I think a quick call to the AA before we're ready to go. Six dark-red milk bottles – a pint each – are ready to be put into me, at the same time as my own filthy, sick blood is taken out. My evil plasma is washed/centrifuged out, and good, five-star, BMA-approved, *Appellation Contrôlée* A negative is gurgled back in. Not to be too scientific, I think the idea is to calm down my hyperactive white cells by taking them on the equivalent of a holiday to Center Parcs. Using so much blood I'm warned there is a small risk of HIV, but then again there's a fucking huge risk of me curling up my toes and joining the choir invisible if I don't try this anyway, so on with the show.

Here's a quick chemistry lesson. It's a bit complex so I'll try to make it brief. This machine also takes calcium out of you. The highly trained operator has to put some in before starting the process. If they don't put the right amount in it really, really hurts. And this process leaches all the painkillers from your system at the same time . . .

Bearing in mind that this is a new procedure, each patient is different and I've got a bizarre condition, there's no blame attached to this, but oh my God this really, really comes sharp. Worse than a lumbar-puncture sharp. Worse than breaking my thumbs as a kid. Worse than coming off my bike and breaking my fall with my face.

The entire procedure takes just under an hour. The first bottleful is removed/replaced OK. There's a slight ache in my left side. Shell and my uncle are here and I try not to upset them by going Ouch too much. Clearly I'm failing cos their faces suddenly blanch. But no, they've just noticed the sheets ooze red and we stop and fiddle with the leaking lines. We continue.

The second bottleful makes my left side stiff and sore. I can take it.

The third bottleful and I stop telling jokes. I start to shake. I snatch a look at Michele. She's biting her lip. She sees me watching and smiles.

The fourth and my bones are cracking. I am being ground to dust. My uncle, a big old-fashioned man-of-the-world seen-it-all-m'lud copper looks like a child about to cry. He's appalled. Michele smiles gently, bless her. Inside, her bones break with mine.

The fifth and I cannot speak because I'm afraid of the sound that will emerge. My body goes into spasm. It's nearly over, but the lines block again and there's more delay, more spurting of blood, more clever manipulation by this woman who *does* know what she's doing but at this moment wishes she wasn't doing it. She's pale, she's sweating, she knows she's my torturer and keeps saying she's sorry, but I can hardly hear her.

The sixth and I am somewhere I did not know existed. I'm begging the operator to stop. Even Dr Matt, the emotional equivalent of a Psion pocket organiser, is shaken. In an astonishing display of passion, he's gone quietly white. He turns to the operator and tells her to switch the wretched thing off. Enough, already. She does. Thanks, Matt.

For half an hour afterwards I'm held by Michele as I shake uncontrollably. Eventually I quieten. I'm given sedatives, painkillers, and the normal pain, the suctioning, the sickness, the headaches, the failing eyesight all seem like paradise. Michele never lets me see what this does to her. She hides it for years, but there will be a time when I will hold her in the same way. As she shakes with the pain that will always be our pain.

I had six more of these procedures over the next couple of months. By the end we knew how much calcium to add, and what sort of painkillers to whack into me before we started to make the time just fly by. I also always stopped after the fifth bottle. Call me chicken if you like. Or a turkey, as we're almost at the season to be jolly.

And I get an early pressie. Instead of taking yet another predictable daily turn for the worse, I wake up one morning from whatever hideous nightmare the God of Making Nigel Have a Shit Night has inflicted upon me to find – Ha! The fingers on my left hand are freer. I'm not dreaming – I once had one exceedingly cruel dream where I was at home, better – I'm awake. I try to wiggle them. They don't take much notice, they give me the surly

'What?' you get when you tap your teenager on the shoulder while they're trying to choose a PlayStation game – get off Dad no I don't want to go to Waterstone's I haven't got Final Meltdown Fantasy Seventeen and it's only 45 quid lend it us I took the dog for a walk two weeks ago didn't I?

I keep tapping and there's an answer from my spastic digits. OK, it's not ideal – my fingers are bending the wrong way for a kick-off, but I've finally got their attention! *This is big news*. When Michele waddles in – God, she's already enormous and not due for four months – I write my news on my pad. I try to show her my new trick. She can see what I can. They *are* moving better. She's thrilled. Fortunately, today is a Dr Lane day. Michele waits for him. He finally appears, like David Niven entering the Monte Carlo casino. This is his world and he knows it. He sits by my cot and we show him my five-finger trick. I wait for the applause. There's a pause. He's not thrilled. He'd like to be, I know, but this is crushing. He still thinks I've got a busted flush, or put all my chips on the wrong colour or whatever it is they do in Monte Carlo casinos. He leaves, a little sadly. Michele grabs my hand. 'You're getting better,' she says.

It's the first time she's said it. It's the first time I believe it.

Now I'm a little stronger, and the suctioning gets less frequent and I start getting physiotherapy. Which sounds odd considering I can't even move enough to turn over. But muscles begin to waste away after only twenty-four hours of inactivity and I've been lying about now for weeks.

This is a thought that keeps me awake at night. Or

maybe it's the hard plastic green box of the ventilator digging into my neck, or the noise of the machine, or the nattering night nurses, or the pain, or – but no, it's my overactive, bored brain knitting problems that's the culprit.

So muscles start to waste away after twenty-four hours of inactivity, do they? Hmmm. There's one muscle in particular that's concerning me here. The inactivity thing has not been a problem since I was about eleven. By the time I was fourteen it was probably begging to be left alone. It certainly got its wish granted by the opposite sex, but that's by the by. All I'm saying is never shake a teenage boy's hand, and certainly never share his packet of Cheesy Wotsits. My bedroom saw more tugs than a Dutch harbour. No wonder my eyesight's going – Mum was right, after all.

I even liked to keep my hand in when I had girlfriends. Men do. Ask your man. He'll lie, the dog, but he does. The average chap might not go to the gym as much as he'd like, but my God his cock'll be more pumped than Arnold Schwarzenegger. I used to be able to hang a towel off mine. And before any ex who might be reading this mutters something about a tea towel I'd like to say for the record I could dangle one of those big fluffy Marks and Sparks towels. Although that did get me banned from our local branch.

However, at the moment not only do I feel as sexy as Michael Winner in Speedos, but I've got a big plastic tube down the end of it and on the rare occasions when there's a bit of a stirring, well let's say the thought of Mr W. comes in very handy for keeping things under control.

But it's a worry. I'm only thirty-seven, even though I'm

not exactly the towel-hanging, über-tugging, drilling-for-oil, whack-it-on-the-table-and-bash-it-with-a-brick-to-get-it-down fellow I used to be. This situation is not going to help. And there's something else. I don't mean to offend, but there are certain images from certain private moments that have a certain erotic resonance, a resonance that, er, resonates perhaps years after the original, ah, certain moment. Obviously mine are all about Michele and they are all quite wholesome, but well, in quiet, private moments, blokes like to give themselves a private slideshow. I can put it no stronger than that. But at the moment if I see even the first slide I'll give myself a fucking hernia so that avenue of pleasure has been well and truly barricaded off. And what about my old fella? What sort of state is he going to be in when he can finally return to active service?

Oh look, it's morning and here come the physios.

There are four or five of them. I'm one of the first on their list so they're not shagged out and they're all chirpy, the bastards, and here's the leader – the proper one who's passed all the exams and knows the names of muscles in places where I don't really think I've got any. She's teaching the others as we go along and I'm startled to learn I have a trapezium, an ice rink, a deuteronomy and an eclipse. All in my left arm. Shame none of them work. Bloody marvellous though, education.

This is what they do:

The leader – who I like – takes an arm and moves it around. Then repeats with the other. Ditto each leg. Job done, frankly. Off they trot. I'm a bit let down. Ah, but that's just day one. Over the next few weeks the regime toughens up. I find myself sitting up. It takes three physios to do this. One's a huge bloke – willing but with no technique. Our little leader, who can hardly weigh seven stone soaking wet, can chuck me about like a Welsh farmer with his favourite sheep. She tends not to bother, though, cos her acolytes are eager to please.

So we begin the months that will turn into years of physio. We start with an arm wiggle and some time, one day, it will stop. Today, though, a couple of weeks after the programme began, a contraption is wheeled in. It's a hoist. Today I am going to get out of bed. This is it. Now we'll really see how far I've fallen. But first, the damn hoist.

The hoist is like a small crane, or a scaffold. Where the little rope noose should be there dangles a blue nylon swing. What happens next is tricky. I have to get this under my arse while the physios unplug and replug my tubes and wires. Finally a switch is pressed and up I go, smoothly. Except I've got my knackers caught under me and I'm sitting on my bollocks while swinging on this thing and my hospital gown falls off so I'm hanging naked in the breeze by my cobblers while the rest of the ward has a good laugh and my face and undercarriage turn purple.

There's shouting and swearing and most of it would come from me but I can't speak. Finally I'm lowered on to a chair and for the first time in six weeks I'm out of bed. It's a momentous occasion.

It's horrible. I'm dizzy and sick, and I never knew gravity was such a weight. My head bows down, unable to support itself. My body sags. The cushion hurts my skinny arse – it feels like solid wood. Surely air cannot be so heavy? I'm a hundred years old. I'm as ancient as the old ladies on the local news who remember Queen

Victoria's christening. *'I've still got six of my own teeth and I've stayed alive due to smoking fifty a day, downing six pints of Guinness and walking the cat. And due to the fact that I'm one of the undead and have given my soul to Satan.'*

I must have aged a decade a week. And it wasn't even fun. When I was knocking about with certain stand-up comics there were weekends that aged me a year or two, but this is taking the piss. What the fuck has happened? My joke turns sour in my mouth as the full impact of this illness suddenly slams into me, suffocates me, unmans me in that chair.

How am I going to get out of here now? While I was in the bed I could hide, pretend, kid myself I was not too poorly. Yes, even despite the vent, the sweats, the paralysis, the suctioning, yadda yadda yadda. I do denial like a good 'un. My God, I've got a great siege mentality. Stalingrad in 1942 ain't in it. Tell me I'm in trouble and watch me prove you wrong, dammit. I spent years with an ex despite – no, *because* she was humourless, paranoid, pretentious, needy, neurotic and had no tits. That and because *everyone* I knew said we were the most unsuited, benighted couple in the history of the world. Up to and including Michael Jackson and Bubbles, Catherine the Great and Shergar, and Julia Roberts and whoever she's married this week.

So I'm sick, am I? Can't move, can't I? Turning into Yoda I am? Nonsense, I'll be up and running about in time for New Year's Eve. Book me a table at the River Room and put on your dancing shoes, honey. That was easy in bed. In bed that was a piece of cake, pal. In bed I was just lying down. Putting my feet up. Having a rest. Taking it easy. But now – *now* I am a cripple, a husk, half-alive. *Now* I'm better off d—

'That better?' smiles the little physio.

Shit, shit, shit, shit, *shit*.

Fatty Michele is chuffed to bits that night about my time out. It was only half an hour before gravity squashed me down so damn hard I had to be hoisted back into bed. This time it was only my left one that got caught. I wanted to tell her it had made things so much worse, but she was right. It was a good first step. It was necessary.

What with the physio, the sitting, the new antibiotics, the plasma exchange – fuck, the Lourdes water, for all I know – the suctioning tailed off to one an hour. The amount of oxygen being pumped into me to keep my lungs inflated reduced. My left hand moved enough for even Dr Lane to smile. If nothing horrible happened in the immediate future, I had every chance of pulling through. Dr Lane gave Michele his most charming smile and, with reference to the possibility of cancer and the insane biopsy, said, 'I'll call off the dogs.' It wasn't a tumour. They knew that because I was alive.

But for what sort of a life? I'm staggered by the wreck I've become. I've been hit by a train. Which then reversed over me. Twice. Whereupon the driver got out and attacked me with a crowbar for messing up his timetable. On the plus side – alive, alive-o, great, I'm not complaining. But what life? I cannot sit nodding and dribbling in a chair, being fed, watered and kept breathing by machines. A life half blind, a life with the room spinning, a head full of helium, bones full of molten lead. I can't inflict this on Michele, my family, me.

People were noticing I looked fed up. It was putting a

damper on Christmas. Even watching the wife's knockers do a Jordan wasn't putting a smile on my face. Some idiot doctor asked if I wanted Prozac. I asked if she wanted a fat lip. She took that as a no, but said huffily that it might soon be NHS policy to give all patients antidepressants automatically when they went on to ITU. Cos studies have apparently shown they do get a bit miserable in there.

Leaving aside the civil-liberties issues and the ethical question, ignoring the fact that these tablets take time to kick in, rubbishing the contra-indications problems, forgetting about the fact that hard-core antidepressants should only be used with therapy, I tried to explain on my pad that it was *perfectly legitimate and sane* to get depressed on ITU, what with all the pain, disorientation, loneliness, uncertainty and fear. Oh, and plus we were all going to die. Or had just escaped death but would probably be left fucked up for years. And patronising twats like her were not going to make it any better. Only I used less reasoning and more swearing. She took agin me after that, and often accused me of 'not trying hard enough' to come off the ventilator. She only said it to Michele once.

Since I've known her, Shell's only threatened to deck a few people: a social worker who suggested she put me in a home, some bloke who parked in a disabled bay and answered her back, and face-like-a-bag-of-spanners, dirty-bed-artist Tracy Emin who tried to interrupt her doing a karaoke of 'Denis, Denis' when she'd been on the Mateus Rosé. The other person was this doctor. Michele means it when she says it. People know she means it. They always back down. I was left alone to wallow after that.

Except Michele wasn't having that. So she bought me a telly. It's unusual to find a telly in intensive care, but if you'd been in Charing Cross ITU around Christmas 2001, you'd have seen one at the end of my bed. I don't want to think about the red tape she had to cut through to get it approved, but she did it and suddenly the world was opened up to me again.

And guess what the first programme that bedridden, knackered, immovable old me turned on? Michael Palin's *Around the World in 80 Fucking Days*. Well, it's on every Christmas, like *The Great Escape*, *Zulu* or Natasha Kaplinsky. Fortunately it was the episode where he's on the slow boat to India and the crew make him supper with their filthy unwashed hands and the silly polite tosser eats it and spends the next two days shitting his liver out into the Indian Ocean. I smiled for the first time in a week. Thank you, Michael. Your privations were not in vain.

I also liked turning the volume up while the shouty consultant was doing her rounds. By this time I was the scary bloke who wouldn't die with the scary space-hopper wife who wouldn't go away, so it was always the youngest junior doctor who was sent to ask me ever so politely if I could turn it down because the consultant was trying to break the news to someone that they had terminal bone cancer and Tinky Winky going 'Time for Tubby bye-bye, time for Tubby bye-bye' was appropriate but not in the best taste.

So I'm now officially a cruel heartless bastard. But I'm not. I've morphed into a creature so thin-skinned, so fragile it's almost impossible to bear. I stare at the TV in astonishment and rage at the stupidity of people putting themselves in danger. Do they want to end up in here? I can't watch a comedy pratfall, can't stomach a shouty cop show, and as for the Winter Olympics, what are these people thinking? There's some idiot girl hurtling down an icy slope on a skeleton bobsleigh, like a quivering condom on a tea tray, her head inches from the unforgiving, fatal ice. Her *head*, for heaven's sake. You need it, you stupid woman. Adrenaline junkie, eh? You want thrills and spills, you want to spend a couple of nights in here. You won't play with a fucking *snowball* after that, missus. I switch over and – no word of a lie – there's a Channel 4 documentary on the history of the guillotine.

I turn it off for the night, but there's nothing next day I seem to be able to watch. There's an arts programme on *The Hobbit* and I'm in terror for stupid fat Bilbo Baggins. Why in Gandalf's name does he want to leave his lovely comfy house at Bag End? Doesn't he know there are dragons out here?

Brilliant. After toughing out the worst the NHS can chuck at me and feeling, sometimes, pretty good about it in a kind of steely-jawed, stoically-suffering-hero kind of way, I realise I am in fact not Bruce Willis at the end of *Armageddon*, but officially a big girl's blouse.

And then, next day the worst realisation. Dull, ordinary people doing dull, ordinary things in dull, ordinary programmes – putting up shelves, drilling holes in some MDF, buying tat, selling tat, talking about their love for their cousin's mother's brother's auntie, are the most amazing, lucky, jealous-rage-inducing fuckers of all.

Odd, this outside world, when you're inside. Or rather, *outside*. I was having my first sickening taste of a feeling that lingers to this day, a feeling shared by thousands, millions of our disabled, elderly, vulnerable, excluded, *unseen*. The TV flashed me images of a world I was no longer a participant in. Every person walking, talking, eating – Jesus, even *breathing* – was a slap in my aghast face, a stabbing, gut-twisting reminder of my uselessness, my death. There are many ways of being dead. Ask the long-term unemployed, the homeless, the newly divorced, the abused, the sick. The forgotten. If, as the song goes, loneliness is a crowded room, how lonely are you in a crowded world?

(And it's the same for your loved ones, dealing with the loss of you. Christmas makes it worse. Michele tells of a time in Sainsbury's when she saw a young couple kissing and smiling in the frozen-food aisle and she wanted to assault them with a Taste the Difference Christmas pudding. Mum walked past an office party on the way back from the hospital and swears if she'd had access to any automatic weaponry she'd now be in Broadmoor.)

Supersized Shell bounced in and asked if I was enjoying the telly. Fantastic, I wrote. Ta. Makes the hours fly by.

Hold me.

Hey, but look, I love being the outsider, right? Always the observer – never really a part of things. A journalist, the classic refuge of the bright and indifferent. My loves – photography: putting a machine between me and the world, my music, reading, and of course my writing – all solitary, the world wrought into some sort of order, some shape, some control. Me on the outside, watching, commenting, staying away. I'm trying to cling to an identity but I've realised too late it's ephemeral. I chucked it away a long time ago. I've shown too many different people too many different faces and now I don't know which is mine. Take five friends and ask them to describe me and you'll get five different men reflected back: a boozy, sober, fun-loving, serious, shagging, faithful, exciting, boring, smart, dull, cowardly, brave, trendy nerd. But that's alright, it's kept everyone at arm's length. How clever. How stupid. Relationships floundered because no one was let in and they smashed themselves in tearful frustration to wrecks against the adamantine hollowness that must have always been there. And I blamed them as I walked away, slightly puzzled but untouched by the guttering fires, or maybe I blamed the weather or the wrong song or the wrong haircut. And it's never gonna be alright. Because now I've seen it. The hollowness that I've hidden even from myself, distracted by distraction from distraction.

Hold me, my love. All these faces remind me of the me I could be, will never be, stripping me until I am nothing.

Wasn't I always? Wasn't I simply one of life's voyeurs?

If so, I was going to love the next five years.

Hold me tighter.

And I write none of this until now. Oh look, when I am alone again, writing, listening to music, putting things in order. But hold on, I can change. Look at this. I have a stack of CDs on my desk. I'm not going to arrange them in alphabetical order. Anarchy.

Shit, I've already put them in chronological order.

Maybe I should have taken the Prozac.

Maybe I should still be taking it. I had a letter the other day from one of my many consultants, saying he was concerned my illness had left me with an occasional inability to engage with reality. Michele pissed herself as I tried to use this as a defence for not getting the car taxed. She said I'd always had an inability to live in the real world and proceeded to give me several frankly hurtful examples of my pre-illness hopelessness, which – unlike other women in my life – she'd seen as endearing rather than a reason for, say, walking out, smashing my guitars and setting fire to my record collection and trousers on the way. Just an example. I reminded her of the time she threw a large wooden horse at my head and she told me to get-back-upstairs-and-finish-this-chapter-you-procrastinating-bugger-and-don't-try-and-pass-this-off-as-some-clever-deconstruction-tactic.

Disorientation's a problem in intensive care. It's the Glastonbury of the NHS. It's down the rabbit hole. It's hard to concentrate. What is there to concentrate on? Where was I? Oh yes, a friend of mine told me this funny story which Glastonbury brings to mind. He and his wife – old enough to know better – have gone along to the festival with a few, ahem, substances to share with friends. Sadly, first night they're there, a Friday, the tent next to them is raided by the old bill. (By the way, what a tricky job, working the drugs squad at Glastonbury.)

Anyway, my mate and his missus are hearing this commotion as some poor hippy and his stash are taken off to be interrogated and smoked respectively and they realise in a paranoid way that they're next. There's nowhere to hide their stuff. No bog, no bedside cabinet, no fake tin of beans. They panic. They come to the only sensible decision in the circumstances. The circumstances being they're already off their trees. They scoff the lot.

They wake up on Sunday night just as Billy Bragg's finishing and the last tent is being packed up.

'Best bloody gig I ever went to,' said my mate.

He's probably the only bloke I know who understands the disorientation of ITU without having been through the tedious business of landing up in it. Although fuck knows how he didn't.

I have mentioned that it was coming up to Christmas, but in here it was only a notion. Like, for example, the notion of a British service industry, a pleasant waitress or a train that arrives roughly at the time you've paid for it to, it was a talked-about concept that never actually, physically materialised. There's no such thing as Christmas on ITU. Because of the risk of infection there are no decorations, no cards, no nurses with silly hats. Maybe a consultant or two wore a tie with Santas on, I can't remember. The only way you can tell it's Christmas is that the staff get a bit slack and it takes longer to get any test results back from the lab. All long-term patients hate weekends in hospital cos the backroom boys – all the lab techies, the people who fiddle with your blood and wee and X-rays, the speech therapists, the physios, etc. – piss off. Christmas is like a long, long weekend. And it makes you nervous.

Plus there's the golden rule, the same as in the outside world, that if you're going to get sick it'll be late on a Friday night. Just before a bank holiday.

Difficult to know which particular turn for the worse I should mention in the run up to Santa's arrival. Suffice to say there were enough to keep the medics on their toes, Doris at the whetstone and my family's nerves on edge. But eventually I lurched and wheezed my way into Christmas Eve and I'd just recovered from a lack of something or too much of something else or a combination of all or none of the above and everything was quiet and it was lunchtime, ho fucking ho, as the liquid squirted into my stomach, but I could smell the stink coming from the heated Welsh trolleys even two floors below so it must have been about midday when Mum turned to Shell and said, aghast, 'We haven't got any Christmas presents for the kids.'

Michele said, 'Bugger that. We haven't got a turkey.'

Or, it transpired, vegetables, cranberry sauce, crackers, tinsel, party poppers, paper napkins with holly on, stocking fillers, stockings, Terry's chocolate oranges, selection boxes, Woolies gift vouchers or any of the billion things that make Our Lord's birthday so great for kids and such a miserable pain in the arse for parents.

Shell paused. 'When is Christmas Day anyway?'

'Tomorrow.'

'Oh, fucking hell. How did that happen?'

They legged it to Hammersmith Shopping Centre. I feel sorry for any poor soul doing their shopping in Hammersmith on 24 December 2001. They would have seen – and probably been mown down by – two crazed blonde women attempting to do an entire Christmas shop – from gift tags to gobbler – in four hours. I wasn't present so I can't give you an authoritative, proper journalistic account of the carnage, um, expedition, but knowing this pair . . . I'm trying to think what might have been comparable, as they snatched the last Harry Potter train set from some poor dear or knocked over a confused granny consulting her list in Topshop. Remember the SAS Iranian Embassy siege? A gentle stroll in the park. The Nazi invasion of the Low Countries? A veritable amble. Genghis Khan's murderous looting hordes rampaging across the endless steppes of central Asia? Getting close.

And bugger me, they did it. They came back later that afternoon, flushed, triumphant and a little smug. They were not unscathed. Mum's hair looked like the wig on one of those scary ventriloquist's dummies, and she had a similar glazed expression; Michele's Zulu genes (long story) had made a sudden reappearance and she looked as if she'd just done a good job at Isandhwala and now had Rorke's Drift in her assegai's sights. There was some ripped clothing, some glitter, some blood, but it wasn't theirs so we didn't talk about it.

Christmas was going to happen. Partly cos Mum, like the festive season, is a bit like the immovable object. More so these days now she's moved in with us permanently and brought her horrible red recliner that squats in our living room like a velour ASBO. Give her a cup of ('*decaff*') coffee ('*black, with a drop of cold water else it's too hot*'), a decent soap storyline, the minutiae of which she insists on elucidating to anyone within earshot up to and including the dog, a packet of digestives, and it would take a major thermo-nuclear device to get her to shift; or one of the kids, who've now worked out what the little lever on the side of the chair does and occasionally creep up behind her and fling her halfway across the room.

This immovability has its up and downs. The downs are bleedin' obvious when you live with it – and shamingly, when you're trying to stop it sitting on the end of your bed every day – but the ups are actually rather good at times – obstinate relatives are very, very useful in stopping you becoming dead.

They also force you to keep in touch with what's going on outside – it was important that I knew it was my birthday or that it was Christmas, just as for some reason it was important that I knew about the new bus diversion around Barnes bridge. But be that as it may, there was something astonishingly comforting about that figure at my bedside each day; something human, something *connecting*.

When she disagreed with anything in the hospital, she put on what we call her 'Woolworths face'. It's a weapon of immense clout, like the ring of Sauron. No mortal can withstand its strange, awful power. Nurses would shrivel, doctors blanch, even consultants agree to get a second opinion.

It's called a Woolworths face because one day while I'm here mucking about in ITU, my boy James bought some awful noisy plastic toy that needed batteries. Mum took him to Woolies to get some. They were the wrong size. On taking them back, she was told by some McDonald's reject foetus that as she'd opened the packet, they couldn't be exchanged. Mum argued, reasonably, as a queue started forming, that she couldn't tell they wouldn't fit unless she opened them. The assistant manager was summoned from the crèche and took the side of the high-street retailer. Impasse. The queue got a bit restless. It was Saturday, you know?

More staff were called cos Mum wouldn't move. What she did do was repeat herself. A lot. I know, shocking. And then came something far worse. Then came silence, and the Face. It's almost Zen-like. It can be read as defiant, noble, indignant, righteous, Churchillian.

Or just blank and a bit simple.

Either way, it was blindingly obvious this mad woman was never *ever* going to leave, and so as if by magic new batteries were thrust into her hand and three shop assistants were sent for post-traumatic stress counselling.

James came back in awe.

Mum and Michele

Mum used to get home after a day at Charing Cross and watch – absolute truth – *ER*. It was her way of unwinding, she'd say, as a horrified Michele watched some poor investment banker who used to be in *Ally McBeal* collapse in a twitching heap next to George Clooney. Mum would sit happily munching her bacon sarnie (or on diet days her grilled turkey-rasher sarnie) while the poor sod got his head trepanned and never flinch. Michele was usually gibbering quietly behind the sofa at this point.

It's the only time they ever really disagreed during this whole rotten period. Or even in the few years since we all got welded together. Mum, who'd been on her own and having quite a nice time of it, ta, for several years, has fitted into our family life like she was born to gran.

She'd always adored Michele, right from the kick-off. It helped that Shell followed someone Mum very much *didn't* adore, but mums are like that. If you're ever going to meet a new flame's parents, make sure the previous one was a complete arse. I always used to follow on from Johnny perfect, who worked in the City and took them all on cruises and could talk to her dad about golf and gave Auntie Edna his fucking kidney for all I know. Either way, I never lived up to Mr Previous. Maybe it was me. Most of the time I was broke, jobless, chippy and thought their gazebo should be turned into a refuge for disabled Albanian asylum-seekers with behavioural problems.

And despite Shell having two kids already, and Mum knowing I was about as promising dad material as a used teabag, she loved my little shouty missus from the start.

She knew Shell was the right woman for me, which is unspeakably annoying. The idea that mums might actually, genuinely know best, or indeed know anything *at all*, is quite abhorrent to any son. It might put some of those teenage rows into perspective, and what you must *never* do is look at your teenage years with *any* genuine perspective *at all* else you would climb under a large rock for a very long time.

And Mum took to the kids pretty much instantly too. Hey, it was easy. Instant family. Like sea monkeys. Just add water. She lived just the right distance away: not too close, obviously, but not so far that we couldn't visit with only a couple of stops for car-sick James to chuck up. After an initial short but unpleasant period as Michele disentangled from her previous relationship, it all began to seem easy, comfy, *right*. Maybe this was a happy ending.

We never really imagined those relationships being put to this sort of fierce, unblinking test. But know what? We're all still here and we're all still talking. Until she puts on the Woolworths face. Then we just let the kids tip her out of her recliner.

But we're getting ahead of ourselves. Dunno why I don't want to plunge into Santa's sack of happy ITU Xmas memories but . . . oh, here goes.

Ding Dong Merrily on ITU. Christmas Day 2001

Today's the day I stop dying. It's as simple as that. If I need to mark a point where I 'turn a corner', as they say, it's today. I don't know that yet, obviously, and I couldn't enjoy it at the time cos I'd stubbornly/stupidly refused to believe I was heading for the big body bag in the basement anyway.

God, why do I make things so difficult for myself? I can't enjoy anything.

I'd got this great new bed. The staff were at pains to tell me how expensive and rare this was, and what a privilege it was to be given one. They made it sound like they'd dragged the previous occupant out by his catheter tube and chucked him on a trolley so that I, star of the ITU, could have it.

It was basically one of those beds that go up and down when you press a button. You can get them from DFS for about five hundred quid. This one probably cost the NHS about ten grand.

You find this in all big state-run bureaucracies. I think I read somewhere once that the Civil Service paperclip budget works out at something like a fiver a paperclip. I'm sure there have been great strides in reducing waste but I'm not always sure the savings have been made in the right place. A bit less spent on the flashy gear and a bit more on the lemony-scented Cillit Bang might be an idea. But I digress.

Either way, I'm not complaining cos my new bed meant I could sit up on Christmas Day without getting a team of physios – who were all at home wrestling with the limbs of free-range bronze turkeys anyway – to hoick me about. So I was sitting up in my nice new Christmas pyjamas when Mum and Shell arrived. (Actually the PJs had been a bit of a bone of contention. Shell had bought me two pairs of very nice, very expensive ones. I was annoyed, saying it was a waste of money as I wasn't going to be in hospital that long. She agreed and made me put them on.)

I decided the nurses who work over the festive period tend to be either the really hard-up ones who need the overtime, the divorcees who aren't getting the kids this year and don't fancy sitting alone with a Bernard Matthews turkey crown and a re-run of *The Italian Job*, or the young poofs who are still in the closet and can't face another row with the boyfriend as to why he never gets to meet the parents. Or people who don't give a rat's ass about Christmas cos their God wasn't born on 25 December. All in all, not a terribly festive lot. So it was with more than the usual pleasure that I greeted Mum and Shell when they arrived with presents.

Presents for me. This'll be something to see.

The poor sods. Never mind what you get the man who has everything, I was a real toughie. They could have bought me a compilation CD of some of my favourite songs – 'Girlfriend In A Coma', 'Breathe', 'My Iron Lung', 'Ventilator Blues', 'Get Up Stand Up' – but they'd decided against it. There's only so far irony will take you.

Chocolate oranges were out, as were shoes, clothes, Michael Palin videos, books, or any vouchers that expired within, say, six months. I did get one tome from a hippy friend about angels and healing and the like. I couldn't read it very well because the print started doing the tango after about five minutes, but I loved the soppy pictures. My favourite chapter was about crystal healing. I love this idea. Rocks heal, you know, if you know the right ones and where to put them. I know exactly where to put them when anyone suggests this as a course of treatment and I'm sure it would do me a power of good. *It's a conspiracy!* cry the devotees of the onyx pyramids or the anthracite rhomboids. *The government doesn't want to admit the truth.*

Do they honestly think that if this government believed they could slash NHS budgets by prescribing a course of gravel rather than penicillin they wouldn't be shovelling up half of Brighton beach within the hour? If you're one of these people who believes in the power of a crystal dangled over your chakra then fine, and frankly, you deserve all you get. You're probably not going to be around long enough to annoy me too much.

And angels? Do me a fucking favour. There may well be more things in heaven and earth than are dreamt of in Horatio's philosophy but that's cos Horatio was a pig-ignorant Danish grunt in a damp castle in the Middle Ages. He knew fuck all about fuck all. If you'd shown him an iPod he'd have burnt it as a witch. Of course there are things we don't know, but give us enough time and the chances are we'll work them out. Like Evolution, or the laws of motion, the role of the unconscious, the special theory of relativity, or even how to programme an iPod. No, we won't be able to disprove the existence of angels, just like we'll never be able to disprove Thor, Viking God of Thunder, but most right-thinking people have quietly written him off as a sort of embarrassing but understand-able episode in mankind's development. A bit like your first shag. Anyone in my position who dares to think an angel pulled them through not only deserves to die through stupidity, but also through lack of gratitude. About a hundred medics, an unknown number of scientists, a lot of blood donors, a loving family and my own bloody-mindedness did the trick and that's a lot of real, flesh-and-blood, here-and-now people to thank, let alone remembering the debt of gratitude to the political giants of 1945 who set up the National Health Service so that ordinary people like me could get a million quid's worth of care, despite successive governments' attempts to dismantle it. So you can take your angels and your pyramids and your pan pipes and shove 'em up your arse. The only angel you want to be thanking is Nye Bevan.

Mum and Michele both went down the pragmatic route. Mum got me a squeezy yellow ball with a smiley face. It was to exercise my knackered left hand. Shell got me a puzzle with little balls you have to put in holes. I still haven't managed to do it. Now I may be wrong, but I bet Mum also got me a jumper. Not because I needed one – ITU was as hot and humid as Ray Mears' armpit in a Borneo heatwave – but because she's bought me a Christmas jumper ever since 1964. I've never worn one since I was thirteen, so I don't imagine she minded me not wearing this one either, bless her. Shell got the best present, though. It was a rubber cow. When you squeezed it, it pooed. Practical and funny. The woman's a magician.

Mum brought a bottle of champagne and some orange juice. It's not Christmas for her without a Buck's Fizz and she wasn't going to miss out now. Come to that, I thought, neither was I. Swallowing for me had become dangerous. It's a ridiculously complex action, the swallow. Several things have to happen at once for it to work, mainly to protect a person from the dangers of aspirating – when food and liquids go down your trachea and into your lungs, rather than into your oesophagus and stomach. Anything in your lungs aside from air is bad. It leads to infection. Weak swallowing is one of the reasons the elderly suffer from pneumonia so much.

To open the oesophagus and simultaneously close the trachea your tongue has to move forward to make the back of it lift up strongly. The soft palate has to elevate, otherwise your tea goes down your nose and back into your cup. The larynx has to move up a surprisingly long way. The vocal cords need to slam shut – the last line of defence. A cough reflex is triggered if something 'goes down the wrong way', just as a gag reflex is triggered if you 'bite off more than you can chew'. Muscular contractions, together with air-pressure changes in the mouth, trigger the double movement of opening and closing. Then peristalsis – or muscle spasm in the oesophagus – pushes the food/liquid into the stomach.

Simple. Except in my case my tongue couldn't move forward, my palate couldn't elevate, my larynx couldn't move upwards, my left vocal cord was paralysed in the 'open' position, I had no cough reflex and my gag reflex was so poor I could have had a career as a sword swallower or gay porn star. Fuck it – when the nurses weren't looking I drank some Buck's Fizz.

Everyone cheered. It went straight down into my lungs. I couldn't feel it, but I figured I was on enough antibiotics to deal with any subsequent infection, so what the hell. Oh, the sweet, sweet tang. The fizz. The pleasure after six weeks of wetting my mouth with water from those rough-pink-plastic sponge lollies. God, that taste was worth a bucketful of Prozac. And if I'd known it would be the last taste I would have apart from bile for the next fourteen months I might have emptied the bottle.

But I was enjoying today. Not just enduring it. The sweats had stopped, the suctioning was tailing off. The room was less inclined to spin me right round baby right round. I still had a tendency to drift off a bit, but I felt good. Fair enough, that's a bit of an exaggeration.

I didn't feel like I wanted to shoot myself in the head with a rusty nail gun. Which, I suppose, means I felt good, I knew that I would, yeah. And just like my MRSA, this feeling was infectious.

I see the strain lift from Michele and for a few moments we are young lovers again, laughing over something stupid like her inability to appreciate the difference between pie 'n' mash from a pie 'n' mash shop and pie plus mash from, say, a Waitrose shop. Or the time we had such a big row over something terribly important probably involving the young Gene Hackman, when she jumped out of bed and told me she was leaving-for-ever-you-bastard but was too small to reach her suitcase on top of the wardrobe. After she had hopped about arse-naked for a couple of minutes we were both killing ourselves laughing so much that she dived back into bed, tears soaking her beautiful face until I kissed them dry, and oh the memories are sweet in my mouth today, not bitter because we will make some more my love, and she reads this in my face and she hops into bed, or rather rolls like a Weeble and I kiss her face dry again.

And the nurse lets the cuff down on my tracchy for a few seconds and I push the air from somewhere and force my unwilling, frozen throat and mouth to work and yes I croak:

'Merry Christmas.'

And wonder why everyone bursts into tears.

Chapter Five

A Life in a Day

Not all of these things may have happened in one day, but they all happened.

5 a.m.

Trouble sleeping. Wake up covered in sticky fluid. Only two options: I've had some disastrous haemorrhage or my nadgers have burst with two months' worth of jizz. In my befuddled state I don't know which one to prefer. Either way I'm clearly in trouble. Again. It's dark. Not properly dark, cos of the lights from everyone's machines and the grubby neon of the dirtier side of the fogged city, seeping through the blinds all the way up here, floating high on the eleventh floor. No, more the sort of dark you get on the bridge of the *Starship Enterprise* when they've been caught in a space spider's megaweb and the bridge is down to emergency power only. Which is OK with me. I'm not a big fan of the proper dark.

I didn't know this until I went to stay on a friend's farm. I turned the bedroom lights out and the blackness hit me in the face like a coffin lid. I grew up on a main road. OK, pedant, in a house next to a main road. I've always lived in cities. I thought I knew what dark was. Dark was when the kebab shop opposite turned off the revolving neon doner. Streetlamps must be like starlight, I reckoned. Are they balls. Proper dark, countryside dark, cows-in-fields, hens-in-pens, sheep-in-lonely-farmers'-beds dark, is an actual, physical thing. Not an absence of light, but an overabundance of dark. I slept with the light on for the first time in thirty years. Which the flying, biting things just fucking loved.

'Restful night's sleep? I bet you did. Without all those lights and cars and stuff,' said Farmer Giles the next day. I hadn't slept a wink. 'Leaving zo zoon?' he asked as I legged it back to civilisation to get some kip, a doner and the cowshit off my Timberlands. Yes, I might own a 4×4 but that's cos I lived in Twickenham, where it was properly essential. Have you tried turning up at the school gates in a Honda Civic?

I didn't hit that kind of dark again until I went blind in Chapter One. So this half light was fine, ta. Although it did mean I couldn't see what had leaked out of me. On the other hand, I wasn't sure I wanted to. Let's just have a quick feel around to see how much there – oh bloody hell, there's pools of it. I must be like Tim Roth in *Reservoir Dogs*. Calm. Think logically. You're not in any pain, which means . . . ? Which means these painkillers are bloody good. Hmmm. Fair enough, see your logic. Panic. Someone should be told. Of course, there not being an alarm, I can't press one. And I can't speak. I rattle my pill box, but the nurses don't hear me. I hear them alright, nattering. Usual thing – pay, kids, holidays.

'No, I'm a grade J now, which means I get eighty pounds an hour. Course most of it goes on buying heroin for my eldest who's on the run from Broadmoor, so it's a good job I've booked that two-week holiday to those poppy fields in Afghanistan. Save me a fortune, that. Oooh and I must get these Jimmy Choos re-heeled, they make a funny rattling sound.'

Course, I might have misheard. And now some odd statistics flash through my mind as I rattle away and the nurses finally start looking around in the gloom to see where the annoying noise is coming from.

It's been bothering me a while, this. According to various studies – some of which I've just made up while trying to sleep, but they sound about right – one in four people suffers from mental-health problems at any given time. One in eight may have a venereal disease. One in three will have tried hard drugs and one in five will have committed a crime. So out of every hundred staff I come into contact with in this hospital, on average there'll be 12 syphilitics, 33 junkies, 20 criminals and 25 loonies. Which leaves 10. Who'll therefore be gay.

This bit of politically correct maths takes my mind off my predicament for a few minutes as I try and work out which is which amongst my medical team. I have my suspicions and I'll be on the case, but here comes a nurse. I like him. He's attached to another hospital down the road, but because of a shortage of good ITU nurses he spends his time off getting overtime here. He nips off sharpish when his shift finishes cos otherwise his chauffeur gets the hump. He's a really nice guy, but he never puts my feeding tube in properly which is why I'm now covered in liquid dinner. Again.

Cleaning me up takes a while. I can still hardly move so it takes two people to undress me, sponge me off, turn me one way to pull out half the sheet from under me, roll me the other way to take it out. Then push a new sheet back in and roll me back over to pull the sheet back under me. Simple. Only a couple of hours to go till dawn.

This nurse is one of the few who ever talks to me about anything other than what is strictly necessary. I found this a surprise at first, but I've got used to being ignored. It's a nice and slightly emotional moment when they do talk. I find myself absurdly grateful. I cannot for a million quid remember what we talked about, but I know we did and cheers, mate. Even if you're probably a disease-ridden mad smackhead on the run.

6.30 a.m.

I doze and am woken by the strip lighting coming on and the cleaners turning up. The nurses do a last body count before preparing for the big eight o'clock handover and hometime. There must be simply mounds of paperwork cos you hardly ever see a nurse between six thirty and nine. In both the a.m. and p.m. So try not to take a turn for the worse then, is my advice.

The neon lights bounce off the white walls and it's hello campers once more. Painfully I turn my head to the left to check out bed twelve, aka the Bed of Doom. For the last few days some cheery old bloke called Alfie has defied all the odds and remained in bed twelve without turning up his toes. He's going for some kind of record. I like him. He's about ninety-twelve, and was once clearly a big man.

He has a kind, lined face and a croaky East End accent like Dot Cotton.

I imagine him as a docker, not a horrible shouty one, but one of those reserved men who came back from hammering the Hun for a quiet life with a steady job and an allotment. A few pints in the old Bow Bells on Friday after work and back home to the Mile End Road for ham and eggs with the missus. Yeah, and maybe Dick van Dyke accompanied him singing Chim Chim Chir-fucking-ree.

Truth is, I've no idea, have I? But he did have dignity. Which was sorely tested, cos every day he'd be wheeled off for some new operation, some new exploratory fiddle about. His wife was tiny. She came every day in a brown overcoat and held his huge hand. She took to my little family, though we didn't say much to each other. She made sure the nurses looked after him. It makes a huge difference. Studies – real ones this time – prove that bolshie relatives save lives.

I look over at his big kind face and freeze in horror. A lurid, purple scar with huge stitches slashes him literally from ear to ear. He's swollen and almost unrecognisable. He's Frankenstein's monster. Sometime yesterday he was taken out again and now he's been replaced by this thing. I can't look away and I cannot even now look away. I had no idea what this image would do to his wife.

Know what she did when she came in that morning? She kissed him on the cheek. She took hold of his frail, huge hand and talked to him softly, like always. I wonder who she saw in that face.

8.30 a.m.

I need a poo. I know it logically, even though I don't feel it. I know it logically cos I haven't been for a week and during that time quite a lot of food's been pumped into me. I'm also aware that my brain damage is probably messing up my I-need-a-poo receptors. No one seems too concerned about it save me. For the last couple of days I've been given supplements of a loosener called lactulose, but for all the good it did I may as well have shoved it up my—

Which, funnily enough, is precisely what's going to happen now. I want to get this over before the day starts – there are always a lot of people in and out and I do like my privacy. When I first came into ITU I was put in a disposable nappy and told just to soil myself or even do it in the bed, it didn't matter cos I could be changed. What the lazy-arsed nurses probably meant was they couldn't be fucked to run backwards and forwards with a bedpan should I need one.

I soon got rid of the nappy. But now it was time for drastic measures. All those of a squeamish disposition, look away now. The little bumhole torpedoes – hold your breath and hey ho, up they go – have been useless. So now we bring out the big guns – the enema. It's just a small plastic bag with a tube on the end. (The NHS would grind to a halt if there were no more plastic bags with tubes on the end. They are everywhere.)

It's not entirely pleasant, but there are a lot of celebrities and neurotics who don't like the idea that the body produces waste who pay a lot of money for this sort of treatment. I have no inkling that very soon people will allow themselves to be filmed having it done – on teatime telly. The world I will finally emerge back into will be a different place for all sorts of reasons . . .

I'm told to hold on as long as possible for maximum effect. Screens are pulled round me. I'm suddenly in two minds about this, now it's too late. It must be like going for a dump in a trendy loft space whilst all your mates are trying to get through their seared tuna and making small talk whilst you're pebble-dashing the porcelain across the other side of the room and wondering whether to shout 'Sorry, it must have been the scallops' or join the polite pretence it's not happening. And Christ knows how bad it's going to smell in here. On the other hand, I'm not the first person to drop a log in this ward and that fat old bag in bed six can make your nose bleed.

Things are moving. I tap on the side of my cot so that the unhappy nurse detailed to wait outside the screens can slide a cardboard bedpan under me. I like this guy. He's definitely in the 10 per cent bracket and is very effeminate. He's gentle and hardworking and means well. I do wish he would stop calling me 'my darling' though. Especially when he's got his fingers up my bum.

8.31 a.m.

Oh dear. This is going to be ugly. I reckon they're going to want to clear the area and set up a cordon quite a long way from this bed. With those 'crime scene – do not cross' tapes. I silently apologise for what we are about to receive and it's amazing, even now, after all the humiliations I've already endured, that I have any shame left.

How can I be embarrassed? I would have thought I'd

have been able to toss one off the wrist in the middle of Tesco's, or take Snow White up the wrong 'un onstage during the kids' matinee at the Theatre Royal, Guildford, or even tell the House of Commons with a straight face that there are weapons of mass destruction in Iraq – and maybe I could. But I am hideously ashamed of the perfectly normal thing that's about to happen.

Oh, if only it had been perfectly normal. God, the noise, the smell, the *g-force*. Nurses dived for cover. Machines stopped. What am I saying? Traffic stopped. I'm sure someone called 999. Given that this was not long after 9/11, I'm amazed I didn't start an international incident.

My nurse cleaned up the filth stoically. I noticed he didn't call me 'my darling' much after that. It's the same with all relationships. You can just know too much about someone.

9 a.m.

In pads a sulky phlebotomist to take my daily bloods. No chit-chat cos she's got a busy day ahead and let's face it no one's pleased to see her and she's heard all the jokes about vampires she can take. They have the same effect as going up to Richard Wilson and shouting 'I don't believe it!' in his ear. And you want her to keep her hand steady. I prefer the needle in my right side because I can't feel sharp things on that side. No, or temperature. There's a line right down the middle of me, as defined as a freshly cut paper edge. On my right side I can feel and identify all sorts of textures – flesh, cotton, wood, etc. – but not their temperature or any sharp points or edges. On my left I can't tell what the hell is touching me, but I know if it's red hot, freezing cold, or jabbing into me. Basically, if it's going to hurt.

This is because – and this is proper science, not made up by me to stop me going doolally on long ITU nights – this is because when you are a foetus, you grow in two halves, spreading out from your central nervous system in what becomes your spine. You meet in the middle at some stage but each half is still distinct, and is given instructions from different parts of your brain.

I know what the quicker and more prurient of you are thinking – does this invisible line run halfway through everything? Astonished you may be after what I've just been sharing with you, but that information will remain off-limits. I think there are some things that should only be shared by myself, my wife and my consultant at the Royal Why Can't You Feel Anything on the Left Side of Your Cock? clinic.

For now, I only exist in the right half of my body. That's where I have feeling, that's where I can move, that's the half that's not dead. I'm huddled, cramped in my right side. I have been joined to this other half, hanging there like a dead Siamese twin. I want it removed. I don't know if I want to go back in there. It's gone rotten. And it hurts.

I snap back to the present as the phlebotomist snaps on the gloves. She has her little plastic tray and all the plastic gubbins and needles and bottles are wrapped in plastic. I listen to the unwrapping sounds that still flit in my ear from time to time. We're going to play hunt the vein. As any junkie – or apparently up to one in three of her colleagues – will tell you, veins collapse if you keep

147

shoving needles in them. I have had cannulas – permanent needles – in my hand and wrist for nearly two months, through which my daily doses of antibiotics or other magic potions constantly drip. I have had dozens of injections and pints of blood drawn. My veins are in a sorry state. This is not what the phlebotomist needs at nine in the morning. She must wake up going, 'Oh bollocks, I've got that git in bed ten again. Can't we move him to bed twelve?' She's just worried that one day she'll have to put a needle in my old fella and that's too much to take on a cup of coffee and a bowl of Bran Flakes. Most women coming into contact with that for the first time have been fortified with half a dozen Bacardi Breezers and a doner supper. Oh, and the Rohypnol. (That's the other great thing about a kebab. If your date'll put that in her mouth, she'll put anything in.)

Today's a lucky day. She's gone in the right side, though I probably don't deserve it after the Rohypnol and kebab jokes, and it's not too long before she has her three bags full. The main thing the boffins are looking at when these are handed over is white cell activity to see how my infections are doing. The more white cells, the worse I am. The results usually come through in time for the ward round. I listen to the numbers go up and down each day and sympathise with Nick Leeson at Barings watching the Hong Kong stock exchange.

9.30 a.m.

It's all go today. Here come the physios, happy as Larry. I should be easier to move about now as I'm obviously several stones lighter.

The first bit of bad news is that it's not the usual team leader. This one's small, fussy, and mistakes officious for efficient. We go through the arm-moving thing without too much hassle, then it's time to sit up. She hasn't got a clue. And without proper guidance neither have the trainees, some of whom are big lads and lasses. I'm being knocked about here. They fall on me like a bunch of pissed mates who agreed to help put up a friend's Ikea bookcase but just popped down the Frog and Ferret for a couple before they got started. It's all 'Left a bit, right a bit, to me to you, to you to me.' Oh brilliant, now I'm starring in the Chuckle Brothers. Ow ow, will you get off? I would have said, if not for the big plastic vent thing. And I couldn't reach my notebook. And even if I had been able to, I wasn't sure this bunch could read.

After quite a long time of this amateur, painful mauling, I'm sitting up, face to face with the lady in charge. She's not happy. She blames me for being awkward. She's heard about me and my awkward ways. I can't argue.

But I can smack her in the mouth. So I do, hard.

With my left hand. Which, as we all know, is unfortunately often clenched inadvertently in a fist. And as we also know, my left arm is prone to involuntary spasm. The timing of what might otherwise be seen as a decent left hook is apposite but entirely coincidental. You're not allowed to hit NHS staff, you have to go private for that. I am in no way advocating violence towards ignorant, rude, arrogant, unhelpful physios, and it was with no satisfaction that I saw this poor girl wipe a little blood from her mouth. I was utterly horrified at how upset she was at this accident, brought on as it was by the stress of my inept manipulation for which she can bear no responsibility, and I was very pleased that I never saw the cow again.

10.15 a.m.

Oddly enough the physios have all slunk away – no doubt to do quite a lot of paperwork and possibly lay criminal charges – when in waddles the incredible expanding woman. She's balancing a cup of hot chocolate on her bump. Look, no hands. Are you sure there's just one in there? I wonder. Actually, now I've watched my greedy little piglet daughter stuff her face for the last few years I think she was triplets. But ate the others.

Shell's a bit stressed cos the stupid fat American nurse in charge today wouldn't let her on to the ward because I was having physio. But the nurse didn't explain why she couldn't come in, so left her outside thinking there might have been some emergency. Then the nurse forgot about her. Shell was left waiting and worrying. Finally she buzzed again, and was let in without so much as an apology.

These seemingly little extra stresses and worries happen all the time. They're like the constant fear that the medicines you're being given are the wrong dose, or being given at the wrong time, if at all, or that your catheter's not being changed regularly enough, or you're not getting enough food and water. When you're in an acute state, tiny things take on gargantuan proportions. Because tiny errors can have gargantuan effects. Deadly ones. And mistakes get made. Every day. Which is understandable. If ten people have to do ten things for you each day and they are 99 per cent perfect, there'll still be one mistake made every day. Which is where the well-informed relative comes in. Oh, I've heard the latest nasty little word coined by doctors about patients and relatives who are now using the internet to help understand things that previously were kept in a closed book in an arcane world controlled by doctors who knew the posh Latin names for things and wielded impossible, unreachable facts in their gargantuan, holy brains.

Cyberchondriacs.

Isn't that great? Doesn't that just sum up the attitude of the entire, smug, protectionist cabal of self-satisfied, self-serving quacks who'd rather see someone dead on a slab than admit to a mistake or, Jesus in heaven, admit that a patient, an ordinary member of the great proletarian unwashed, may be more informed than they are, the fucking fuckers.

Sorry, I think I dropped off. I've had a busy morning. Shell's reading something from the *Daily Mirror* to me. It's either about the humanitarian crisis in East Timor or Kate Moss's new cat. It doesn't matter a fuck to me either way. There's nothing I'm going to do about it from here. Bollocks to East Timor, and North, South and West Timor, come to that. And bollocks to the cat. Same goes for global warming, battered baby seals, battered wives, battered husbands, battered cod, immigration, emigration, North Korea, South Korea, the shouty cleric with a hook who wants to smash the state apart, presumably from his local dole office, the new Jaguar XKR – actually I'm a little bit interested in that – Kylie, Madonna, Desert Storm, Shield or Orchid, *Coronation Street*, Tony Blair, something called an iPod that'll never catch on, Ricky sodding Gervais, Chris bedwetter Martin, new films, new restaurants, New England, Newmarket 3 p.m. going good to soft, David Beckham, Sven Goran E. or Wayne Rooney. (Apart from that stuff about the Auld Slapper, which would make a corpse sit up and laugh.)

But I love Michele's voice. So I let her burble on, while I wonder what my magnesium level's going to be today.

And as I look across at the old, brutalised man in bed twelve and his tiny wife holding his hand and burbling just as inanely to him, I write on my pad:

'If it's a boy, let's call him Alfie.'

Michele smiles and agrees. At this time we were under the impression the baby was a boy only because the nice lady who did the last scan told us it was. And now it's time for Shell to go. Her clients really, really understand about her personal problems, even the ones that have just left.

11 a.m.

A couple of physios toddle back in with the hoist. I'm going to be put in my chair. I'm surprised they haven't brought an armed guard with them. Actually they seem pretty cheerful, for whatever reason. But they're in for a shock. Here's the thing. The hoist, like a lot of procedures inflicted upon the long-term disabled, is not for the benefit of the patient, it's for the convenience of the staff.

It only takes two people to operate the hoist whereas it takes four to carry me out of bed. It's much more comfortable for me to be carried. It's much easier for the physio team to get the hoist. The other thing is, the hoist is supposed to be operated by experienced, trained staff. Even when it is, it's still a difficult, painful procedure.

When you lie there watching some nump reading the instructions on the damn thing for what is clearly the first time your heart shrinks, as do your cobblers – as far inside as possible.

This nonsense has to stop. I go on strike. I refuse the hoist. This causes much head scratching, and an hour or so where ever more senior people are called in to tell me with less and less patience, and with less and less speed and syllables, why I need to sit in the chair. It's good for my lungs, for my muscles, for my bedsores, for me. I agree. They smile at this point. Then I explain, again, that it's not the chair that's the problem, it's the getting into it.

I still have the piece of paper with my most coherent and least sweary argument on. It says, in the original capitals:

I AM NOT GETTING IN THAT FUCKING HOIST ANY MORE. IT'S PAINFUL, IT'S HUMILIATING, IT'S DEGRADING. AND IT'S FOR YOUR BENEFIT, NOT MINE.

By this time doctors were involved. They were perfectly aware that my getting out of bed was a big step to my getting off ITU and freeing up the bed for someone else who needed it. And as I clearly wasn't about to die and there was no room in bed twelve, they had to get me better. So my very nice ITU consultant Mark, who has more than a touch of the Goodfellas about him, had hustled his way into the scrum like Joe Pesci in – well, every film Joe Pesci's been in – and said something quietly to the effect of – and I'm paraphrasing here:

'You fugging with him? Does it amuse you to fug with

him? Cos when you-a fugga with him you fugga with me, capisce? So you take dis hoist and you sleep it with the fishes you sonsabitches and you lift this poor muddafugga by your own sweet hands even if it takes ten a youse and you put him inna de chair, you unnastand? Or you gonna incur my extreme displeasure. Which is something to be avoided, you bunch of zabaglionis. Now kiss my ring.'

Or something similar. I'm on a lot of drugs, remember?

Mark's great. He's on a weekly rota and he's clearly under pressure from someone to get me off ITU asap. But, as he says to me when they all leave, 'I'll keep you here until you're stronger. If you go downstairs now you'll only bounce back here twice as hard.'

I think I understood him better as Joe Pesci. What he meant but wasn't allowed to say was, staff on the less hardcore wards wouldn't be able to look after me properly. Which was fair enough – not to cast aspersions on other staff, but because, overall, the care here was exemplary. And very complex. There was so much science involved. They love their science up here. If you haven't got a double first in organic chemistry from a very good university – a proper one that got its charter before, say, 1315 AD and not 13.15 p.m. – you weren't going to work in this ITU. Doctors here knew what my numbers meant.

The physios take the hoist away. Victory. They don't come back to get me out of bed. Hmmm.

While they're here, the eagle-eyed medics notice that the cannula in my right hand is bleeding. From the inside. Thin feathery trails of blood fan out under my skin. Time to move the cannula. 'It's granulating,' they say, with their usefully euphemistic language. Great. I'll need a new one.

Cannulas go in with a big needle, which then guides the semi-permanent thick plastic tubing under the skin to allow various other tubes to be attached, sometimes for days. They use them mainly for drips, of which I need a lot. They're useful because having a screw-top opening into your blood system means it's easier to change drips, introduce medicines, etc. Which is fine for short-stay patients.

A thirteen-year-old doctor approaches with a new cannula. I refuse to let anyone who's not even allowed to watch *Dr Who* on their own stick one in me. But I know a secret. The best people to put needles in are anaesthetists, cos that's all they do all day. They're a much more highly trained bunch than you might think. The art of keeping a patient unconscious enough to be pain-free and unaware that some ham-fisted surgeon is removing his spleen with a pair of pinking shears, and yet somehow not killing them, is an arcane and extraordinarily difficult one. During an operation they monitor minute changes in the patient's heart rate, oxygen levels and brain activity. If a doctor has to go under the knife, the first thing they want to know is the name of the anaesthetist. Despite this, anaesthetists still get a bad press in medical revues, similar to the reputation of drummers in musical circles. To wit:

Q: What's the difference between a drummer and a
    drum machine?
A: You've only got to punch the rhythm into the
    machine once.

Or this:

> Drummer, fed up with all the jokes, decides to become a guitarist. He goes to the shop and says: 'I'll have a Les Paul Gold Top guitar, a Marshall JCM 100 lead amp with a 4×12 speaker cabinet, three dozen plectrums and some spare strings please.'
>
> Bloke behind the counter says: 'You're a drummer, aren't you?'
>
> The drummer's aghast. 'How did you know that?'
>
> 'This is a fish and chip shop.'

My point is anaesthetists get similar treatment. This is by way of apologising for a scene in a comedy programme I wrote where an operation is taking place. The surgeon asks the highly trained, on-the-ball anaesthetist if everything's OK. The anaesthetist takes a quick look up from the crossword and goes:

'Yeah, whatever.'

OK, it's a visual gag. You had to be there, and as it's quite clear from the ratings that most of you were watching *TV's Filthiest Language Ever! Part 23* on the other side, you were not. Worse, I remember chatting to an anaesthetist before the show went out and he said, 'Oh, I hope you haven't portrayed us as lazy sods who just put people under and then do the crossword for six hours.'

Either way, I demanded my new cannula be put in by a proper anaesthetist. As lovely Mark was on duty and was used to patients on ITU going slightly round the bend, he acquiesced. So, some time later, a frazzled anaesthetist was dragged from some hideous twelve-hour heart-lung-liver transplant/bypass/resection operation to put in some bolshie git's cannula.

She was not best pleased. She was less pleased when even she couldn't find a vein. An hour later, she finally shoved it in my foot. Several times, like a dodgy darts player desperate for a double finish and bouncing off the wire half a dozen times before smacking it firmly in. I still have a scar to remind me.

12.30 p.m.

A trundle on the ward. No, not the food trolley all the way from the valleys, look you, and not the plasma exchange, thank God, but my daily chest X-ray. Most patients on a vent have these, to make sure they still have lungs. I used to have two X-rays a day, but now it's just the one.

I won't describe the kerfuffle to get me sitting up, the cold plastic plate against my back, the moving of all the wires and tubing, cos you can imagine all that. Just as the little man was about to snap my lungs, I asked about a bit of lead shielding. Most patients are only in intensive care a short while – for one reason or another – so the X-ray people get a bit lackadaisical over the lead shields. They figure, I suppose, that patients generally won't get enough strontium-90 to do any harm. I was begging to differ. You know how in comics radiation is usually a useful thing, giving you the powers of a spider, or invisibility, or the keen hearing of a wombat? In real life, radiation just makes your hair fall out and gives you cancer. And Baldy Cancer Man ain't gonna sell many comics.

Directly in the firing line under the camera were my poor, bruised, hoisted, knackered knackers. Shoving a bucketful of gamma rays into them repeatedly might, I suppose, give them the curious powers of – oh, I dunno, vision and speech or something, but it was more likely to make them shrivel like unpicked grapes in an unexpected Bordeaux October heatwave. And I didn't want talking knackers either. They get to see terrible sights and I really wouldn't want a running commentary.

So I get the lead lap cushion and breathe in and away snaps the snapper – another one for the family album. Down I lie again to read my mail.

I'm not really allowed post cos of the risk of infection, but the nurses have grown either to like or hate me and let me have some. My absolute favourite, which I treasure to this day, is a huge get-well card from all James's class-mates. Of course, the teacher's made a project out of it and it will probably go to her final Key Stage 2 assessment, but stop being cynical, it's a lovely thing. Obviously it's rubbish cos it's made by seven-year-olds, just like cave paintings are rubbish cos they're made by cavemen, but they have such lovely meaning, such great intent that even I am won over. By the card, not by cave paintings – they are still rubbish. Did these people ever see a real bison? They don't look like that. And hello. Perspective? It took until the Renaissance for people to work out that things further away *look smaller*. How our race survived is beyond me. No wonder the Vikings were so successful. You've got a bunch of Saxons on a hill going:

'Oh look over there, Ethelred, it's Viking longboats.'

'Don't worry, Brythnoth, they're really tiny ones this time. We'll just stamp on them. In fact, let's not even bother getting our swords.'

The chimps must be really pissed off we got the genetic nod.

The card from James's school has little pictures of all the children which they drew themselves. In one sense it's beautiful, in another, it's disturbing. Especially the ones with the giant heads. It got stuck up on the wall and was OK as long as I didn't look at it at night. When they came down from the wall, waving their little stick arms and, and . . .

The other post I had was from a mate who'd bought a packet of hilarious postcards all featuring unpleasant toilets of the world. He wrote a lot. Michele used to pop the cards up on my bedside tray so I could get a good look at some squalid Guatemalan bog all day. The other side was worse – it was full of him moaning about how terrible it was to be at the Royal Shakespeare Company getting paid for dicking about two hours a night in tights and getting pissed and knobbing pretty actresses half his age. I just about preferred the shanty-town shite houses. God, but I could smell the stench. It ate into my nostrils. My imagination must be—

No, I'm not imagining it. It's me. I stink.

Even the nurses have noticed.

1.30 p.m.

I'm getting my hair washed. Great. My neck hurts when I bend it back; my tracchy cuff digs into my throat; my skin is hypersensitive to water; the smell of the shampoo makes me gag and my little Filipino house boy is doing the honours. And I know where his hands have been. They think they're doing me a favour. I refuse to be shaved because I've decided to grow a beard as a protest at being kept in here against my will. It's unhygienic, it's ugly, it's piss-poor logic, but it's something no one wants me to do. So doing it makes me feel better. My hair is getting long – apart from the receding bit at the front – and I'm starting to look like I should join a 1970s prog rock band. Probably as a drummer.

2 p.m.

I'm in the bloody chair. Four physios turned up, waited sulkily for my lovely flowing locks to be rubbed damp with a thin towel, and the previous half-hour painful embarrassing performance with the hoist now takes five minutes. I was right. They know it, I know it, they don't like it, I don't care. I turn on the TV and, saints preserve us, it's him again. Palin. This time going round the world back to front. Or doing it with only one shoe, or on a bike, or by camel or something – basically another travel show with some specious modus operandi tagged on to give it a unique selling point. Impressed? Well I used to work in TV too, you know. I turn it off.

And look at my notepad. I've not done this before. I try to make sense of the sentences. I can't make head or tail of them. They're like David Bowie lyrics. Here's a page, at random. Unedited.

Loose cuff – air in cuff
On and off/less and less
It's stopped.
Are they safe?
Park permit?

I'm happy just sleeping
What's the date?
Not as bad.
Not so fierce
How were your do's?
Long distance ×2 vision (end of war)
Ashes to ashes, funk to funky, we know Major Tom's a—

Alright, I made the last one up. But tell me there's not a hit single in there somewhere. Here's a page that makes more sense. I've added my own notes – like I did for my fantastically useful English degree, when you learn that everything you've been reading up to now is wrong and actually no writer actually means what he wrote or what you might think, thicko, and you need well-paid fat drunk tightly wound professors who have more time off than the unemployed to reveal to you what is *actually* being written. Well thank God for them, or we'd all be stuffed if all we had to be going on with was just the boring old ability to read.

How do I find a way to get home – just for a couple of
days – even if I have to come back?

This appears several times in Nigel's later Charing Cross work. Many scholars have seen this as a reference to the divine. It's almost as if the hero is here appealing to a higher power to lift him out of the ordinary into the transcendent. Note the 'couple of days' and compare with Christ's harrowing of hell and later return to the world. The hero is clearly suffering from delusions of grandeur.

What's happening with my white cell count?

On the face of it a simple enough question, but *cf.* Melville's *Moby-Dick* p. 978 (Parsnip edition), Ahab: 'Where's my fucking leg you overgrown goldfish? I'm gonna fillet you, you see if I don't.' (Unpub. first draft.)

I prefer tracchy mask to whisper.

Only the most literal reader would ascribe this to a preference for one of the two methods being used in an attempt to wean Nigel off the ventilator. The whisper-flow reduces the amount of oxygen going in through the trachea in an attempt to strengthen the lungs to make them work harder. The mask works on the same principle, but when applied, Nigel breathes through his mouth. Most modern interpretations now see this as a fairly straightforward rebuttal of Cartesian Dualism. Which is stating the bleedin' obvious when you think about it.

Thanks for coming down again – it's a long way. And Shell said you were off tonight?

No, this is pretty much as is. He's talking to his uncle, who feels he's done his bit now and is legging it in case something else unpleasant happens and he has to muck in some more. His uncle will soon move permanently to France to get right out of the firing line.

You're a bit double.

Poor eyesight, or are we back with playwright and wit

Sean O'Casey in the Sailor's Fist pub in Dublin and his celebrated bon mot: 'Youse. You at the feckin' bar there. Oi'll be having a large one and if you can see your way to putting it on me slate then – oh hang on, I'll just be falling off me stool now so I will.' I think we know where we stand.

> Bed of doom and bed of a loon. Mind you I've only just started to see people sicker than me. He's 40. His wife broke her heart in here the 2nd night when he took a turn for the worse. Think it's blood escaping into the brain.

A difficult one this. Best move on. It won't come up in the exam.

> Can you chase me down a pair of small teds please?

'Teds' could be a reference to the useful but uncomfortable elasticated surgical stockings which patients with limited mobility have to wear to prevent Deep Vein Thrombosis, but only a dullard would take this at face value. I mean, come on – he's in a cot, he's infantilised – teddy bears' picnic? Is it making sense yet?

> Cramping down left side – difficulty in breathing – I can't sleep with this in – am I due some painkillers? – I feel quite breathless – yes I'll start earlier tomorrow, but I'm uncomfortable NOW – loose cuff – suction please – could you flush my tracchy, it feels there's secretions there – am I due can I have some painkillers yet? – when can I have paracetamol through tube? – can I have

suction – actually I'm secure on this ward, particularly at night – how long will you be? That was the most stupid thing I've heard for months – when can I go home? Can I go home? Send me home.

2.15 p.m.

. . . And here comes Mum. Bugger. She's seen that I'm awake. And I'm in the chair so I can't pretend to be asleep so she'll sod off outside for another fag and a cry to put off the evil moment when she *tells me about her day*.

Don't get me wrong; I dearly love my mum and I owe her big time for the love and support she gave unhesitatingly to me and my family through this crisis and well into my rehabilitation. I know, you're waiting for the but. Mum, reading this, is waiting for the 'but'. I'm avoiding writing the 'but'. I do feel bad about the 'but'.

But –

I know about her day. It's the same as yesterday's day. And the day before's, and so on. And on. To be quite honest, Mum's days didn't have much variety about them before I was ill, but since then the wow factor's really taken a nosedive.

She came in on the Number 33 bus via Barnes. She likes to get the one before the kids get out of school because kids today have no respect, etc. . . . She sits by my bed for the next lots of hours redefining the concept of small talk. She leaves when Michele heaves up after work and goes home on the Number 33 bus, puts the kids to bed and puts a ready meal on. Michele gets home; they watch an hour of TV and discuss my progress. She goes to bed, gets up, potters about, and gets the twelve-thirty Number 33 bus via Barnes. She likes to get the one before the kids get out of school because etc. . . .

Now I know James Joyce could get a big old novel out of one bloke's day, but Mum got three fucking months out of it. She is the quantum physicist of conversation; nothing is too small to warrant her attention, or indeed endless comment. Even running out of things to say presents no problem for this mountaineer of the mundane – she just tells me it all again.

Fortunately she is nicotine dependent and also fortunately the lifts here are shit. So a fag/weep break can take up to half an hour. Problem is, when she gets back, she's met someone with a terrible sob story. Mum attracts these people like footballers attract Chingford glamour models.

'. . . So one minute she's getting some veg in Iceland, the next thing she knows she's being rushed in here with a suspected stroke and a bag of frozen peas stuck to her face. Only thirty-five. Got nine kids and her husband's just been made redundant from that chemical works so they don't have to pay him compensation for his accident. She said it wouldn't have been so bad if her mum was still here. She ran off with the vet who put their Jack Russell down . . .'

4.30 p.m.

'. . . via Barnes. I get that one before the kids get out of school because . . .'

I'm now hoping for a medical emergency, up to and including something fatal. I look out at the darkness, idly wondering if there's a 747 hurtling towards me, but it's just rain. I remember Alidz is Iranian so with any luck George W. will send a couple of cruise missiles over to take her out and any other civilian getting in the way of the War against Terror. I'm volunteering Mum as a human shield.

The physios return, just as I'm getting very uncomfortable. I'm nice to them because it's easy for them to get very, very busy and forget me. Not on purpose, but it would still be unpleasant. And I'm sure they'd feel very bad about it and everything. Hey ho and back I go. Now I do need to sleep.

6 p.m.

Brilliant! Someone's turned up to take my catheter out. It's going to hurt but it gets rid of Mum for another half-hour. I've been toying with the idea of bribing Dr Lane to tell her I've died but wonder if it's unnecessarily cruel. Can't quite decide, but either way there's a nice man here who's just about to—

– Whoa. Steady on there. Ow ow ow.

There's a squeaky noise like chamois leather on a wet windscreen, a soft 'pop' and it's out. Time will tell if it works.

Time. It's slowed down since lunch, and not just cos of Mum. Most things in hospital happen before about 2 p.m. You get an overcrowded morning when you wish everyone would piss off, and then they do and you're left with the afternoon and evening stretching out like a desert, an eternal double chemistry lesson staring at a periodic table just wishing some of it would make sense. And wondering when you'll ever get to put iron filings in a Bunsen burner again, cos that was fun but it seems a long time ago.

We're all just waiting.

Which is bad, because that's when the fear can creep up on you. 'The waiting's the worst part' is such a cliché that it must be true.

Especially in hospital waiting rooms. I think they don't bother with appointments; they just call out the funniest names. Staff have competitions to see who can read out the most ridiculous name loudest, without cracking up. So when you're sitting there, reading last month's Closer *and worrying about whether Eric from* Big Brother 65 *is going to dump his gay lover Bruan from* Boyz R Us *for that hussy Spangle who was in those mobile-phone photos with that central defender from Blackburn Rovers, you'll hear this:*

'Eureka Zebra? Massalla Gestapo? François Petit Morte? Patrick Pudenda?'

And sadly you're called Greg or Susan or whatever and that's why your appointment is always an hour late. Straight up. Heard it off a porter who was told it by a cleaner.

7 p.m.

A spotty female doctor is talking to me. God, is there nothing remotely shaggable in this place? I was brought up on *Doctor at Large* and *Carry on Nurse*, but this is more Hammer Horror. My old man's free at last and he could do with some encouragement.

Whoops, writing out loud again. Sorry about that. So, what do you want, Sebum Face? She wants to know how

167

I'm getting on with getting off the vent. Not bad, as it happens. I'm spending several hours a day on reduced oxygen, and it's uncomfortable but manageable. But I don't like it at night. I keep waking as I drop off, gasping for breath like a funfair goldfish. But now there's a new ITU consultant on call who's determined I stick with it. Maybe they think I'd rather be on a ventilator than not. Maybe some doctors think secretly we all love being sick, and if they could just convince us that being better is better, there'd be no more illness, they'd get a Nobel prize, and we'd stop writing rude things on our pads at them.

8 p.m.

The wife weebles her way in. Hoorah, I can finally hear something interesting. But –

Another bloody but.

First she wants to hear about my day. Sadly there's only Mum, the Bernard Levin of ITU, to tell her, so that's half an hour gone. Mum clears off to the canteen for some chips and a rendezvous with a limbless ex-tree-surgeon with a drink problem. Then Shell says she doesn't really want to talk about her day cos she thinks it was boring and doesn't want to bore me with it.

But I'm desperate to take my mind off my own body, full of crap and piss and pus and blood, and it's all I get in here. I'm in the gutter, looking at the gutter, wallowing in the gutter. Please talk to me about the stars.

But she's looking at me like Alfie's wife looks at him and I notice he's missing. I promise her I won't go anywhere and she tells me I'm being silly and recounts some meaningless industry nonsense and that tells me everything's OK today. We're both here. Which means I'm not here.

Until I need a wee. My legs have been crossed, but now my fingers are. There's a plastic bottle. Shell manoeuvres it into place. The neck is wider than a milk bottle. I make the obvious joke that it's too narrow. Michele makes the obvious joke that I could use a Coke bottle and it wouldn't be too narrow. And now we're ready, both nervous.

And yes! It works! My Lord how it works. It's coming out like the piss of a full-bladdered stallion and for a moment I'm elated. See me, see me wee. I am a man in charge of his own urinary tract! How great is that?

Well, *not very* kicks in the miserable/sensible voice in the back of my head. I mean, in the great scheme of things, Big Deal. The bottle is removed. Naturally, it's half empty. Shell thinks it's half full.

We're both right. And even now I seem powerless to determine how to view this, day to day. Some days still my piss bottle is half full – hey, sometimes even three-quarters – and others, it's very, very empty indeed. I don't know this yet, but as Michele kisses me goodnight and I watch her bump leave the ward five minutes before the rest of her, somewhere in my bruised psyche I am starting to realise this.

Nearly Midnight

Trouble sleeping. Thing is, the doctors say I'm allowed to put the ventilator back on full power when I choose, but they forgot to tell that to the nurses. There are many good and sensible reasons for not letting nurses so much as fart without written instructions from a doctor, in triplicate, as to duration, timbre and perfume. But blimey, sometimes they should be allowed to take some initiative. Because now the nurses are refusing to tinker with my equipment despite the irritating fact that I'm suffocating. They eventually send for a doctor, I plead my case, the doctor argues I should try harder, I start writing in large slow capitals. No one likes being called a cunt in capitals. The machine is turned up.

Apparently it's New Year's Eve. Oh whoop oh joy. Some staff seem to be pleased about this. Presumably because not only are they on triple time but they haven't got to go to another hideous New Year's Eve party.

Someone who presumably thinks I give a shit turns my bed and the machines around to face the large windows overlooking London, to see the fireworks over the Thames. I wait a while. There's the odd sad rocket in the gloom.

I suppose it's appropriate to reflect on the year just gone. Maybe in the manner of one of those cheery outside-broadcast presenters who've been cued a couple of minutes too early cos they've just lost the link to Edinburgh, and are desperate to fill in time but make sure everyone knows what a momentous, amazing, incredible night this is:

'*We're here at the bedside of 37-year-old former human Nigel Smith. Nigel, how was 2001 for you? Sorry, he can't speak but he's writing something down. F – U – must be Fun! What an amazing man. Still joshing despite the utter collapse of his livelihood and bodily functions.*

'*And it started so well. OK, most of the people he knew in the TV comedy industry were insecure, shallow, ambitious, grasping arseholes, but as he could do a good impression of an insecure, shallow, ambitious, grasping arsehole, he was doing fine. He had a more than usually eventful Edinburgh Festival, to which his now pregnant wife will attest, had written several jokes over the course of the year, and was looking forward to an eventful redundancy when, sadly, fate intervened.*

'From big banana to cabbage in a few days, a sobering thought as we hear the chimes of Big Ben and etc. etc. . . .'

Turn it off. Turn my stupid head off. That's my New Year's resolution. To stop thinking. The past has gone. Fuck it, my future's gone. Accept it. But my child?

Oh my child, what will your world be for you? When Alfie's wife looks at the wreck of her husband, I do know what she sees. She has sixty years of the man to cling to. If I am here when you are born, what will you see?

What will you know of your father? What remains?

After half an hour staring into darkness I'm wheeled back into place.

All the time I'd been facing the wrong window.

Chapter Six

The Fine Art of Surfacing

January 2002

New Year, new me. Bollocks to both of 'em.

Well, they're both going to be rubbish, let's face it.

Maybe I should try some resolutions like any normal person. I have no idea if I did make any at the time, but I know what they would have been. In no particular order:

1. To be able to see, read, eat, walk, run, breathe, feel, be pain-free, hold my lovely beautiful new baby and give the wife a right gentleman's excuse me. (After her stitches have come out – I *am* a new man, after all.)
2. Failing any of that, to top myself.

That seems fair.

Meanwhile, some early Happy New Year facts to face – my swallow is seriously knackered so I'm going to need a permanent stomach tube – a PEG – fitted. At the moment, I have a naso-gastric – NG – tube which goes up my nose, down the back of my mouth and into my oesophagus. I'm quite PO'd at the NG. The PEG – a percutaneous endoscopic gastronomy tube – will go directly into the stomach, and leave me with a two-inch limp tube thing dangling from my mid-section. And not for the first time, sadly.

The PEG will be more comfy than this tube up my nose. There's been a delay in fitting it partly because PEG fitting is unpleasant and invasive – what a surprise – so they waited to be sure I was going to need it (official version) and cos of the Christmas and New Year party season, which meant that at least one of the three-man team it's going to take to fit this thing has at any given time been off skiing/sick/drunk in a ditch somewhere for *weeks* (unofficial version). I'm looking forward to the change in my culinary arrangements for another reason. Currently, to check my digestive system is working, nurses syringe up my dinner through my nasal tube and splash it out into a kidney dish for a poky nosey. Then, horribly, they squirt it all back in – so I don't have to produce more gastric juices. I'm snorting down vomit, which is quite rock 'n' roll, but not nice. On the plus side, it's my first hot meal for weeks.

I have some time on my hands now. I might try and sort my head out. Why not? Things have been so busy lately what with one thing and another I just haven't had the chance. But it's all settling down into a nice routine now. So. A bit of spring cleaning. Be nice to know where I stand. Let's have a quick delve into me. Am I going to be calm and dignified, the perfect model patient, a joke here and there? Am I going to be the class fucking clown for the staff's benefit? An Uncle fucking Tom in a nightie? Or at war? Mouth like an Uzi? You fuckers. Get me out of this fucking bed. I'm getting this fucking tube out of my throat and I'm walking out of here and you can all kiss my white fucking ass. Now laugh that off, motherfucker.

Hmm. So that would be anger then. I need a 'Parental Advisory' sticker. Shall I take another quick peek?

AAARGH!

. . . and that would be fear. Know what? I might leave the dark recesses of my mind in the dark. There's a reason I've not put a new light bulb in.

I've often felt that about psychiatrists. Always desperate to firk about in the filthy unconscious or subconscious or wherever it is that's not actually conscious. Know what they're doing? They're calling you a liar. You go in and say you're scared of snakes and they'll basically tell you after months of expensive and traumatic therapy that you are not scared of snakes, you lying little arsewipe, you're scared of your mother's penis envy. So now you're a liar, you're still shit-scared of snakes and you can't go round your mum's for toad-in-the-hole ever again. Brilliant.

But sod it, I've gone and looked and now I can't play the dignity card any more. I'm not dignified. I'm a mass of hate and don't know where to put it. Of course, I know exactly where it will end up – it's all going inwards. Outside though, hey, I'm fine. Fine fine fine. That's it, don't let them know. Yes, that's the thing. That'll show 'em. What a trooper. I'll play that game and I'll keep this hate and this rage to myself and I won't let anyone see, he he he, and I'll tell jokes and everyone'll think I'm such a great guy and when I get out I'll, I'll . . .

OK, I'm turning into Charles Manson. Best get a shave. One day I get my PEG. I can't be arsed to write about the fitting of it cos I've stopped paying attention by now and I'd hate you to do the same.

'What's happening in that book you've been reading?'

'Oh, the bloke's having something horrible shoved in him.'

'What, *again*?'

'To be fair, last chapter he was mainly having stuff taken out of him. In a horrible way.'

'Hmmm. Bit samey, isn't it?'

'Bit. And I did prefer his earlier, funnier chapters.'

So let's move on. I developed the theory about two minutes ago that if something is forced on you long enough there must be a point at which you get so de-sensitised that they can do anything to you and you accept it as normal, no matter how warped or inhumane. Which explains Thatcherism, *EastEnders* and several of my exes.

I'm not entirely exaggerating. Here's proof: when I told our one mutual friend I was writing a book 'about my horrible experiences', she immediately blurted out: 'Oh please don't write about Carol.'

So I won't. But I'm really tempted. Five years with her made ITU seem like a weekend in Center Parcs. There's an American phrase, coined I think by John Updike, 'pre-disastered'. That was me. I think for a couple of years afterwards I walked around looking like those haunted Vietnam vets in Larry Burrows' photos – secretly praying for a bullet to put them out of their fucking misery. Maybe it wasn't too late to go back to Tipu Aziz for that hysterically dangerous brain biopsy. I could bung him a few quid to slip and get rid of her altogether.

I shouldn't dwell. Perhaps I just need a hobby. My catheter's out so I suppose I could go back to my previous favourite, but somehow things just aren't the same between us any more. Annoying the staff isn't getting me anywhere. They either think I'm joking – what a trooper, isn't he brave? – or occasionally a nurse will bite back. And not suction me, for instance. And then who's got the power, you little fucking rude cripple, squirming in your bed and turning purple? Think you're funny now?

I have impotent rage. Not good. In the First World War, spotters from both sides were sent up in tethered hot-air balloons, in daylight, to spy on the enemies' trench formations and movements. A little while later a squadron of fighter planes – the ones that look so quaint in airshows or on telly – would come tootling along, and more often than not, before the balloon could be hastily hauled down, rip the poor bastard in the basket to bloody chunks with a Maxim gun.

The life expectancy of these benighted souls was not high. But to the annoyance of the top brass on both sides of Flanders fields, many of those who did survive quite rapidly went a little odd, claiming to be General Haig's auntie and hiding under tables with a teapot they called Desmond. Or some such. Presumably these people were either shot or promoted. But an answer was found. If they armed the spotters with a handgun so they could fire back, no matter how uselessly, they didn't go mad. They still died by the cartload, of course, but that was par for the course and much less of an embarrassment.

The *idea* they were fighting back was the key thing.

The problem I had was in identifying the enemy. Truth is, I was aware it was my own body. The enemy within and all that. I've often had the notion that I'm my own worst enemy but now it's true. *Look, I've got to get out of here*, I write to Michele. I argue they could now take me home. They gently raise some sane objections but, ha ha, I've thought it through. Obviously we'd need the machines, yes, and some nurses I suppose, but we'd remortgage and I'm sure I've seen a second-hand ventilator in the *Twickenham Exchange and Mart* and . . .

It's not going to happen. I'm being cruel just asking. I see pain on Michele's face when she has to say no. So now I'm lashing out at her. I might as well be some chemo kid asking my bankrupt mummy to find five grand to take me to Disneyworld before I join the big Mouse House in the sky. 'But can't you – cough – organise a quiz night at the Frog and Ferret, Mummy? Or a celebrity fun run? And I think you can earn up to – hack – five pounds a time giving hand relief behind King's Cross station. Oh I do so want to see – bleeeagh – Cinderella's castle and I have got leukaemia, you cheap bitch.'

I need to get out of here.

So Michele gets me out.

Course she does. I'm taking it for granted now that I can ask her for pretty much anything and she'll deliver. It's a rod for her own back, the silly cow. (She's just come in and read that bit over my shoulder and called me a cheeky fucker. The rod's on the other back tonight, I suspect.)

So I get to thinking about what extreme circumstances do to relationships and I can't think of any happy endings. There's, ah, let's see – Tristan and Isolde (you won't know it but put it this way, Shakespeare nicked the ending for *Romeo and Juliet* but made it more upbeat), Heloïse and Abelard (he had his nuts cut off and she was locked in a nunnery), Leo and Kate (*Titanic* selfish unshared-door situation), that really boring couple in *The English Patient* (he got fried and she went mouldy), and me and my art teacher when I was eleven. You may scoff. She was lovely. All fresh out of college, with fuck-me boots and long hair and, well, I can't remember much else bar a tight leather jacket and a long, long scarf. First art lesson I'm blindfolded, she stands behind me and puts something round and yielding into my hand. She holds my hand in hers and guides me, teaching. She made me stroke it. She told me to caress it with my finger, to feel the ridges, the smooth waxy flesh, to press with my thumb just *there*. My finger went moist. She said I would never be able to draw if I couldn't feel. Draw? By now I couldn't fucking stand up straight, let alone *draw*.

It was an orange, by the way, and her sudden departure several months later left me with an ache until my O-levels and a desire to hang around the greengrocer's at chucking-out time. I blame the age gap. Ten years. But no one minds an older man and younger woman, do they? The world just didn't understand. And as I went to a Catholic school I suppose I should just count myself lucky it wasn't the male art teacher showing me how to colour in two kiwi fruits and a banana.

All tragic endings. The omens for me and the missus were not good. The point about adversity is it makes things that much harder, so why people bang on about it as something to be relished is beyond me. There are, I freely accept, people for whom adversity is a draw. People who get up in the morning and think, 'Right, before breakfast I'll hop to the South Pole naked tied to a bouncy castle.' But even they might baulk at getting tied to a human wreck like me. In their emotional lives, people tend to play it safe. I would recommend that the next white middle-class Protestant twat, the next bored, root-less, over-stimulated useless twenty-something with an iPod and PSP and a snowboard and indulgent parents who's considering bungee jumping in Thailand to spice up his life should simply marry a disabled Muslim lesbian single mum in Basra. And then see how much adrenaline he's really addicted to.

I was in bed with the wife the other night and just as she was finishing yet another book about a troubled LA forensic scientist hunting down a serial killer in a quest that threatens to engulf him and his family – sorry, almost dropped off there – before finally confronting demons from his own troubled past – gosh, is that the time? I have to be up early tomorrow no no I am interested it sounds marvellous – she turned to me and said, 'You know, it's never been boring.'

So that's the answer for all you bored folk wanting to live life on the edge. Get yourself down to your local intensive-care unit and bag yourself a good 'un. But hurry, they're going fast.

So was I. Out of there. Before I know it I'm being plonked in a wheelchair with a portable ventilator (OK, an old dented oxygen bottle) slung over the back, unhooked from all my monitors, and me and my gear and my drips were going out. Out into the big wide corridors. Oh fuck, stop, stop the chair, you're going too fast, I feel sick I'm so dizzy, who put me on this rollercoaster?

Ungrateful I know, but my eyes were so buggered and my balance mechanisms so impaired that moving forward was like the end sequence in *2001*, where that astronaut gets to Jupiter very quickly indeed. The corridor was going past me at warp factor twelve and I couldn't take it, captain. How fucking perfect. Beg for weeks to get out and then can't bear the sensation of movement. Ho de fucking ho.

Poor old Mum was pushing me. In reality, I know she wasn't hurtling me round the corridors like Stirling Moss, as she has the top speed of a one-legged Womble with a bunion. It just felt like it. We were heading for *outside* and the famous fish tank. The ground floor of the hospital is like a beige bus station: huge, crowded, noisy and draughty. There's a gift shop, escalators, lifts, etc., a bunch of shifty smokers hanging about outside who look like extras from *Boyz n the Hood* (and that's just the staff), the odd geezer in an overcoat and pyjamas shuffling grimly to the pub next door, hoping no one will notice his drip on wheels, a cancer information centre (I always thought there should just be a big sign inside saying YOU ARE FUCKED, MATE) – and smack in the middle, a bloody great fish tank. Maybe there's something metaphorical about these poor creatures swimming pointlessly around until the day they get to the big bog bowl in the sky, or maybe they're supposed to be soothing. But trust me, no one going into the hardest of hardcore inner-London hospitals as a visitor or patient is going to be soothed by a couple of bored rainbow fish hiding under some plastic coral.

Same goes for the shit art that hospitals put up. Maybe they're donations from local schools. Special schools. For the blind and emotionally disturbed. Or maybe they're from the psychiatric wing. But they're always utterly rubbish. And worse, you always suspect they were expensive. Some poor bugger's on a trolley for want of a bed, but look, we've got a seven-foot-long puce splodge entitled 'Peace' next to the cancer drop-in centre. It makes the hours fly by. And between that and the goldfish, I've almost forgotten about my sister's brain tumour.

I'm trying to write this all down, but even Mum's aware how depressing the ground floor is, especially on a late rainy January afternoon, and anyway my eyes are almost jiggling out of their sockets as it is. So. Off we hurtle to the canteen.

Which is the only place in the Western hemisphere even more depressing than the lobby.

There have been very few times when I've been glad I eat through a tube in my stomach. This was one of them. If the food they serve to the patients was terrible, at least it had the saving grace of being free. The relatives and staff have to pay for this cack. I sat quietly while Mum gamely tackled some chips and my feeding pump whirred and dripped another few calories into me and the oxygen hissed and I stared out of the large, grimy, glistening windows on to the large, grimy, glistening street. The trees scratching the window were bare and looked like they would be bare for ever, sharp, spiky and somehow inorganic, brutal, coated in filth from the endless unstoppable traffic. A small flower shop opposite was the only splash of real colour in the road, otherwise full of greys, browns and dirty fizzing neon which was just flickering on, shouting adverts for doners, pizzas, chips and dysentery.

I wanted to go home.

But they wheeled me back to ITU instead. Where I got a surprise: if it's a bit scary being in bed looking out, it's fucking *terrifying* seeing ITU from the relatives' perspective. It is an inhumane place for doing humane things. It is white and mechanical, and work goes on inexorably on the prone bodies of the sick. *My* prone sick body, more to the point, as I was unhooked and rehooked back into my cot.

Michele and Mum thought it was another step forward. I agreed. I thought it was a step forward off Beachy Head. But over the next week or so, there was no doubt I was making progress. Picking up speed. Infections lessened. Suctioning stopped. Doctors were itching to wean me off the machines. I was on the whisper flow more, I was encouraged/cajoled/forced to cut down my oxygen even at night. I was left in the chair longer, and my bum hurt less. The physio got more intense. I went for further trips in the million mph wheelchair. As I stared at the blurry fish tank feeling a cold, moist wind on my left side one afternoon, I knew I was surfacing. I was looking at a horrible case of the bends but my head was soon going to be above water.

And one day, like Jacques Cousteau bursting from the deep, like a whale sounding, I took my first breath of proper, unfiltered, hospital air. The ventilator was turned off. My lazy arse lungs were on their own.

I should have marked the day, but by now I was fixated on total recovery, and I hardly noticed. They left the tracchy tube in just in case, but I knew I wasn't going back on the machine. Best of all, by holding my hand over the open tube sticking out of my neck, I could now speak. It wasn't going to get me into RADA but if there were any openings for really scary James Bond villains, I might have had a chance at the auditions.

I still needed a little help from a nasal oxygen tube – the sort that all soap opera actors get in soap opera hospitals no matter what's happened to them. But come *on*, breathing, talking, surely now it was just a matter of weeks before I was giving it large to 'Rhythm Is A Dancer', playing a flaming stratocaster like a demented Jimi Hendrix, wolfing steak and chips, downing fifteen pints of lager, knobbing the wife into the next millennium, and doing 100 miles an hour down the A40 on jet-propelled rollerblades. All at the same time.

There's a fine line between ambition and delusion. You only need to watch the first few rounds of *The X-Factor* to see that. I was the misshapen hare-lipped tuneless fifty-year-old nut job in a tiger-print leotard saying I could be Michael Jackson with just a few pointers from Simon and the gang and singing's all I ever wanted to do. Apart from cleaning out bogs, which I'd been doing for the last thirty years, and where I'd perfected a rather unusual dance routine called 'Whoops that's slippy' – did they want to see it?

You might laugh, at home safe on your DFS sofa, but this is a world where Jade Goody's *mum* became a celebrity, so we are not living in normal times.

And when the day came on which I was to leave ITU, it came with the swiftness of the midnight knock on the door. I was rolled out of my very nice expensive bed on to a trolley and down a floor. That sounds odd. I mean I was taken down to the tenth floor. Further away from God, which I've always thought a good move. Now this is where my MRSA infection came in handy cos it meant I got a room of my own. The ugly cheap garret I'd always longed for. (When I say *always*, we had in fact recently bought a nice little house in Twickenham, but look, that was only for the kids' sake, got that? Otherwise I'd have been off. Oh yes – Paris, Barcelona, New York – as soon as the kids grew up I'd be, um, oh bollocks, nearly sixty. Shit. It was all going so well . . .) But I could pretend. I had the dodgy lungs, strange clothing, was on lots of drugs and had rotten personal hygiene. I was finally an artist!

This room, with its peeling two-tone cow-sick-green/dog-poo-brown colour combo was progress! This move *meant* something. I was on my own at last. Just me, my oxygen bottle, a drip or two, my feeding machine, nurses in and out taking blood pressure, blood, ECGs every hour, but hold on, I was nearly better. I mean, there are doctors who'd write me fit for work now, aren't there?

Actually those sort of doctors work for social services and insurance companies, and they were to turn up a little later, bless them.

Tenth Floor

And a regime change. It was noticeable on my first morning. My meds were left on top of the bin by the nurses at 6 a.m. as they prepared for the morning handover at 8 a.m. The morning nurses threw them away at 9 a.m. cos they'd been lying about, but by now they'd been ticked off as having been given to me so I couldn't get them. They were mainly painkillers.

I sorted it out later that afternoon. But this happened every other day. Sometimes to liven things up a sleepy nurse would come in, open the pedal bin sharply to chuck in someone else's rubbish and spray the meds all over the room.

And then there were the new staff to get to know. The

second morning, a nurse came to give me a bed bath. He was a young tall Antipodean dude with a shark's tooth necklace, and within minutes I was wishing the tooth was still attached to the fucking shark, along with several hundred others. He clearly hated the idea of bed-bathing me, slapping the flannel into the bowl with a sigh. He tried to haul me up the bed. I was still a dead weight and it hurt.

'I'm not Superman,' he hissed nastily. He was right. He was a cunt.

His tender ministerings were nasty, brutish and short. Each morning he was on duty it was the same thing. I dreaded these mornings, and was relieved on the days he wasn't on duty. Despite my growing reputation as a 'difficult' patient, he scared me – we would be alone in a room.

I tested the waters with the nurse from Chapter Two who looked like a more butch Tommy Cooper. I was probably being quite demanding, asking for, I dunno, perhaps a space shuttle, a unicorn horn, a philosopher's stone or some water – it would have been one of those, and she just turned to me before walking off and said, 'You're not on intensive care now.'

I told Alidz and she advised best not upset the nurses as they could make life difficult. For her, I think she meant. She also told me to be careful of a certain female nurse who kept being turned down for jobs as a prison officer, presumably on the grounds that she might frighten the inmates. Perhaps she'll be OK now there are a few posts going in Abu Ghraib.

Visiting Time

Happier things. I was now accepting gentlemen and lady callers. Cuh, I almost got knocked down in the rush. The names are concealed cos the legal people would stop me having quite so much fun else. But I do like to be truthful, so let's say these are the *types* of people who came to visit.

The ex-girlfriend who was around so long when I was younger she became part of the furniture – the part in question being the doormat
'Well as you know I'm seeing that bloke you always hated and see you were wrong it's going really well now I've got this ring I wear it on the third finger but it's not an engagement ring he said it's a friendship ring which I don't mind in fact it's perfect cos we're both free to see other people only I don't get chance to go out much and he works away a lot but that's fine as well and I don't really want to see other people cos I was always more the faithful type you might remember unlike ahem but anyway fancy you being in here like this all helpless and pathetic and I was going to buy you some fruit but they told me you couldn't eat anything and you can't really read any more and obviously anything like shoes would have been exceedingly inappropriate not that I'd buy you shoes anyway you never wore that pair I bought you just before you went off with anyway so I did get you some flowers which are in the sink and that oxygen's coming through alright is it? Just checking. I think that nurse fancies you.'

The ex-boss
'You're well out of it in here. Um, not *here*, exactly, but

186

out of the business. Not that you'll be out of it for long, naturally, but you wouldn't want to be in it anyway. Even if you were able to – I'll put it another way. I went for a job at the BBC, didn't I? Job was mine. All but in writing. So I went for my usual month in the Seychelles without a care in the world. Came back, the bastards had given it to someone else. I had to work elsewhere. On contract. *Me*, on contract. Course, it's bloody good money, it's fantastic money, but I still feel cheated. For example, know I said I'd take you with me if I went somewhere else cos I really rate you? They won't let me. That's how cheated I am. Terrible business.'

The mate who's made a really shoddy effort to keep in touch or help out and has one eye on the clock in case Michele catches him in here and he gets the withering stare

'I rang, I texted, but there's something wrong with my phone. And my car broke. Then the dog died. And Mum broke her teapot – hip, she broke her hip, picking up the teapot, ha ha. I've been thinking about you a lot, mate. Honest, non-stop. Couldn't decide whether you dying – getting sick – so young means I should cut out all the bad living – which I did for a week – or say fuck it and cane it while I still can – which I've been doing ever since that really boring week I had. Oh, I did get my first celebrity shag and that was – ah, not as good as you might think. And the fall-out was shocking. Took up days. I was hiding out. That's it. I couldn't go out cos of the press in the box hedge. And I don't suppose you heard about the Hackney tsunami?'

The really shit agent who I saw once despite her working ten minutes away and the hospital being on her way home

'Can't stay, I've got another sick client I have to see. What a bore. Get well soon so I can get some more commission out of you without getting off my lazy fat arse and here's a book written by a relative of mine. You should think about turning it into a screenplay. A spec script, obviously, I haven't got you a job in four years, I'm hardly about to start now.'

The real mate

'Alright you old cripple, I bought you some kids' books. Big print and pictures. Tell me about your day.'

I admit, there were a few more good eggs, but they don't make for as good copy. They know who they are, the people who made me laugh, the people who hid how affected they were by how affected I was, who pretended they could hear what I was saying and gave a shit in the first place, who told me what was going on outside the hospital, who bought me films, who wheeled me about a bit or just sat and chatted about bugger all. I've already said thank you, so I'm not saying it again.

Oh alright. Thank you.

My new bed does not have cot sides so I feel very grown up until I fall out of it one morning and can't get back in. The door to my room's open and I'm clinging to the sides of the bed, sheets tumbling round me, useless legs jerking spasmodically on the shiny floor in my slippery surgical stockings. My pyjama trousers are falling down around my bare bum and there's a puzzled electrician come to fix some fuse or something watching me and mine from the corridor. There are no nurses about. He's not unconcerned, to be fair, but is utterly paralysed with indecision. Yes, there's not a difficult decision to be made but his brain was programmed only to fix a broken switch this morning. He's brought his tools and everything. Now, in front of him is a mad bloke with an ever-widening Dagenham smile who can't get back in bed. No. Does not compute. He stares a bit longer. I wave at him feebly, which makes him more nervous. I put my hand over my tracchy tube whilst still hanging to the bed to stop me sliding completely off and breaking the fall with my nose.

'Can you get a nurse?' I ask, remarkably politely I think.

This really confuses him. I mean, where is he going to find one of those? But he still can't leave. He's not going to go anywhere near me, but he *so* doesn't want to get involved. He wants this not to have happened. Well, that makes two of us.

'A nurse. Get a fucking nurse you moron.' Is probably what I said next.

He looks about and licks his lips nervously. Perhaps he doesn't know what a nurse looks like. Perhaps he's seen the nurse who looks like Tommy Cooper and thinks it *is* Tommy Cooper so doesn't want to bother him. Perhaps he's a nutter from the psych wing dressed up as an electrician and the real one's in a white coat that does up at the back with a needleful of Thorazine up him – I don't know and I don't care, but we've both been here for ages now and something's got to give.

It's both of us. He ambles off to get help and I slide gracelessly to the floor.

As I lie there I reflect there's still a lot of work to do. If my recovery is the top of Everest, and say there are ten camps on the way up the mountain, I'm in Waterstone's buying the maps. And then discovering I've left my wallet back in the car. Perhaps I should just go for a coffee and look in Thomas Cook's for brochures on a nice Rhine cruise.

Everest's all very well but it's a long way off, it's a bit nippy and there are no decent pubs.

I'm bundled back into bed by someone or other and even as I try to talk myself out of it, I know somewhere inside I'm getting my crampons on. I don't seem to have a choice in the matter. Perhaps that's why all those idiots climb tall things in the first place. Dunno. I'm tired, confused and a little beaten. S'alright, in a couple of hours Mum'll come in and tell me about her day.

Oh fuck.

So I lie here and I can't work out why the soppy electrician bothered me. OK he was a dozy eejit but there's something else, something that was in his face. And then it hits me and I am sickened at both of us. It's the outside world. That's who he is – not just some berk with a Black and Decker. And today was our first proper look at each other. Everyone else – staff, relatives, visitors – had in some way prepared themselves for me. But the real world was going to stare at me with pity and disgust and simply wish I wasn't there. You know, the way I used to.

And for a long time part of me was going to agree that I shouldn't be there either. I was finding out that fighting for your life is a damn sight easier than fighting for a life.

All I had to do in intensive care was not die. That was it, my daily job. And I did it. Well done that man.

COWARD WINS FIGHT FOR LIFE COS HE DIDN'T WANT TO DIE. What a headline. How much was down to me, how much to modern medicine and how much to my plastic bottle of Holy Lourdes water and ju-ju beads is a matter for philosophers, scientists, theologians and meta-physicians to fight over, if they could be arsed, which is unlikely unless there was a good meal involved.

But now I had to *live*, and fuck me that's complicated. There's more to it than you think. Certainly more to it than I thought, but maybe that's because I didn't spend much time thinking about it and quite a lot of time just getting on with it. Oooh I was good at it. I suspect you might have liked me, had we met socially. I'm not saying I'd have instantly become your bessie mate and you'd have given me the keys to your Kensington pied-à-terre, or your season ticket to Chelsea, or dumped Brad Pitt for an evening of short bald fat passion, but I reckon we'd have got on OK. I'd have told a few jokes, regaled you with some cunningly self-deprecating but actually self-aggrandising anecdotes, and as time passed, I might have been invited to your house, had your spare ticket to Stamford Bridge, or you might have, well, you *might have* . . . Depending on circumstance, gender, and the absence of Michele.

A few weeks before I became ill, there was a reading of a sitcom I'd co-written at the BBC. It went quite well and afterwards in the BBC bar I got very drunk with some of the cast and some good mates who'd come along for moral support and had been primed/bribed into laughing at the right places. That night, getting walloped on licence-fee-payer-subsidised lager, I think I was about as happy as it gets. My life was pretty much on track after the odd bumpy decade and things were alright with the world.

I don't see most of those people any more and I cannot recall being that unthinkingly, easily happy since. Just so you know.

So what, I wonder, will you think of me now, new person I've not met yet? To my eternal shame, and when I was old enough to know better, I called a kid at school – who I actually liked, and I'm going hot recalling this – 'spakka'. As a joke, you see. People laughed and everything. It was because he talked and walked funny and because everyone else called him it. Well, if he wants, he gets first dibs at calling me the nastiest things he can think of. But I know, if I meet him again, he never would. He was a kind boy with large, hurt eyes and I betrayed him. He won't remember it. It was what his life was.

Today I'm glad I was cruel because I'm glad of my shame.

February, Part One

My tracchy tube – a Shiley, size six – came out with a nasty sucking noise one sunny afternoon. Gerard my favourite nurse did it. There was blood and all that but he just whacked a big square plaster on Doris's hole – now there's a sentence you won't find in many other books – and job done. The only tube now in me was my PEG, and blimey, that won't be in for long, will it? I'm going to stop writing now because it's lunchtime and I've a nice 500ml bottle of Jevity – I think the 2007 – to shove into my stomach via a syringe.

Yum. That's better.

I have a new physio team to take me to Everest base

camp one. That's the camp where the minibuses park up and there's a Little Chef and souvenir shop. What I'm trying to say is, it's not a long way up the mountain. But have you tried walking to Nepal? It's a bloody long way.

These are physios for people who can generally get about a bit so I'm rather dull, especially as I keep asking when I can have a go on the parallel bars. Every so often I'm wheeled down to the gym, which I vaguely recognise from my wheezy asthmatic days at school hiding behind the vaulting horse and hoping I don't think about my art teacher in the showers.

I'm quite excited by the promise of all the equipment but oh no, not so fast. I'm to spend weeks perfecting the fine art of 'the transfer'. That's basically getting from my bed into a chair without ending up in a crumpled heap on the floor hoping a passing electrician might take pity on me.

My left arm doesn't work, my left leg doesn't work and my right leg looks like Gandhi's after a particularly thorough fast. The sensible option would have been to say, 'Bugger this for a game of soldiers, I'm going back to bed with a big pile of Michael Palin videos. Silly sod's sure to end up in the Himalayas sooner or later.' But I keep heaving myself backwards and forwards until I make safe landings nine times out of ten and I'm allowed the luxury of not having to call a nurse for assistance every time I need to get in or out of bed. If only my left arm would work I could get in a wheelchair and be free! Free I tell you, but as it is I just keep going round in circles like a one-oared rowing boat. Frankly that's how my life is going to feel for several years, but I don't know that yet.

My eyes are getting better. I know that because each

morning when I open them, and after that small internal scream to greet the new day, I look at a mouldy patch on the wall. Recently it's been getting smaller, which is nothing to do with better hygiene and everything to do with my double vision improving. Also, it doesn't spin around quite so quickly. I'm now pottering about on the waltzers rather than the Big Huge Massive Scary Cyclone of Doom. I can also read a little. It's a race between my eyes giving out and my weak hand dropping the book on my head, but I'm getting a few pages down in a session.

What I'm not getting my head around at the moment is how *long* every improvement is going to take. Neurologists talk in terms of years in the way an orthopaedic surgeon talks in weeks. It's like waiting for my first girlfriend to give in. This is simply not acceptable – as I may have mentioned on many a sulky bus ride home with said first girl – and any time Alidz tries to explain this, I refuse to listen.

Look, it's very simple. I want to get better, right? So I'm going to get better. What's not to understand?

You *are* getting better, she'd say. It's only taken you a month to get in and out of a chair.

Only a month? Do you know how long a month is? Are you mad, woman? A month of gym work and I expect to look like Arnie bloody whatsisname, not Stephen Hawking. A month of practising the guitar properly and I reckon I could work out the fiddly bits in Sultans of fucking Swing, you Iranian bint. It's all I can do to *hold* a guitar at the moment without turning into Pete Townshend doing an impromptu spot of fine-tuning using the floor.

Do something *better*, Alidz. Yes, you've saved my life and everything and I don't want to come across as, like, really ungrateful, but fucking hell, you got me here, you can't leave me like *this*. It's first-year art all over again.

This sort of conversation always made Alidz uncomfortable. It still does, so I still do it when I feel a bit naughty.

Then one day Alidz brought her little girl in to see the nasty shouty man and my God, she was – is – heart-rendingly beautiful. She has this incredible mop of impossibly curly hair – in fact I thought at first Alidz had brought in an actual mop to help out with the cleaning problem, but no, it was her poppet. And she looked at me from somewhere under the hair like a Crufts champion Lapsang Suchong Boutros-Boutros Bin Laden we just call her Dibble, and she was *life*. And looked at me with nothing but shy curiosity. To my astonishment, I didn't resent it. It was the outside life I was so scared of and so hated and it was going to go on with or without me but I was still part of it and oh I was so glad I was still part of it and I should have hugged Alidz but I think I just held her hand while I stared at her child. That night when Michele squeezed her bump through the door I held her around our little growing thing and I was connected again. Just for a moment.

Michele wondered if they'd changed my medication cos I was smiling and she went off to shout at someone while I knew, I just *knew*, I was in the Himalayas now.

I was going to need a better coat.

February, Part Two – Goodbye To All That. All That Shit

I've found a great way to get my (low) blood pressure up without drugs – the *Daily Mail*. It's fantastic. Now that I can read for longer I get Michele to bring one in every day. It's a double-action treatment. First you read the story, headlined something like:

IMMIGRANTS SPARK GLOBAL WARMING AND WILL FLOOD 90% OF ENGLAND'S GREEN AND PLEASANT LAND – YOUR HOUSE PRICE HAS COLLAPSED! RUN FOR YOUR LIVES!

And that gets you started. Then after a while you reflect on the utter tosh you've just read and bingo! Blood pressure restored. There should be a health warning, though – you can overdose. Symptoms include nausea, irrational fear of your neighbours and, in extreme cases, moving to the Cotswolds.

So next time you see someone on the bus reading the *Mail*, perhaps discreetly tucked inside a copy of, say, *Razzle* to avoid social embarrassment, remember appearances can be deceptive: it might be for medical purposes. (I can write what I want about that paper from here on in, no *Mail* reader's going to get past the earlier Disneyworld stuff anyway.)

Hang on, something's happening. Behind my back, wheels are in motion. They want me out. Great, *I* want me out, can I go home? Ah, there's the problem. I'm not sick any more, *as such*. But I can't go home cos I'm something else.

I'm disabled. And now I'm a bed-blocker.

There were a couple more weeks of desultory physio, some occupational therapy which pretty much involved watching me try to squeeze a ball of putty, some difficult speech-and-language therapy – difficult because I was learning to speak all over again and because I hated the fucking speech-and-language therapist and she me, but it was getting clearer that I was out of immediate danger and needed specialist treatment for my – fucking hell – *disabilities*.

I'm finally off oxygen but I'm still off my feet and, if I'm honest, a bit on the fragile side. Breathless, knackered, dizzy and infectious. Not much of me works – Michele says that's par for the course but she's just being smart. But I *have* to get better, I have a deadline. I've had others and I keep putting them back. [*No surprises there – ed.*] I would be home by my birthday, then Christmas, New Year, some arbitrary date in January I made up to gee myself along a bit, my uncle's birthday in Feb, but the one I was not going to miss was the real birth day; the mini-me birthday. Alfie. The big lump.

So I get the sales pitches for the various high-class establishments in which I can experience the joys of rehabilitation. That's where I'm heading. Out of here and straight into rehab. Now you should know this about head injuries. No matter what their cause – stroke, lesion, blunt force trauma by a wooden horse cos I'm home a tad later than planned – and a wooden horse which I bought you as a bloody present, by the way, and let's face it it's not like you've never crept in in the wee small hours pet – ahem, like I said, head injuries. Doctors will try and tell you there is a 'golden period' of rehabilitation, lasting approximately six months. That's to say, after six months, chances are you're as good as you're going to get, lame-o.

When they tell you that, take out this book and shove it up their arse. Don't worry, I'll buy you another. Because what they are saying is complete and utter shite. Bollocks, baloney, rubbish. It's *not true*. People keep recovering, basically for ever. Yes, it may slow down sometimes, and perhaps the biggest strides in recovery do take place earlier rather than later, but the brain *wants to get better*. And it has a nifty way of re-routing signals around the knackered bits. OK, you might be in for a wait, and you might have to work bloody hard, but it's all possible. Do not let the bastards convince you otherwise.

Which is what they are currently trying to do to Michele. Who didn't believe it either. So, where to go next? If I had to go into a rehab unit, I wanted a good 'un. I've paid for this, me and my stamp, over the years. It was like going on holiday. We looked at the glossy brochures, read round the subject, you know, bought a few of those quirky travel books like *Driving Over Windowlickers* or *A Year in a Provincial Nuthouse* or *Up Shit Creek Again*. Oooh we had a lovely time. Came down to a choice of two resorts: the Arbeit Macht Frei Dribble-o-Rama in north London, or a lovely concrete bunker of a place near Wimbledon called the Wolfson Neurorehabilitation Unit. That sounded just the ticket. Very cosy. And within electric scootering distance of my house.

Which reminds me, I was almost run over by an electric scooter today. It's pension day and I'm not too nimble on my feet, as you might have guessed, and I was on my way to get the *Daily Mail* cos the dog kept being sick and I needed something to keep the Pedigree chunks out of the sisal matting, when the usual Thursday squadron of flying grannies came whizzing down my street on their little machines. They don't give a rat's fuck about road safety or pedestrians, they have right of way because they are all

106 years old and they're on the scooters. They ride four abreast and it's like a geriatric version of the chopper scene in *Apocalypse Now* where they're taking out the Vietcong, except it's pedestrians being flung in the way of cars as they charge down to the post office at 12 mph – which is a damn sight faster than me, let me tell you.

Best is, the scooters all have names like the Rascal. Which is hardly appropriate, although more appropriate than the one the Americans tried to introduce last year. No word of a lie, it was called the Spaz.

Was that the life waiting for me at the other end of this Wolfson place? A Rascal with a shopping basket? A bed downstairs? A bottle for a wee? A life watching the hours tick by in front of daytime telly? I'd been a student, I'd already done that, thanks. Then the horrible thought struck me that I was too damaged even to ride a bloody scooter. What could I do? And who was I?

When the NHS puts its mind to it, things happen very quickly. You wait ages for something to happen, then when it's your turn everything's done in a rather unseemly rush. Like your first bonk. So it proved with my move. One day I was counting the blood and dirt stains on the walls as per, then halving them cos of my double vision, the next I was packing my trunk – or what was left of it after the nurses had been through it. (Note to legal: can we get away with that? Legal: no, we're working double shifts as it is.)

I was procrastinating. I'm doing it now. Against all rules of writing, at a time when I should be taking you forward with excitement to the next chapter, I'm banging on about some geriatric nonsense and the like. But I didn't want to leave. I still don't, writing this. I don't want to go back to the Wolfson and I did not want to go then. I knew where I was in Charing Cross. As unpleasant and difficult and frightening as it had been, I was in good hands, on the whole. Even though I hated it for turning me into this helpless monster, because I had come in those doors a man. And now it was goodbye to Alidz and Dr Lane, to Mark Palazzo on ITU, to Doris (though somewhere she's always with me), to Gerard, to the others I've not named but who know who they are, and I was in my outside clothes and in a wheelchair with the inevitable pale-yellow knitted blanket and now I was in the waiting room at the back of the hospital and the electronic doors open on to a damp February morning and the ambulance is backing up and the ramp descends and I'm bumped and rolled out of the hospital but now strapped into the ambulance and the journey makes me sick with the motion and I'm being taken against my will and I can't see out of the windows because of the drizzle and my sickness but I know the roads and I know when we get to the roundabout that turning right will take me home.

We turn left.

Chapter Seven

Welcome to the Monkey House

The Wolfson Neurorehabilitation Unit, in leafy Wimbledon, was very much like my primary school for many and varied reasons, the main and unvarying one being I hated it and still do. It even looked the same: brick, single-storey 1930s Adolf-bunker style. You could hear the terribly modern architects of the time thinking they were doing their bit to bring Le Corbusier's revolutionary designs to the great unwashed when in fact they were just helping municipal councils bung up shitty cheap Legoland affairs that even the thickest building team could manage to assemble in about half a day.

Needless to say, it was a square, with a quadrangle in the middle. This space was supposed to be a garden, but several factors prevented it from being one of those sylvan glades that might have gladdened Alan Titchmarsh's little heart. First, it was mainly concreted over for ease of maintenance and ugliness of appearance. Second, it was still winter, and no one had ever thought to plant whatever it is that doesn't die and go horrible and spiky and/or brown and mushy in winter, and most importantly, because the unit was non-smoking the only things that proliferated out here were piles of fag ends. There was more tobacco in that garden than in the average plantation in eighteenth-century Virginia.

I had stepped back in time: there were drab classrooms everywhere, noticeboards with yellowing announcements, safety posters, a crappy gym with a climbing frame and the like, daily lessons in reading and writing, a big emphasis on plasticine, and staff who generally talked to you like you were *a – mental – five-year-old*. So, hello teacher. Which didn't bode well for me. My experience of schoolteachers in general – and I have to say it's pretty limited to state jobbies in the arse end of the West Midlands – is that the kindlier they are, the more stupid they are. Which is frustrating. The kind ones are those you want to spend your time with, but you know that they haven't got an ice-cube's chance in hell of explaining why $x = 2$ and not, as they originally suggested, Borehamwood.

But unlike my school, you'll no doubt be amazed to hear, this establishment is for boarders. Most rooms are twins, but I soon play the MRSA 'unclean, unclean' card and get a single. Hoorah. It's in the basement. Shit. A dirty, sludgy bank rises in front of the nailed-shut window, blocking out most natural light. What light there is is brown. It's convenient as it matches the decor. The room is pretty bare, with a lino floor, and looks like the bastard love child of a misguided drunken Travelodge that humped a borstal for a tenner.

But before I can settle in, I am to meet the headmaster – sorry, governor – sorry, unit director, who tells me that famous actor Rik Mayall, after his quad bike accident, once sat in that very chair I'm sitting in. Well, ahem, he'll rephrase that, not *that* chair cos I'm in a wheelchair, ha ha, but that spot. I later learn that Rik spent about twenty-four hours here before legging it and checking into somewhere else, presumably a damn sight nicer. Like, I dunno, Strangeways. The director reminds me of the late actor Charles Gray, in one of his more sinister roles. After he died.

The power of celebrity. This man's not proud of his physios, his resources, his success rate, his heated swimming pool, but of the fact some madcap comic once parked his sick backside in this office. Albeit briefly. While I'm on the subject, and while I'm thinking about wheelchairs, a thought's just struck me. One of the worst things about being in a wheelchair you are unable to self-propel is that you're never alone. Which is unspeakably annoying. The same appears to be true of celebrities, cos on the rare occasion I see one, they're always surrounded by at least ten really, really good mates only too eager to help them, say, order champagne at £300 a pop. The celebs seem to enjoy this. Perhaps they'd be just as happy in a wheelchair? The average carer that you get to shove you about wouldn't need anything half so expensive as a bottle of Cristal to keep 'em going. Usually all they want is a nice cuppa and a chat about their Raymond in Bridport with his own hairdressing business shame he never found a nice girl to settle down with though he was cut up about that one – Sandy or summat – that broke his heart that's probably it ooh my bunions . . .

If that is the case then there are several celebrities whose legs I would be happy to break for a small remuneration. In some cases, gratis. Call it giving something back.

But still, rotten as this place appeared, as far as I was concerned it was there for one purpose – to get me to walk again. Once I was out of the chair, everything would be better. The exercise would strengthen all my muscles before they wasted to nothing and I looked even more like Mr Muscle from the cleaning advert, the movement would help clear my labouring, continually infected lungs, and I would be *normal*.

'Ah, but what's normal?' asked a very smug, very modern physio one day, as I answered her puzzling question as to what I wanted from them.

To be normal, of course, I'd said reasonably, trying not to add 'you stupid twat'. What she was trying to tell me was that I had between Bob Hope and no hope of being normal and that I'd better get used to it buster, and quick, and settle for a life that quite patently was less – was worse – than normal, and yes, before you start, you sort of people who look for these sort of things, I have disabled friends who'll be offended by that and I'm sorry but being unable to walk is *worse*, not just *different* from being able to walk.

I'm sure people who've had their cock shot off in a war can go on to have happy and productive – if not *re*-productive – lives, but it's not as good as having a cock, is it? Same with legs. We are products of millions of years of evolution and, barring the appendix, we have ended up with what we've got for a bloody good reason. We need all of it, dammit. I know there are some feminists who argue that the clitoris is the only biologically unnecessary part of a human being, and go on to make some very important feminist point out of it, the main thrust of which escapes me for the moment, and there are times when I've had a few light ales and I'm tired and I'm inclined to agree with them – about the unnecessary bit at any rate, but even that's wrong. A woman's – um – love button is there to help facilitate orgasm, which in turn helps propel sperm to where they're supposed to go. (Safely into a French tickler if either of you've got any sense, but either way . . .)

I can only speak for myself and God knows it's hard enough coping with a disability and most of it's a mind game, but I knew I'd rather finish last in an egg-and-spoon race against a bunch of three-year-olds than win a dozen Olympic golds for having the fastest wheelchair on the planet. That's just me. Call me a walkist, I don't give a shit.

The dreams I have in here, starting tonight, are some of the cruellest. I've not been upright for five months but here I am walking again, usually around the place where I grew up. Which is odd, cos I spent most of my time there running. And crying. And dodging things – badly – hence the crying bit. But in my dreams I'm strolling like a pimp king past the Ford Cortinas and the post office run by the woman who years before tried to get me to fetch my ink pen from between her prepubescent breasts and I shrank away in ten-year-old horror and sorry love I still feel the same way and in any case I'd never find a typewriter between those saggy old dugs now. And now I'm at the sheet-metal factory that backs on to our garden and I'm hopping – no less – over kerbs up by the electrophoretic coating plant at the top of our street and for the first time in my life I'm having fun here and why would you leave a place like this? Up by the old gutted house and the new flats already looking drab and I might try and run across the island by the new Asda and I wake with a clang cos the night nurses here *have put my meds on a fucking pedal bin as well, for fuck's sake.*

And of course *here*'s normal. Shitty room, endless lines of nurses, carers, therapists, prodders, pokers, movers and shakers, pain, sodden pillow and saliva bubbling in my broken throat, electric strip lighting and, next to my single bed, a wheelchair. But still in the hard light the dream won't leave. I swing my legs out of bed until dizziness and nausea hits. If I put them on the floor . . . I know the muscle memory will kick in. Half asleep, but I'm sure I was walking a minute ago. Now I'm sitting up. I grasp the chair next to me for support. I heave myself up with my right arm. I'm rising, standing . . .

The chair shoots off cos some idiot forgot to put the brake on and I'm back on the floor, hard. It would appear my legs still don't work. The dream has fractured with the crack of my head on the lino. I'm awake, at any rate. I lie sprawled, temporarily beaten.

Tempo-fucking-rarily. I should just lie there, I know, but that thing in me, that annoying, nagging bastard little voice that's made up of Michele and Mum and the kids and everyone who thought I was great and strong, just as much as everyone who thought I was shit and weak, and most of all the secret little bump inside my wife, but inside me now and always that voice, that feeling, that pressure, that presence won't let me lie there like a fucking smashed insect even though I know that's what I am and I know my right arm is already grabbing on to the bed and my right leg is pushing and I'm edging up now with my *chin*, for fuck's sake, let me go and Christ I'm already half on and my centre of gravity's over the edge and a heave and a claw and a spastic roll and I'm in the fucking cunting blessed bed. By myself.

And the voices. Which I'd best keep quiet about.

When a nurse wanders in soon after to get me up she wonders why I'm making funny noises between laughing and screaming and wonders why she's been told to fuck off. I've done my bit for the day. I close my eyes. Normal is nearer.

Timetables

I get a timetable. No, really, day by day, with squares you can fill in. My lessons are:

Occupational Therapy (OT)
Speech and Language Therapy (SLT)
Physiotherapy (Get off me)

I liven mine up by writing things like:

Monday 10 a.m.: Sexual Healing with Mrs
Maguire, broom cupboard. *Memo to self –
move brooms out this week.*
11 a.m.: A beginner's guide to frotting, with Jane
from physio. Meet Wimbledon Tube station, or
if wet, the vicarage.
Tuesday 11 p.m.: Advanced devil worship. Bring
your own virgin.

. . . and deliberately leave them lying about near the front desk for the visitors to find. Some of the wives later spend the day giving their old men some very old-fashioned looks . . .

Each of my real lessons is for an hour per day most days, sometimes one-on-one, which is bearable, sometimes in a group, which is not. There's an hour extra lunchtime gym if you feel really keen, and a Friday dunk in the swimming pool after they've let it out to a prenursery group of toddlers. 'Little tiddlers', the group's called. The staff refer to them as 'little piddlers'. Cos they pee in my pool. Geddit? Oh, that NHS humour. I hear this joke every Friday as I'm being lowered into 4,000 gallons of warm piss on a mechanical chair.

I am to follow the piddlers late on Friday afternoons, cos my MRSA means I have to be the last living thing in the pool each week. Knowing how hard up the health service is I wouldn't be surprised if they also rent it out to pet owners or the local car wash. The pool is sterilised over the weekend. No matter who or what's done what in that water, I'm considered more filthy.

But who the hell would take their two-year-old to this unit for a swimming lesson? The sights those kids are going to see . . . it's like *Dawn of the Dead* in here. I mean, I guess it's cheap but what parent wants their little Aimee to come across a stroke patient on a bad day looking like fucking Lurch?

Middle-class twat parents, that's who. The kind that think it's good for kids to experience all aspects of life – even if it's a six-foot dribbling maniac with knitted trunks who's late out the water and is suddenly bearing down on them like the creature from the black lagoon. Or maybe they just liked it when Aimee got home cos she was quiet.

I've got news for you. She wasn't quiet cos she was tired, she's been fucking traumatised, love. Give her a couple of years and access to some power tools and see how she repays you for that little day out at the pool.

Testing, Testing

Oh they love their forms, their charts, their bits of paper, their assessments, do the NHS. And so here I am in the physio room, which is full of tables and benches and mats and equipment and *stuff* and I'm on a padded table with nowt on but my pants. I don't care that I haven't got any shorts. I am so uninhibited these days that I'd be in the nudd if they wanted. The little lady physios do not want beardy shouty man in the nudd, they don't even want him in his dangerously baggy boxers. But they are doing tests today.

The first one's rather nice. I'm blindfolded by the first physio I've met who doesn't look like a struggling middleweight in drag. We'll call her Sporty Spice. Then it gets all *9½ Weeks*. They are trying to find out where on my body I can feel heat and cold, sharps and softs, how much of my sense of touch has been damaged. This will be something of an education for me as I've had other things on my mind. To facilitate this, various objects – hot, cold, sharp, soft, you get the picture – are placed or rubbed on various parts of my anatomy. By a girl. While I'm blindfolded. In my pants.

I can only apologise for what happened next but I'm only human. It was the first time I'd been touched by a woman in months who hadn't wanted to hurt me in some way. Actually, given my track record with my exes, make that *years*.

You'd think physios wouldn't get embarrassed, but they do. The final bit of the testing, around my upper thighs, was carried out in what can only be described as a rather hasty fashion. I was quite disappointed when the blindfold came off, but enjoyed seeing a very red-faced Sporty and three other physios pretending they were not killing themselves laughing.

'We'll do some bending and stretching next,' said Sporty.

'Righto.'

'Let's leave it a minute, shall we?'

So we left it a while and I studied pictures of the musculature of flayed people on the walls, which worked until I thought of that poor sod in Greek mythology Marsyas and that brought me back to the Sistine Chapel, cos he's in there, and from there it was a short leap back to my old art teacher and whoops, proceeds were held up for a bit longer.

I liked Sporty almost instantly. She probably guessed. She was a karate champion and must have been good at it cos she was still pretty. Her friend and senior partner, who we'll call Fergie cos she was a ginge, was also good company. And between the two of them they started to give me a right good testing. It was a bit like that American WWF wrestling, except with smaller breasts. They soon found something they liked. A big problem. Physios like problems cos they can generally fix them, in a way oncologists *don't* like problems. It's the difference between the mechanical parts of your new sporty motor, and the electronic wizardry that's there to stop you driving it into a tree when you run out of talent.

When bits of the engine play up a mechanic can give it

a wallop with a spanner, charge you £500 and you're away. When the electronics go, twelve people in white lab coats from Düsseldorf have to do major surgery on the car and your wallet.

In this place, the physios were the mechanics. They were bloody good, too. My left leg was 'interesting'. I thought it just looked like a piece of white knotted string. My foot pronated, whereas my knee supinated, and as for my hip, well, that was just buggered.

Basically, my left foot bent one way, my knee the opposite way, and my hip didn't know what the hell it was supposed to be doing. We soon found out that a major obstacle to sorting this lot out was going to be lack of what's known as proprioception. I'll explain. Close your eyes. No, idiot, read this then close your eyes. Oh, for fuck's sake. I'll start again. When I say 'go', close your eyes.

Hold out your hand, close your eyes and move it about. Somehow, without looking, you know where it is in space. Unless you've got PMT, in which case you've just knocked over your coffee and it's all your boyfriend's fault.

Go.

See how that works? Isn't it great? Right, you smug bastard, my leg did not have that. I could not tell you where it was. I think I've seen Bill Clinton try and get away with this defence once or twice, but anyway . . . Unless I looked, I didn't know what my foot, knee or hip were doing; this made exercises doubly difficult. It was like having an artificial leg. Except it hurt.

Say aaah.

Now I'm being tested by my new speech and language therapist, who shall henceforth be known as Patti, as in

Smith, seventies art/punk queen, cos she thought she was still a bit rock 'n' roll, had a loud voice and I couldn't work out whether I liked her or not. On the plus side you've got 'Because The Night' and 'We Three', on the other – well, there's all the shouty nonsense rest of it.

Patti the SLT's job was to get me to swallow. You already know she failed, so I suppose that colours my view, harsh as that may seem.

Today she's assessing what needs to be done about my voice and swallow. Basically, everything. She's highly trained and I can tell she knows what she's about. Sessions with her are good but I only get her for two hours a week.

Patti has long dark hair, a trim figure and is not as young as she'd like to be. She has a look of a sixties bird who's been passed around a bit by sixties blokes and still likes to think she could hit Glastonbury hard if only it wasn't quite so loud and muddy and they had Molton Brown in the bogs. You know the type. The type who has joss sticks at home but wishes she could afford Diptyque candles and owns the complete works of *The Who*. She buys CDs but prefers vinyl cos the sleeves are easier to roll spliffs on. She wears cheap silver jewellery from Camden Market and dresses in black. She lives in an unfashionable part of West London and hungrily checks the property pages of the *Standard* each week to see how much her house has gone up. Her and her old man consider themselves sexually adventurous cos they own a vibrating egg and had a regrettable night of retsina-fuelled wife-swapping on a villa holiday in Paphos with friends they haven't seen since. One day she'll move to a smallholding in the country and run off with a pig farmer from Attleborough who makes her feel twenty-one again.

Back in the real world, today she diagnoses me with dysphagia, which means I can't speak very well. My tongue is heavy, stiff and flat in my mouth, and is numb and unresponsive. I often bite it and spit blood regularly. I'm used to spitting. Even now I cannot swallow my saliva. This makes me, I reckon, even more unpleasant company. My soft palate won't lift up so that adds a hare-lip tone to things. My left vocal cord is still paralysed open, so I'm breathless and breathy. Altogether it's a bit Frankenstein's monster with a spot of Igor chucked in. Which fits my self-image, so that's fine.

Playtime

Occupational Therapy is held in a room that does look just like a reception class in a failing inner-London primary school. And the form teacher we'll refer to as Mrs Bunny-Wunny, as she's round, kindly, docile and I'd like to empty both barrels of a Purdey 12-bore into her floury apron just to liven her up. Kindly. Hmmm. Remember what I said about the kindly ones?

Her job is to get my left arm and hand working again. My hand is the main problem because fine motor skills are hard to acquire in the first place, let alone when half your brain's disintegrated. I started trying to play guitar when I was eighteen. A couple of years later, with money from a summer job, I walked into Rip-off Music Ltd and bought the first red electric guitar I saw. I saw it thirty seconds after the owners saw me coming. It was probably called a Spender Flatocaster or a Fibson Des Paul or something and was made in Burma by blind fingerless WWII prisoners who couldn't manage

213

the railway that day. And then an odd thing happened.

I was in my third year at college and had decided to hate it when an old mate turned up and blagged the box room next to me. He was a bit of a dope-fiend to put it mildly and constructed a bong bigger than the bed. I remember walking in one October day and accepting one end of this hideous smoking, bubbling contraption and taking a good lungful just to see what would happen.

What happened was I remember nothing else until the following January, when I found myself playing guitar in a reggae band. Absolutely true. Best of it was, I'd learned to play the bloody guitar in the meantime.

Even so, I like to think I'd put *some* work into my musical studies at some point and it was bloody annoying it had all disappeared.

I am unable to make each finger touch my thumb, I have so little control. I try this every morning. I still do. Here, my left hand is numb, stiff and sore. When I hold my hand out straight the fingers curl painfully back over themselves – hyperextension. It's the hand of one of those nightmare-story creatures that Germans like inflicting upon their kids, presumably in the hope they can desensitise them enough to explain what Grandpa did in the war. I have no proprioception in this hand, but it can feel temperature and sharps, which my other hand can't. Hoorah.

Mrs Bunny-Wunny has absolutely no idea what to do with me. She suggests basket-weaving and I suggest what she can do with that. I play with plasticine for a bit and then she brings out a large wooden puzzle. There are coloured movable pegs in the wooden board. It's like a simplified Solitaire, and you have to end up with one peg.

The idea being you get so caught up in the game you don't realise you're in rehab. Oh, go on then. I take the pegs out with my left hand.

It was, in fact, doubly frustrating. Not only did I keep dropping the pegs, I never did manage to complete the fucking puzzle.

Can't Get You Out of My Head

Gym. Three letters that always scared the wheezy fat kid who was so smart at everything else. Cos it was going to be revenge time. Hah. You can remember the date of the battle of Borodino, can you? Well, you can't remember how to dodge this. Pow! Oooh, conjugating 'être' again, smart-arse? Conjugate the side of this wall! Smack!

It was worse now. The gym had various machines that cut-price gyms have: old exercise bikes, stairs, bouncy balls, a basketball hoop, and a complete tosser in charge.

Let's get this out in the open: I didn't dislike this guy because he acted like a screaming homosexual. Actually, come to think of it, that *was* part of it. The *acting* bit, I mean. Because by all accounts – and by his account not least – he *wasn't* a screaming homosexual. But bugger me he tried his hardest to look like one. Barring wearing a T-shirt with 'I'M NOT GAY BUT MY BOYFRIEND IS' printed on, or actually sodomising the unit director in the quadrangle one wet afternoon, he could not have set his stall out clearer.

I don't know why he pretended to be that way if he wasn't that way. I don't pretend to be an Italian Mafia Don, cos I'm not. Unlike several well-known white DJs, or kids from the estate near me, I don't pretend to be black.

On St Patrick's night, I don't pop down to Kilburn wearing forty shades of green wielding a shillelagh and shouting 'to be sure, to be sure'. So why pretend you're gay? My car is not a Ferrari. I could stick as many badges with 'Ferrari' on it as I like, it would still do 0–60 in about ten minutes and have the pulling power of, well, an old Mitsubishi covered in Ferrari stickers.

No, I didn't like him cos he acted as though he didn't give a shit about us. He was too busy shaking his tight little booty to the latest pop shite he'd brought in on CD and chatting to his little physio chums, distracting them from watching over us wobbly folk. So here were grown men, dignified men, men who'd not tuned in to *Top of the Pops* since it was *Juke Box Jury*, being vaguely ordered about by some mincing twat playing Kylie at full volume and not noticing they'd fallen down the stairs.

Please God when he gets old let him end up in the twilight home for retired anarcho-punks and spend his final years enjoying singalongs to 'White Riot'.

I'll call him Cliff. As in Richard. Cos he's not gay either.

The Drugs Don't Work

Oh but they do, they do. That's when I manage to get them and they haven't been chucked up the wall. I was told by someone I suspect knows about these things that it only takes five years for a prisoner to become institutionalised. Bollocks. Maybe I was simply weak-willed, but I became aware of this process happening to me after less than five months when I found myself going mental at a nurse who was ten minutes late giving me my 2 p.m. meds. I'm sure ten past two would have been fine, but it's hard to explain why these things matter so much. Maybe it's control, maybe it's that you're aware you *do* need them on the dot, or maybe you've just become a smoking beagle, running back to your cage gasping for a Benson and Hedges.

The main drugs I was on were: good old paracetamol, baclofen – a painkiller and muscle relaxant – and my beloved amitryptyline. The latter was a green viscous medicine. A painkiller, a sleeping draught, and – I later learn – one of the first antidepressants. Whatever it was, no Parisian dauber pined for his nightly green fairy as I did for my amitryptyline. 30ml I had at night, which guaranteed sweet sleep if not sweet dreams, a dose which I've since found out is a relatively low one. I found that shocking as I was also very much aware that I liked it a little too much and it was not a toy. If doctors are, as I suspect, dishing this stuff out like Archers at a hen party then there's a lot of doped-up people out there somewhere. Actually, I know where. Outside the bloody school gates every morning.

All these were administered through my PEG, so had to be in liquid form. Occasionally a nurse would show up with some tablets and get very confused. My feeding regime had changed since I moved as it was impractical to have my feeding pump on all the time. Well, *I* said it was impractical, the local dietician was very keen for me to have the bloody thing on 24/7. I compromised. I would hook myself up to it every night from about 8 p.m. to 8 a.m. In the day, I would have 'lunch' by what's known as bolus feeding – i.e., I filled a syringe with goop, hooked it up, and waited for it to get sucked into my stomach. This took half an hour or so, which was not fast but better than eight hours. I thought it was a good system. But no. Apparently I was breaking with routine, making trouble. Again.

The Inmates

I'm not an expert on my fellow patients cos I spent most of my time alone, avoiding the fuckers. Most were older than me – stroke patients mainly, or people recovering from brain haemorrhages. I didn't find them a particularly friendly or inclusive bunch, but then this was a very unusual club I'd joined. I mean, if you go along one rainy Thursday night to the Newport Pagnell and District 00-gauge-steam-railway-modellers' sect – sorry, club, and you bring along a nice shiny bit of 00-gauge steam train, or a piece of track or a tree or whatever these saddoes wank over all night, I suspect you'll be welcomed in as 'one of us'. They'll be happy to see you because they're happy to be there.

What was I bringing to the party? Disability, rage, self-loathing and anti-social tendencies. OK, I fitted right in, but that doesn't make for a cheery party atmosphere. People, especially men, like joining groups because they can recognise fellow travellers, people like themselves, whether it be the 00-gauge modellers or Wolverhampton Wanderers supporters or the Nazi Party.

No one wants to recognise themselves in here.

Every shuffling, mumbling, dribbling wreck being patronised by a stupid nurse reminded us of what we had become. The corridors were a hall of mirrors in a grotesque freak show.

'Why don't you join in a bit more?' asked a particularly

brave nurse one evening as I lay in bed alone, watching the telly. 'There's a TV room upstairs.'

Yes, and it's always on *EastEnders* at ninety decibels cos none of us poor fuckers can reach the telly to turn it over or down. And anyway, I don't want to sit with these people, nodding, twitching, lost in their own pools of misery. I want to be on the sofa with my fat little missus and our noisy kids arguing over – OK, probably why they have to have *EastEnders* on so loud. But either way, this is not what I call a good night in.

Lunchtimes are possibly the worst. There's a canteen that belongs in a run-down provincial garden centre, where I have my syringeful and my meds. I sit near, but not at, the little Formica tables while the rest of the lucky bastards stuff their greedy little faces with food I can't have. They often stare at me with my tube. Jesus, even in here I'm weird. What the fuck am I going to be like when I'm let out? I feel on display. No one ever talks to me. After half an hour I gratefully finish my lunch and escape.

But not everyone's no fun. There's a young lad in here, let's call him Kyle Asbo. He's tall, thin, favours chunky gold chains and has a smile that will get a checkout girl on a night out into trouble at twenty paces. Or six Bacardi Breezers. Kyle has frontal lobe damage. This makes him poorly but big fun.

Science lesson:

Little children say the first thing that comes into their little heads. This can be cute, like 'Who painted the sky blue, Daddy? And where did he find such a tall ladder?'; it can be embarrassing: 'But you said Auntie Sharon shouldn't have any more trifle cos she's a big fat piggy, Daddy.' It can be dangerous: 'Daddy, why does that man look like Golly? And why are we running?'

As they grow older, they develop a little copper inside their heads that tells them when to keep their gobs shut. This is known as learned behaviour. The strength of this policeman varies from person to person, and of course some people, particularly famous ones who go on reality TV shows, sometimes leave him at home altogether.

But generally your copper will say to you, 'Stop! You may well just have bumped into Camilla Parker-Bowles in the ice-cream queue at the Odeon, but do not mention tampons or call her adulteress, Diana-killer or horse-faced parasitical whore.' He is stationed in a lobe at the front of your brain. Hence, *frontal* lobe.

Now, when you go through the windscreen of a stolen Vauxhall Astra at 60mph it's quite easy to damage your little copper. Knock him right out. Good news is, he comes back pretty quickly, but the even better news is, for the time he's not there, you are the most entertaining mother f%^&*er on the c^&ting planet, boy.

Kyle Asbo has had his frontal lobe knocked about. I think it was in a ruck, so chances are he wasn't very good at keeping his gob shut beforehand, but he is *fantastic* company now. The staff hate him. I think he's brilliant. He's the one person who makes going to the gym bearable, cos the days he's there are a riot. They go something like this:

'Kyle, you're supposed to go on the stairs now.'

'Sorry Sporty. You know, you've got great tits, innit?'

'Thank you. If you'd just try to get to—'

'Fancy a shag? Wanna see my—?'

'Now come on, Kyle. Concentrate on—'

'Look, it's that poof Cliff just come in. Oy Cliff, you a

bender? Alright mate, how you doing? Nah, he's queer, definitely man. Hey, where you going?'

'*The stairs. Get on the stairs, Kyle.*'

'Yeah. You like my mum, tellin' me. 'Cept I want to fuck you which is diff'rent. These stairs are hard. Know what's for tea?' (*Whispers*) 'He's a poof, in' he?' (*Shouts*) 'Hey Nige, alright man? Saw you with your tube at lunch. Bad shit. Look man, I had a peg like yours, see the scar? Gone now. You'll be alright. Hey, look at Sporty's arse, she's bending over. Nice. Hold on, she might have heard me. Keep it quiet, keep it quiet. Do you think Cliff's a batty boy?'

Etc.

Brilliant. If James Joyce had had Kyle and a tape recorder in 1910 he'd have banged *Ulysses* out in a couple of days tops. The great thing about Kyle was he was the most honest person over the age of five I've ever met. Wasn't it Jesus or someone else with long hair and sandals who said that unless you thinketh like a child, you won't getteth to heaven? He'd obviously not metteth Kyle. Unless heaven's full of maniacs shouting obscenities, in which case I'm almost sorry I missed out.

Kyle even fancied my pregnant missus, which I could only take as a compliment. She waddled into the gym one day just to laugh at the sight of me *in* a gym, and he clocked her in all her roly-poly glory. This was going to be interesting.

'That your missus, Nige?'

'Uh-huh . . .'

'Nice tits. Pleased to meet you.'

Fortunately for Kyle, but sadly for the comedy gods, he started recovering quickly. I missed him when he went – things were never the same.

I liked the misfits, the fighters, the scratchy buggers who kicked against the shitty hand they'd just been dealt. I saw very quickly that most of the inmates were a docile bunch and the staff liked it that way, and I felt in my gut that acceptance and docility were not the way out of here. Yes, the nurses would be nicer to you, but so what? If all you want is something to be nice to you, get a Labrador.

There was a small, neat Italian man in his late fifties who I only heard speak once. I knew the staff didn't like him much because they talked to him politely, the way I made them talk to me. We were in a speech group. I went cos it was that or *Countdown* and the twitchy contestants and Richard Whiteley reminded me of the people in here, so I thought I might as well give the speech group a go. It was early days and I thought I should make the effort. I got someone to wheel me there.

He was clearly a man of great bearing and dignity. He held himself well, despite his failed body, he was clean-shaven and wore a suit and tie and looked like he ran a small business making roofing tiles, or some such. You could tell from the way he looked at the majority of the staff that he wouldn't have given them jobs washing bird shit off his roof tiles. Recently, he'd had a stroke.

One of the less funny aspects of a stroke is, I suppose, the opposite of the terribly amusing effects of a frontal lobe injury. This man knew exactly what he wanted to say, but he could no longer find the words. They were behind locked doors, lost under cushions or down the back of the sofa in a room turned upside down, hidden amongst the jumble of language and memory, and because of this he was genuinely infantilised. As in an infant, in stroke patients the connections between words, pictures, emotions and language are foggy, unformed. Like small children, they often become angry, tearful and have tantrums. This is a good thing. It means they are recovering. They know something is wrong and they are grasping at smoke. It's not easy to handle, though.

This problem with language happens frequently with stroke patients and I'm afraid to say it often leads to them being treated like genuine infants by the less well-trained members of staff – the non-nurse carers in the main. There's a lot of being – talked – down – to – slowly, as if one's inability to speak is in direct proportion to one's inability to think. Whereas as we know from watching *Big Brother* or Prime Minister's Questions, there's actually an *inverse* relationship between the two.

I can't recall what the group was talking about and it doesn't matter anyway but I remember it was this man's turn. He could not find the words. He struggled like a man in chains as we willed him on. Tears of frustration were waiting but he was holding them back, holding it all back. Finally he burst out:

'This . . .'

'Yes?'

'This *fucking* illness.'

With passion. It was a magnificent, triumphant moment. I applauded. Well, I would have done but my hands missed like some spastic seal, but the thought was there. I turned to the young speech and language therapist taking the group and saw she was horrified. Not at his predicament, but at his *behaviour*. She began to *tell him off*. For swearing. This gentle man who had so articulated with his small profanity the huge profanity perpetrated upon him and his family was being scolded by some jumped-up buttoned-up little bitch of a girl who did not have one ounce of his wit or grace, and damn her I got my revenge when I sent her crying from the same roomful of people weeks later because I had found the power to belittle her the way she tried to belittle this man.

I didn't see him much afterwards. I think his family took him home. I have still never heard anyone so effectively sum up their predicament. Actually, I tried handing those three words in to my publishers a while ago and saying it was sort of a Zen-like work, but they told me in that case I'd get a Zen-like advance and to pad it out a bit.

There was another young lad who was going through a rough patch. He'd had a brain injury ten years before in some kind of pile-up and the medics at the time had done the saving-his-life bit, which was all well and good, but had then given him very little rehab and sent him home. To community rehab, aka bugger-all rehab. Where, to no one's surprise, he didn't progress at all. Now his desperate parents had finally got him back in here. In a few weeks he'd progressed more than in the previous decade. He walked at a 45-degree angle. I was so jealous.

He looked like Liverpool and England striker Peter Crouch, but without the balletic grace. He wanted to be a writer. He'd have been better off replacing Peter Crouch up front for England, but anyway he was going to go to Los Angeles and write films. He wasn't sure what about. He wasn't even sure if he could write. But he had these ideas in his head, and besides, what else was he going to do? I sympathised with him on that one.

And it raised some ugly questions. I wasn't going to die – fair enough, that was a good thing. I was sure I would walk again at some point, but even in my most deluded moments I knew it was going to be a long time, if ever, until I fully recovered. I would still have to *do* something with my life. That had always been a bit of an issue cos I'd never had much in the way of what you might call actual *skills* in the first place. I'd always kept myself busy, but looking back I couldn't for the life of me figure out doing what. Bits and bobs, mostly. I enjoyed most of it, whatever it was, but it was less of a career path and more of a random-drunken-stumbling-upon-something-fun sort of thing that I did from time to time. I suspect I'd do it the same again, stupidly, except for all this illness bollocks.

I had got into TV late and had only just produced my first show. No, think, you must have seen it. It was on regional telly and featured loads of comics you might recognise from voice-overs and a couple of Australian blokes who made funny shapes with their willies. No, honestly. They went to the West End and everything.

Stop it now. If you don't fucking believe me look it up on some TV guide website thing. The review says something like:

'Even for late-night, regional, cheap chickenshit programming this was surprisingly poor.'

Which Mum printed out and stuck up above the telephone table cos it was still the best review I'd ever had. Bear in mind I wrote something once about which the review said:

'Not only the writer but whoever commissioned this should lose their job.'

Well, we both did so there you go. Happy now?

I'd finally inveigled myself into a career, but there were 40,000 younger, hipper, brighter meeja people all coming up behind me wanting to do what I was doing, and not only had I been knocked out of the race at pretty much the first hurdle, I was being wrapped in a silver blanket, given oxygen and a mug of Bovril and told to take it easy for the next, say, twenty years.

Sod it, I'm not going to think about that now. It's nearly bedtime and there's 30ml of amitriptyline calling. And with a bit of luck Kyle might be in the gym tomorrow.

Michele

Michele had this dream. It was early morning, that space between sleeping and waking, and she was curled up with one of my T-shirts. She liked the smell. It says something about her that she did this and something about me that it took quite a while for the smell to fade, but there were still traces of me on it when she felt a body curl up beside her. It was me. She smiled in her dreamy state and she pulled me tighter into, around her. She felt peaceful, home.

She woke with a jolt. I was gone. Something cold and unpleasant trickled into her heart and she rang the unit. She thought I was dead. I wasn't. I was asleep. I hope I was dreaming I was holding her.

Because bad things started to happen.

I'd been in the unit a few days when Shell took the day off work because she didn't feel well. Which means she must have felt like dogshit. Working mums have learned never to take days off when they are ill, because they know they have to take days off when the kids are ill instead. They pass these off as days *they* are ill, and go to work when they are sick themselves so their chauvinist bosses don't go, 'See, told you we shouldn't have employed a bird with kids.' Chauvinist bosses, by the way, are usually other, older women. Women who had to give *everything* up for their careers in an even more un-enlightened era and really resent women who want it *all* – i.e., knackering job they're worried they're not giving enough time to, plus knackering home life they're worried they're not giving enough time to. Oh, those lucky, lucky women.

At any rate, even though Shell was now big boss chief etc. she was programmed never to take a day off. Despite the fact that not all of her lovely supportive actor clients are childish needy fucks who can't bear the thought that their agent/confidante/confessor/mummy might be so selfish as to be poorly when she should be thinking about *them*, yes *them* all the time.

Add to this all the worrying that she'd done trying to save my life, and there was not much left of Michele by now. She was stretched too thinly, too tightly, she functioned like an automaton. But she was breaking down and that afternoon her contractions started. This was very bad because she was just around seven months. At first she put it down to wind due to too many microwaveable midnight meals, but when the wind kept coming on at regular ten-minute bursts, Mum rushed her to hospital.

The ride to hospital was silent, I've been told. Michele was sure the strain of the last few months had brought this on, and the baby – our little Alfie – might not be viable. She was going to miscarry an almost-formed child.

Her link with me destroyed, then buried. And it would be her fault. She'd not looked after him. He was so helpless and utterly dependent and she should have loved him please let my baby be alright and she did love him but there was so much love she needed to give to me and the other kids and please let my baby . . . and she was all used up and would she ever be forgiven and could she forgive herself? She'd failed her unborn baby and was paying the price for her failure with her baby's life. Which she would have to watch ebb away. She was tearing at herself silently, screamingly, when the car pulled into Kingston Hospital.

Inside, the doctors were sorry but there were no incubators free at the hospital – our baby would urgently need an incubator if he was to be born now. They frantically rang round to find a space at a special care baby unit while Michele was admitted, put on a drip, and basically advised not to have Alfie just yet.

'So I just cross my legs, do I?'

The doctors came back after a while and told her they'd found an incubator. In Brighton. And sorry, but they were too afraid to move her in case she gave birth on the way. The decision was made to wait and hope she could hold on to him. The baby's heartbeat was monitored. It was still beating, but only because he was safely inside her. Once outside – that damned hard *outside* – who knew?

So Michele lay there, breathing gently, not moving, loathing herself. Holding on, like she'd held on for the last four, five months. If there was a time for her to break it was now, but she would not, and yes there would be a price to pay later but let it be later. She *was* weak, she had been wrong, she was failing everyone. She waited, she – I have no idea of the thoughts she had at that moment, with the man she loved lost to her, and his child just clinging to her, to life. There are some doors in my wife's mind that she will keep closed, to herself as much as to me.

Mum came through. She made Michele smile a few hours later, when nothing awful had happened. She said, 'If you have him now, we haven't got any baby clothes.'

It was true. The normal happy frantic running about buying stuff for baby that happy couples do had been put completely to one side. If the baby was born – and if he survived – he was going to be nappiless, Babygro-less, dummy, bottle, wet-wipe, layette, bonnet and bootee-less, the poor little bugger.

'You come into this world with nothing, you leave with nothing,' opined Mum, the René Descartes of Kingston maternity. I'm not sure this helped Michele, but at least Mum wasn't telling her about her day. Or maybe she did. Maybe over the next few hours Mum dibbled on about daily life in a way that made our baby decide coming out wasn't so exciting after all, or else she just put him in a coma. Either way, by evening the contractions had stopped. Michele and Alfie were out of danger, but she was ordered to stay in hospital.

Mum then had to find her way back home from a place she didn't know, in the dark. She's hardly the best navigator at any time, even when she does wear her glasses. Our house was fifteen minutes away. An hour later, she was parked on the main runway at Heathrow, terminal one, lost and sobbing.

But, as I've learned through meeting Michele, if you take enough wrong turns you end up on the right path eventually, and a tear-sodden pensioner finally made it home. That's become one of Mum's great travel stories and she tells it fresh every time, like Columbus delighting Ferdinand and Isabella after making it back from that Caribbean beach holiday everyone gets so excited about. I bet even they got fucking bored after the 567th time as well. No wonder he ended up in the nick.

My mobile phone does not work in the basement. I hardly notice because most of my friends have stopped ringing by now. Perhaps the barriers put up when I went into intensive care have distanced them, perhaps they are waiting for me to emerge, all better and ready to go out on the razzle again, perhaps they can't comprehend my mangled voice, perhaps they've realised they can get on with their lives just as easily without me. I don't care. I have Michele. She's all I want. The call about her comes through on the telephone on a landing. The caller has to have patience because it can ring for a long time. If they're lucky, Kyle answers.

The call comes the following day, when it is fairly clear the danger has passed. Michele has been allowed home and ordered to have complete bed rest. She is not allowed out to see me, and Mum will only be able to visit infrequently.

I put the phone back into the slot and I'm wheeled back to my room. As usual I say nothing to the nurse, who's in the mood to ask questions. I'm a puzzle to them; perhaps because of my age, my job, my wife, my anger, my silence or my reputation for smacking physios in the mouth. I will remain a puzzle. I like that role. It is better than any other I can see for myself. Patient, client, sufferer, marked, crippled, dependent, helpless, vulnerable, alone.

I am scared for my child, scared for my love, but

awfully, selfishly scared I am going to have to face the next two months in this awful place in rooms full of strangers, alone.

Alone.

So. I will become as hard as a pebble. Unbreakable, unreachable. Surrounded by others but unconnected, untouchable, alone.

And as I'm dumped back in my nasty little room in my nasty little chair I heave myself on to the bed and stare at my nasty little legs. I'm going to walk out of here.

Alone.

Chapter Eight
Get Up Offa That Thing

First thing I wanted: a Davros-king-of-the Daleks chair. There was a small cache of large, black electric wheelchairs at the Wolfson. They were operated from a lever on the right arm, a knob that looked like one of those Pac-Man controllers. I'd never been very good at Pac-Man so I didn't reckon I'd be all that hot at operating a great big wheelchair and it was going to be Whoops lookout wobbly people, but by God I was determined to get my hands on one.

Shame sometimes that life isn't a *Carry On* film. Because in the *Carry On* version I presumably overcharge the chair one night – or better still, my rival for the chair – almost certainly Sid James, who doesn't really need one in any case – overcharges it, and I shoot off down the corridor trailing sparks like Richard Hammond, and in a clearly speeded-up film sequence take out three doctors, a cleaner with a mop and bucket, a handily placed flower stall and the apoplectic unit director (Kenneth Williams), before narrowly missing Hattie Jacques and ending up with a half-naked Barbara Windsor (or preferably a young Joan Sims, but that's just me) on my lap. In the fishpond. I spit out a goldfish. Barbara/Joan looks like a dumpy pale Venus rising from the waves in a nod to some kind of artistic pretension, with strategically placed seaweed. Cut to Sid J. laughing along to a farting bassoon. Fade.

Or better still, a Woody Allen film, cos then I'd have been smart and rich rich *rich*, been in a New York (and therefore clean) hospital, and no matter how unlikely a hero I'd still have copped off with Diane Keaton. Which would make putting up with all the rotten jazz music a lot easier.

Life at the Wolfson was a *bit* like a film, to be fair – *One Flew Over the Cuckoo's Nest*. And I was increasingly being looked upon as Jack Nicholson. But Jack Nicholson in *The Shining*.

Either way, one fine day I get my leccy chair. It's not the electric chair that the majority of the staff would like to see me strapped into, but it's the best they can do before the other one arrives from Texas.

Freedom. Only of sorts, I know, but who's complaining? It's quite exciting in a way. My distance/ balance/eyesight combo's still not brilliant, so my slow trundling through the corridors feels like playing network *Doom* on speed. Only I'm not allowed the rocket launchers, which I do miss.

News of the World

Visitors become more important as I can no longer see my family. And probably to stop me worrying *all* the time about Michele and the baby, I start to wonder about what's happened in the big wide world whilst I've been out of circulation. I don't want to hear anything about my old career because that's crashed and burned, leaving a trail of blazing wreckage down the mountainside. I'm sure someone will clean up the mess, just not me. I have other wreckage to worry about. It's only taken a couple of months, but the shallow, venal, essentially unimportant world of TV comedy has stopped having quite the allure. Which surprises me, cos I'm still pretty shallow, venal and essentially unimportant too. I know I should have changed. We still have that fundamentally medieval idea that suffering is somehow, deep down, good for you. It's not. That's why it's called *suffering*. Otherwise colon cancer might be called Center Parcs.

And odd, isn't it? Our insatiable appetite for news. Because unless we're one of the very, very few people able to influence events or actually in the news, or perhaps, say, a serial killer looking to see if they've found the bodies yet, the news doesn't really matter. We like to talk about news items at work or parties, we like to feel informed, but mostly I think we're just a bit nosy. Or we like being distracted from our own news . . .

Maybe it's also that Huw Edwards giving you his all at six o'clock saves you having to get actually, genuinely involved. Cos in a way you are – simply by watching. You're glad cameras were there and people know about it, whatever it is, but it's almost time for *Corrie* and will-you-kids-shut-up-there's-nothing-wrong-with-those-Asian-turkey-twizzlers.

I knew I was too late to get involved in much that had gone on in December 2001 *et al.*, but I still wanted to know. Context is everything. So here's what I'd missed.

Bear in mind I never saw the original newspapers, so what follows is made up from thoroughly shoddy research using Google, an iffy memory and lies.

November 2001

Saturday 27th: FA Cup fourth round. Wycombe Wanderers 2, Wolves 1.

Fuckity-fuck fuck.

According to some tosspot on the official Wycombe website: 'A simply marvellous day was had by all Wycombe fans at a packed Adams Park as a Sam Parkin goal just five minutes from time took Wycombe through to the last sixteen.' No wonder I went into a bit of a decline.

More cheeringly, it was announced that the palm pilot will now be available in Latvian. Notwithstanding the fact that the device will shortly be experiencing the same sales dip as a Baghdad estate agent's, it's impressed *Sun* page three girl Keely (21). Page three girls now get to comment on the news to show they're more than a pair of hooters. Keely is pleased that our new European neighbours will shortly be enjoying the same hand-held digital information advantages as the rest of us. Whilst showing us a pair of nips that look like a blind cobbler's thumbs.

December 2001

Scientists at Cambridge have declared that the most sought-after particle in physics, the Higgs Boson, which is so crucial to our current understanding of how the universe works it's been dubbed 'the God particle', may not exist at all. Apparently it's been used as the scientific equivalent of Dad going 'Cos I said so' when asked a tricky question. They'll have to make something else up now.

Food riots in Argentina. Fortunately there are four million tins of corned beef left over in the Falklands.

World's smallest lizard found on a Caribbean island. David Attenborough has been informed and will be flying over immediately for a three-week holiday and to film it having tiny little lizard sex. *Celebrity Love Island* producers hit on new format.

And according to the journal of unexplained phenomena the *Fortean Times*, rumours that the Nazis were experimenting with killer sonic weapons like invisible death rays are popular because 'It sounds like something the Nazis would do.'

January 2002

President Bush almost chokes on a pretzel.

Ha ha ha ha ha ha ha ha ha ha . . .

February 2002

. . . ha ha ha ha ha ha ha ha ha ha. No stop it, a pretzel.

Wolves 6, Man Utd 0.

March 2002

War on terror. There are apparently pretzels of mass destruction near very valuable oilfields – sorry, oppressed people, and oh bugger it's all going to end in tears.

Whatever. There's tons of this awfulness but I'm not really concentrating cos even if my boy's born safely, it's obvious the world sucks. I'm not sure I've missed much being away from it.

March/April 2002

Except, except my family's in big trouble and not only am I not there to help, I've got the nastiest feeling it's all my fault. This will come to be known as the Bush effect, but much, much later.

Hang on. No, listen right, I have to break in here to write this down. It's a perfect example of why being an NHS patient is so frustrating. And why you have to *always* make a fuss. Phone just rang interrupting my oeuvre – my GP surgery. Usual bitch secretary they all have.

How do you reckon they advertise doctor's receptionist jobs?

WANTED: One slow, mean-spirited, desiccated/hugely fat misanthrope with God complex to fuck up sick people's lives and prevent the GP from seeing any poorly people if at all possible, whilst building up his list so he can afford a second yacht. Must be computer illiterate. Menopausal women and/or the undead will be given preference.

Apparently they can't give me one of my asthma drugs because they didn't give it me last time. No matter I've been on it since 1996. And no matter they didn't give it to me last time *cos they made a fucking mistake*. It's now on the system that I don't have it. Last time I should have gone: 'Why haven't you included this asthma drug, you incompetent fucks?' I didn't because I a) had plenty spare b) realised they'd made an error and assumed – ha – they'd rectify it this time, and c) couldn't be arsed to have my ten millionth NHS ruck.

Sorry, I'll justify that passage as context or deconstructionism, whereas it was just a frustrated, helpless rant, but you've stuck with me this far so you can't say you've not been warned. No idea if you've seen *The Godfather Part III* (and if not, don't on my account), but there's a particularly badly acted scene where Al Pacino, trying to go straight for the nth time, goes something like 'Da fudda fuggas. You tink youse out of it, den dey drag you back in.'

That's the NHS.

So imagine, if you will, being in the actual, physical clutches of these good people, here in rehab. Robots servicing other robots. And I thought working at Carlton TV was bad. But through gritted teeth I make a decision to try and play nicely so I can get out of here quicker and back to my upended turtle of a missus. I think that makes matters worse. When I smile at staff in my twisty smiley, I-hate-you-really-but-I'll-pretend way, it freaks them out more. I can't win.

But my visitors – fewer now I'm further from the city, from their lives – do their best, though I suspect by now I'm a terrible afternoon's entertainment.

Here's a good visitor: at the risk of being a name-dropper, I happen to know that the banker in hit TV game show *Deal or No Deal* is not a git. Despite resurrecting Noel Edmonds. At the risk of ruining his evil reputation, I'm going to state that he's not anything but a really nice bloke. I know cos he came round a few nights for a game of pool.

Which was a sight in itself. The pool room in the basement of a tatty neuro-rehab unit. It was grimmer than any other pool hall in the country, which I know is something of a statement, but there you have it. This bloke, and remember this is before the *No Deal* gig, was a slightly out-of-work actor. He was, and is, one of the funniest blokes I know, and one of the kindest. The fucker still didn't let me win though, can you believe it? I'm in the bloody chair trying to get to tricky reds with 74-point turns, using a spastic arm to steady the cue, seeing 300 balls at once and the sod still goes ahead and beats me. And I swear he hid the cue rest.

We talk about the Curry Cup. Over a few light ales in a pub we'd once agreed to organise a kind of pub Olympics, to prove to our deluded flabby selves we weren't getting on a bit. It would be an annual event and disciplines would probably include darts, pool, bar billiards, the slot machine and/or quiz machine. There would be points, rules, tie breakers, possibly a committee of like-minded individuals, all of which would need to be thrashed out during long evenings in the pub in the build-up to the big day itself. The tournament got its name because the loser – the lager-sodden eejit with least points – would buy the lager-sodden winner a ruby in the post-tournament celebrations. Hence, the Curry Cup.

I think I'm just about fit enough this year to give it a go without taking the barman's eye out when going for double top. Sadly, I'm not sure I've got any friends left. Time is a cruel mistress.

Now if that's not an inspirational story to make you seize the day, I don't know what is . . .

You wouldn't want to seize any of the days in here. In fact if you had one in your hand you'd drop it quicker than hot dogshit. Some days I look and see most of my timetable's blank, so that'll be about twenty-three hours in solitary, which is what I'd get if I'd knocked off a succession of Romford off-licences at gunpoint. But at least I'd have a cartload of dirty fivers under the patio and a dishwater blonde waiting in the Blind Beggar for me. And I'd be fit enough to do something with her. The only slightly worrying thing would be shower time, but I never washed that much and after a while you probably take what you can get. Even if it's Big Eric the Northants Nonce.

And on the subject of washing, today I get my first bath! I never thought the words 'bath time' could be so pleasurable. I used to be more like our dog, who is very stupid, but does recognise some key words: 'Ollie' (his name), 'dinner', 'walkies' (or actually 'oh-come-on-then-stupid,-alright,-stop-barking-I'm-getting-my-shoes-on,-oh -I-can't-take-you-if-you've-run-off-with-my-shoes-you — where's-the-bloody-lead-gone-now?'), and, far more impressively, 'bath'. At this point he disappears in a doggie blur and you spend the next half-hour looking for him until he's found whimpering in the airing cupboard.

But today, months after my last plunge into the hot soapy stuff, I'm getting a bath. Because of the sensible and helpful rules designed to help patients and not, I repeat not, for the convenience of the staff, I'm only allowed one a week at about 7 a.m. There's a very, very good reason for this, which I forgot as I was being told it cos I do that when I'm being told a load of balls. Now, 7 in the a.m. has never been a brilliant time for me. I've always preferred to see the morning from the other end. Plus now I'm on industrial-strength knockout drops, so mornings have been a bit of a movable feast for months.

At the appointed hour I manage to come round and Dalek myself down to the bathroom. I don't bother with clothes cos it takes about an hour to get them on and I don't give a rat's bumhole who sees Wee Willie Winkie. I drive around a bit trying to find the bathroom door among all these identical doors, but mentally I'm effectively about eight pints of Theakston's Old Peculier in at the moment so I probably ended up in the garden, which would have given the early-morning smokers something to think about.

Nice surprise when I get there – no hoist! This is one of those baths you can walk into, the sort Thora Hird would have at the top of her stairlift to heaven. You have to sit rather than lie, the door's closed and sealed, and then the bath's filled. This time there is a six-foot geezer with tattoos holding the soap for me, so it really is like doing a seven-to-ten stretch with time off for good behaviour. I reject his kind offer to wash my back and he leaves, relieved. I am alone in a hot bath. I'm probably supposed to be monitored but I've told him to get lost. That's the legal bit sorted out. So . . .

I close my eyes and swish the bubbles. My body, for so long weighted down, is light. I move my left arm. It's graceful. I've finally become the swan from the fairy tale. Fair enough, it's a bit odd, only being able to feel the heat from the water down my left side, but at least I can move my right arm properly. I can also scoop chips out of boiling lard with it but that's just another bonus of this lesion, this gift that keeps on giving.

Great place to think, the old bath. When I'm in, I always wonder why I don't do it more. Which is what the wife says about sex. No, only kidding. I'm half floating. I'm actually starting to relax. Steam tickles my nostrils. I remember our bathroom at home, which Michele has turned into some kind of Moroccan bordello by using more terracotta than the Chinese army. If I concentrate and get the stench of cheapo institutional detergents from up my nose I can get – that's it – the lavender from the French market I bought her one hot Saturday last spring. She loves lavender and sometimes I crush some buds under my fingers and the scent bursts through and takes me to her, wherever she is. And I am crushing some now and yes I know she is smiling, resting, holding our baby safe, and a sleepy warmth fills me, rising from my toes to my face and—

– and fuck me I've slipped off the ledge and I've gone under. I'm back to the night in ITU with green water folding over my head, only now there's a soapy flannel on my face and a bar of Dove up my arse. Drowned *and* humiliated. I could have joined the Tory party for this.

But no, I haven't come this far to expire in three foot of Radox. I struggle, squirm, squeak my way upwards until I get some purchase on the slippery sides and heave my head out into the air. I swallow a lungful and gracefully descend again. This happens several more times before I finally wriggle my way on to the ledge, just before the nurse comes in to see if I'm OK.

Fine, I choke, lying. No problem. You can do my back now.

I'm nice and clean for my physios now, which I think is a relief for them. Unfortunately, now I'm clean, I realise this place smells like a Congolese municipal lavatory. God knows what I'd smelt like to cover that up. Sporty and Fergie are there already in their shiny tracksuits, with smiles like the one a sculptor has when a big lump of marble arrives and he reckons there's a Venus de Milo lurking in there. They're rubbing their hands and getting out their chisels.

But sod me, they know what they're doing. They work as a team. I'm on my back while one pushes my leg some-where – God knows where, I lost sight of it five minutes ago. After about half an hour I have to stop. They've been doing all the work but I'm knackered. I fall asleep on a bench. They wake me after ten minutes to do some bum lifts. Sounds promising, whose bum am I supposed to—? Oh. It's my bum and yes I have to lift it myself. Strike two. But hang on, they've got a video camera. They want to film me taking my clothes off. This is the closest I'm going to get to appearing in a Ben Dover film.

The days are so long. There might only be two sessions in any given day, and for the remainder of the time I'm lurking in my room or haunting the corridors or some-times, if it's free, on the unit's one internet-access computer. I'm lucky, most people don't go in that room. And the ones who do generally leave shortly after I whizz in and start hawking and spitting.

So here I am online, with the whole world at my fingertips. But all I want is to go home. There's no smut control on the computer so I go on the sites you'd expect, but I find them depressing. Perhaps I always did. Maybe it's context again: it's one thing to have a drunken laugh with your mates or a cheeky look with a partner, then there's staring, in the harsh light of day, at a drugged Lithuanian prostitute pretending she's enjoying what three hairy fat blokes in their socks are doing to her. Everyone looks hurt, broken, fractured. I see myself reflected in the glass.

I spent most of my time on Auto Trader afterwards, ogling Ferraris. I mean, look at the pininfarina styling on *that*.

But I've been shaken. I start to enjoy hurting people, but hate to see people hurt. I'm like a child, wilfully doing and saying what the hell I like, you shits, but wounded and uncomprehending when I see the shits upset. I have an urge to smash everything and sometimes I begin with myself because I'm there, hitting my useless left hand when it refuses to work. Hitting it with my other fist until the pain makes me gasp and makes me laugh. I never cut myself, but then I'm never around knives and I wonder sometimes. I enjoy watching people as I smash my hand into a wall. And I enjoy watching people as I smash words into them.

I have no feelings for anyone else because I am losing sense of myself. Something nasty clicks and something shuts off and in this place one day I change and I disconnect or

I would scream and never stop screaming

and so I am safe. I will no longer be happy though the

244

price is fair and I will pay though I no longer see another's happiness and I will no longer be human

and this is what has been done to me. There will be years of going through the motions and there are holes dug in my memory when I was home and acted normally and talked to the people I love and made the right noises at all the right times but I was not there. I was not there then, just as I am not there with my loved ones now in this place and I am hardening. Crystals grow in my fracturing veins but I will no longer suffer and you cannot touch me any more. I am adamantine. I survive, but my God I am going to pay one day for this.

Because you cannot leave being human. Because I have been to that place and to visit that place of nothing is to carry it with you always.

Not Drowning But Bobbing

Inspired by the bath, and with my new-found status as unit psycho nail-gunned firmly in place, I look forward to the pool. And I am not disappointed. Mainly by Sporty in a swimsuit. Sadly, Cliff's there too, but I suspect he's no threat, if you know what I mean, gents. There's an electric chair by the side of the pool to lower me in and all the little piddlers have gone. The physios are a bit restless cos it's Friday afternoon and they want to get home to wash the stench of us and this place off them, but I'm booked in and I'm not missing this.

I'm descending and suddenly nervous as the water laps higher and I find I'm trembling, silly old sod, and then I'm in and it's fucking *brilliant*. I'm standing up. I'm standing – no I'm underwater – but whoops Sporty's there, do you come here often oh shall we dance? I've got more floats than a May Day parade. Up and down the faintly pissy water I bob, covered in Woggles. I'm inspired. I kick my legs up to float on my back. Everything goes a bit funny and blurred and I'm dragged out by Sporty. She's trying to tell me off but I'm infectious – and not just from the MRSA. My joy, my delight at my movement is so enormous that even a couple of tired, stressed-out physios catch the mood and like kids chucking snowballs on the first morning of a snowfall, we're lobbing floats and bags and splashing. I'm taking in a lot of water now, but who cares cos I'm upright and that means that absolutely means I will be upright for real soon.

I hold this memory tight to me that night as the unit empties and the other feeling, the one that will win, creeps up again. I'd pushed it away with the intense delight of standing, but now, in the horrible peeling room, aching and sore, still in a chair, still held down, still alone, sick with worry, I just switch off. I learnt a long time ago, during interminable nights in Charing Cross, how to make hours move. If you lie very still and think of nothing the night is endless, but passes in a moment.

Nice trick. I can still do it, especially when Mum's watching *Emmerdale*.

I liked all my new-found skills, presumably as much as the baddie enjoys his new methods of disposing of the evidence, and would have got away with it if it wasn't for those pesky kids. I wasn't going to tell anyone about my ability not to feel pain or emotion, or to time-travel, because they might have thought I was a fruit loop.

Suddenly it's Monday. How clever am I?

Taste

I'd lie if I didn't admit there were moments when the outside world still had the ability to crash in on me and flood me with delight. Like that moment in the pool, and like this, my first taste in months.

The last thing I ate (and this sadly still holds true at the time of writing) was either a grape, a spoon of Weetabix or a paracetamol tablet, I can't remember. At least it wasn't anything from the Charing Cross canteen – unlike several other people, but they've hushed it up (joke, joke). This morsel was consumed with difficulty in my first few days in hospital and I've not been allowed anything by mouth since then – Christmas champagne being the rather foolish exception.

All I've tasted is a bit of toothpaste, carefully monitored, and various varieties of my own secretions. None of them taste great, by the way. As most of my exes will testify.

Before my illness I'd loved to eat. And cook. But mainly eat. I wasn't one for subtle, you may be surprised to hear. I liked big fuck-off flavours. If I was having cheese, I wanted it to hurt – blue, maggoty, stinky and tangy, that's the stuff. If I wanted a curry – which was regularly – it had to be vindaloo-hot, minimum. If I was eating something, I wanted it to tell me what it was IN CAPITAL LETTERS.

HELLO, I'M YOUR DINNER! I'M PENNE AL ARRABBIATA WITH SO MUCH CONCEN-TRATED SUN-DRIED TOMATO PUREE, FRESH CHILLI AND RAW GARLIC MOST OF YOUR FELLOW DINERS HAVE PASSED OUT FROM THE SMELL ALONE. BUON APPETITO!

I was brought up near Wolverhampton in the late sixties and seventies, the year zero for food. We used to have dried soup from a box, Angel Delight in a sachet, curry in tins, noodles in buckets, meat from a shoe, day-glo pop that came from the outflow of Dounreay nuclear plant, same as everyone else. When I discovered, in the mid-eighties, what real food tasted like, it was a revolution for my mouth. Bollocks to the miners, I've discovered tenderloin of pork and £2.99 Bulgarian claret. That's social change enough for me.

And food is not fuel, it's social bonding, it's celebration, commiseration, it's sympathy, it's society, it's bloody expensive from Waitrose, which is where I used to shop but it was lovely. And the nineties came and everywhere you looked up popped a chef, telling us how to do it better. So we did. Thank you Rick, Gary, Jamie, Gordon, Sophie, Keith and the rest, you made my life better. Even though you can all probably fuck off now, you've made your point.

And I'd recently replaced Michele's wonderful chicken-liver salad with garlic and orange dressing, her seared scallops and Chablis, her enormous roasts and amazing lasagnes, I'd exchanged the meat thalis at Les Portes des Indes and that weird thing with kidneys at Café Spice Namaste – you must have had it – and a full English with black pudding and builder's tea with three sugars at Chezza's Caff, and angels-descend-and-take-me seafood cassoulet at the Brasserie Bofinger, for blood and spit and infected phlegm.

Sorry, forgot the odd bit of Colgate.

So when Patti the SLT let me lick the tiniest bit of lemon curd off a tiny spoon to trigger a swallow, she triggered far, far more.

It didn't bring back any specific memories; it wasn't like the famous memory-jogger madeleine biccy dunked in tea that made boring old Frog writer Proust write about *ten billion words* of arse-aching delicate prose about his fantastically dull life, or this would be volume one in a Terry Pratchett-length sequence and frankly neither you or me need that. No, for that she'd have had to feed me a spoonful of strawberry Angel Delight, or Vesta curry with sultanas, or a fucking rusk.

And so, as the Farley's crumbs dribble from my rose-bud lips to fall precipitously on the crepuscular smear of Vesta beef dhansak with pilau rice hanging mordantly from my shirt, the mists of time clear and I see myself, all scabby-kneed and snot-nosed – sorry, with a delicate dew-drop poised pendulously from my upturned proboscis – about to embark on a doomed and very long love affair with the unattainable Annabel, beautiful but tragic daughter of the owners of the Rough Hay chip shop, our hidden passion communicated only in the way she gave me extra batter bits which I masticated one by one, as the sullen sun sunk low over the gasometer near the tinkling canal and fucking hell I've dropped off.

Talking of proper books, why is it no one likes them? We only buy them to whack on the shelves to impress our mates. We might have the new Monica Ali or Zadie Smith or Norman Mailer or Thomas Pynchon on display, but we've all got Patricia Cornwell by the bed. Actually, I've just looked in the interests of honest reportage, and the wife has la Cornwell, I've got a history of China, Plato's *Republic* and a rather rude Kingsley Amis. Guess which one I'm actually reading? Correct.

The problem with starting a journey is it's only when

you're in a ways and you're tired and bored and covered in cowshit that you realise that nice hill with the lovely view is a fuck of a long way off and you wish you'd brought the Mondeo. Same with books. And same, he said, masterfully bringing himself back to the topic in hand, with recovery. Now salivating like a dripping tap in this little room, my swallow reflex trying to reflex like mad with nothing doing, this day I realised just how broken my broken swallow was. But yes, this taste!

It flushed and filled my being with it, sour and sweet, as Gerard Manley Hopkins, poet, recluse, middle-name misnomer and Victorian religious weirdo might have put it. It was a staggering pleasure and my ecstatic moaning response surprised Patti. Fair play, it was just a smear of SuperSaver lemon curd. But it was also a bitter sense of loss, mingled with this unexpected pleasure. Because as I gulped uselessly I could see exactly why food was going to be as unattainable as that bird from the Rough Hay chip shop.

Which brings us back to Plato, and his explanation of Socratic logic. No, really. Basically, Socrates would go around asking Athenians what they meant by such common terms as 'goodness', 'bravery', 'justice' and the like, and showing them that they didn't actually have a proper understanding of them, na-nah-na-nah-nah. They did, however, have a very proper understanding of what makes an annoying git. So they killed him.

Which should have been the end of it, except a whole raft of other philosophers liked annoying people in the same way and kept his memory and his logic alive. The point of all this – and yes, I'll do some more jokes about swearing and falling over in a minute – is that Socrates very cleverly shows us that we know . . . fuck all. Which is annoying when you've shelled out a tenner and spent several weeks wading through the damn thing, thinking you're getting an education only to realise it was worse than a waste of time.

That's what the fucking lemon curd was. Got it?

(Quite possibly it's what you think about this book, too. But as it was almost certainly your third choice in a Waterstone's 3 for 2 offer, you can stop moaning.)

And the lemon curd did something else. It forced open a chink in me which I let Patti in through. She was the woman who had given me this gift, this taste, and therefore she was a good thing. Fuck those doctors who'd blown half the NHS budget on exotic drugs for me, I was bonding with the bint with a 25p jar of plasticky lemon curd.

I needed to talk. I started talking to her.

Brilliant Mistakes

It had to come. Someone had to get it – me, I mean. It was appropriate – she was trying to get me to speak, after all. Most nurses just got grunts. They probably thought that's all I could manage. We do something difficult to begin with – she tapes my voice. Now no one likes the sound of their own voice played back to them. We all think we sound much nicer. I had this inkling I sounded a bit like an English Clint Eastwood. Something underpinned with a gravelly bass, but with the occasional higher register for when I ventured into light action comedy romance.

Tragically, first time I heard myself I realised I sounded like Johnny Rotten with a sinus infection. There was this horrible, wheedling nasal whine. I thought the tape machine was on the blink. And I mumbled. Lord, how I always could mumble. I spent several years thinking the majority of the population must be suffering from some mass industrial hearing accident, given the amount of times I heard the words 'pardon?', 'you what?' or 'eh?' On the plus side I was never Mr Tact, so it probably saved me from the odd beating. It's all swings and roundabouts.

The passage you're forced to read out is pretty much something out of Janet and John, which shows what this bunch think of patients. And sadly not the Terry Wogan versions – for those of you unfamiliar with that particular pleasure, let's just say it elevates the humble double entendre to high art – and of course here we all are back in nursery school.

I complain about this shite, obviously – and am told the words have been specially selected. I specially select some back and to my surprise Patti laughs. She actually gets it. She agrees with me. But it's a standard text and her hands are tied, so I do it anyway. But now I'm happy cos I'm proved right. Go me. It's a bit like a knackered pony on the way to the abattoir going, 'You know, those rusty nail guns aren't very nice,' and the bloke with the shiny red apron going, 'Sugarlump love, you're absolutely right. Couldn't agree more. Shocking, isn't it? Now, head just . . . here. Mind your mane . . . sharp scratch . . .' You're so happy to be told you're right you forget your chitlins are about to be stuffed into six hundred tins of Winalot.

First thing I notice is that I'm gasping after about six words.

John is out of breath.

Concentrate. I take a deep gulp of air and try again. Seven words.

See John go red.

I take a run up. Six. I try coming at it sideways. Seven. I try it quietly. Seven and a half. I try it very, very loudly. Two.

John is getting angry.

SHI— Wheeze. FU— Wheeze. BOLLO— Wheeze. CUH— Wheeze cough spit.

John is hitting the desk. Naughty John. See John get told off. John is ripping up his piece of paper.

I demand to read a newspaper. We find one. Unfortunately it's the *Daily Mail* and I'm so incensed after five minutes I can't speak at all. I think I might have found out Gordon Brown caused my brain lesion. Or something.

See John give up and try to wheel himself off. See John hit the wall. A bookcase falls on John. Silly John. Does that hurt? Yes. John says a rude word.

But I'm coaxed back and calmed down and given some more sensible exercises, and some material that looks like A-level biology on how breathing works. Patti asks, finally, in the uncomfortable silence, if I know any poems, and I can sulk all I want but it's this woman who's going to walk out of here tonight and talk to her husband and kids and eat and drink, so who's winning? So I begin.

The rhythm of the poem helps, and the memory of learning it for a performance at school is back and my breathing relaxes and I struggle to the end, the rich round words filling my mouth, the force of the lines lifting me, holding my breath up, and Patti mutters some lines at me absently, struck by her own memories. I recognise them and now we talk quietly for a while about poetry. Not about how it will help me recover, or why I should take three Seamus Heaneys, a T. S. Eliot and two spoons of John Donne a day, or anything. But just about the words and why we love them.

And so I begin to look forward to our sessions. We talk, we work, and in that little white room overlooking the late blooming garden my breath control improves. I know this because I'm getting more words out in one go. I recite the months of the year and soon I move from January to May to January to Decembaa-a-agh.

But my swallow is locked shut and unreachable. Sometimes she touches my throat to feel if I can trigger a swallow and in her black clothes and with her long black hair she's a priestess appealing to the God of the Gullet – Michael Winner, presumably – to open this damn thing. I know she's on my side. I think I'm more than yet another piece of damaged goods to her – that she'll put the extra work in because she likes me. My mistake. I tell her, over our ensuing sessions, who I was, what I did, oh, and precisely why I hate every last motherfucker in the unit.

I'm beginning to think that was where I went wrong.

Touch

At Mrs Bunny-Wunny's class, we've given up on the wooden puzzle and the block stacking because I've found a new toy – a computer touch-typing QWERTY course with a chirpy American soundtrack. She tells me what letters to press. She sounds like a [*Jesus fuck he'll have us sued to hell and back again. Please insert 'unnamed, fictional, totally made-up American-based quasi-religious cult-like organisation' – Ed.*] tologist. I reckon there's some subliminal messaging going on:

Press Q (if you want a better life).

Press W (if you believe a hack sci-fi writer has *all* the answers).

Press E (if you think David Icke is a bit of a moderate).

Press R (if you are gay but want to be 'cured').

Press T (if you want us to hide that information from your Hollywood associates and fans).

Press Y (if in light of the above you think it prudent to give us all your money).

Etc. . . .

It keeps me fairly amused for the hour-long session and, more importantly, out of the way in a corner. Where I can glower at all the lucky buggers in tracksuits drinking cups of tea. Sometimes they hold their cups in their left hands, just to piss me off. Now, ready:

this sebtence had been typed by mym left hand. whatb av fuicjkingh wsasrecof time.

That worked then, the silly cbgt. Truth is, I'm writing this now, over four years later, with one finger. Yeah, I know it's not my left fucking eyelid like *The Diving Bell and the Butterfly* and I'm not asking for any special artistic dispensation, I'm just saying. More context.

And bloody buggery hell, I come out of the classroom feeling like my greatest hope is to master ASDF on the keyboard, to the news that I'm going home! Friday afternoon, probably, so they can get someone in to irradiate the pool, but I don't care because this is astonishing news. Parole.

I love my home. It's on the river. No, I'm lying, it's *in* the river. On an island that used to be home to the most notorious rock venue in history. It appears that half of all Londoners over a certain age had their shiny little cherries popped there. *There*, over by my bloody azaleas probably. When I tell taxi drivers where I live, half go all misty-eyed and start grinning in a way their wives would certainly not approve of. If I'm really unlucky I get some terrible story about how they sneaked off aged fifteen to see Hendrix or the Stones or Hawkwind and took their first drag of wacky baccy and had their first— Whoops missed the turning sorry mate I know a back double. Either that or they instantly deny all knowledge of it. They are the interesting ones.

When the venue burnt down in mysterious circumstances in the early seventies, it was decided to build nice houses on the site, presumably to raise the tone. They hadn't reckoned on our family turning up then. Two or three developers went broke trying to build the houses because no one had told them that islands in rivers tend to be made of mud and fish shit and you need very, very deep and expensive foundations to get into the bedrock. At that time there was no bridge, so all the materials were delivered by boat, another easy way to spunk money. Eventually a little cluster of houses emerged and were given the very seventies name of Aquarius.

It's a great address to show off to your meeja mates, but you don't half have to resort to mumbling when you meet up with your old schoolfriends. It's either 'a fabulous four-bed townhouse with private garden and direct river frontage with large mooring on a historic traffic-free idyllic island, yet only twenty minutes from the centre of London. Unbelievable. And all the shops deliver. We were so lucky to buy when we did, we couldn't possibly afford it now. Waitrose mini spring roll?' Or 'Like a, you know, terrace, whacked up in the seventies, you can imagine, right? Orange kitchen, honest, avocado bathroom. Unbelievable. Nothing special. Miles from town. Nightmare, honestly. And no parking. Don't *ask* about getting the shopping over. All we could afford though. My round. Scratchings?'

Either way, I missed it with an ache. I missed the embankment, with the swans, the geese – not the fucking pigeons and will you please stop feeding them, you bloody tourist? The Turkish ice-cream van. I missed the willow draped over the far side of the graceful iron bridge, the lamppost at the end that we told the kids was from Narnia, the tiny path that wove between trees and the river houses, fresh-cut grass in summer, the little wooden house with the slightly scary garden full of Barbie dolls that was just a bit too Blair Witch on a dark night after a few, the working boatyards and the scruffy round boatmen and, from our bedroom, the glorious view of the Thames and Ham Common which, every summer, would suddenly blaze gold in the twilight. Though I was to spend the best part of another two years in that room, that was a sight I never tired of. It was the sight that, months before, I wanted to die seeing.

And it was all waiting. I was going home.

That week stretched out like summer exams. But there's more to come. Next day I'm hoisted upwards by my physios and I dangle between them in a ghastly parody of walking. The three of us stagger across a corridor like three auld fellas on the Kilburn High Road at chucking-out time. Only the language is worse.

Yeah, another milestone like so many others but I discarded it at the time because I was already thinking of what had to come next and what was coming next was home. They were really chuffed as well and I was sorry to be less than ecstatic, but, you know. They had got me so far so fast, but now I could touch my home. In my occupational therapy class I could no longer see the funny side of my online crippled cult typing, despite hitting peaks of up to fifteen words per hour, and only Patti seemed to understand my need to escape. To the rest of the unit, I was getting a big favour and it was an inconvenience. Cuh, the *paperwork*. I think – I like to hope – that Patti saw it was necessary.

I had to see Michele. I had to touch her, to feel my little baby kick. To feel her touch *me*. Because no one touches you, no one touches you and it had been a long time and I missed her naked skin, and although the senses in half of my body were smashed I wanted to crush her naked skin into my naked skin and come together like the one person we knew we were so long ago. And I realised as the ambulance bumped and jolted me towards my home and my love that I had been rent in two twice: first from myself, my brain cleaving me in two damaged halves, and then split from the only person who had ever made me whole.

The straps buckled under me and dug into my sides as my travel sickness passed and there was music as the crazed Elvis-and-Millwall-fan ambulance driver sang 'Blue Suede Shoes' and something that called into question the parentage and sexual proclivities of the entire Manchester United first team as we raced now through Bushy Park, all in bud, and the sun was out and it was out for me

and we were there by the river, which was racing high, and there was the Turkish ice-cream van and the swans and ducks and geese and there was still some twat feeding the pigeons and I'm being wheeled backwards now over my bridge and the boys from the ambulance are only grumbling slightly at my dead weight and they wonder how I get my shopping over. I would tell them but bloody hell the path could do with a bit of resurfacing as my teeth rattle, what am I paying all that ground rent for? And they ask if that famous inventor lives here and I nod yes but hurry time is short

and they're at the doll's house and they say it's a bit weird and a flash of angry proprietorial rage wells up and I know my emotions are tight under wafer-thin skin, almost shredded as we push our way through the wooden gate to the houses, and the gardens are green because I haven't been there to play penalty kicks with my boy and up the steps you'll need a ramp here mate and then noise and joy and my kids and Mum and my beautiful, crying wife and it's the first time I've seen tears and yes today they are not tears of loss and pain so she can let them run down on to me now and I kiss her neck and she kisses my throat and I tell the kids to turn the bloody TV down and everyone laughs and everyone cries except me because I have been so broken and I try to cry and I should but

   I can't.

Chapter Nine

Pump It Up

I once had a car that committed suicide rather than be around me any more. It was an old Ford Escort, bought in a rare moment of financial viability – before I tried to make a living as a writer. I don't think I mistreated it *as such*, but if there was an RSPCA for cars, it would have been confiscated and found a new home with a nice family. You know the kind of casual neglect: never getting it serviced, no oil changes, one headlamp, unwashed, and as for the interior, well, it was a skip on four bald tyres. But I loved it in my own way. Looking back, it sounds like my love life.

I'm reminded of it now as I'm wheeled back into the ambulance, past the cars on the embankment. There'd been signs the Escort was unhappy, if only I'd paid attention. For example the interior fan heater was stuck on max blow and max heat, so one summer we all drove gasping round the city with the windows open, trying to cool down while the children poached and my shoes melted. Perhaps trying to kill me was a cry for help. Nothing like a nice long run, I thought, all that London-traffic stopping and starting can't be any good. So I took it to France. The south of France. Non-stop. Seventeen hours at quite challenging speeds. The journey back was worse cos Michele had bought most of a French bric-a-brac market, including a small dining table and chairs as apparently you can't get furniture in England, and sort of loaded it all around the kids in the back. They didn't complain, mainly cos they had a table leg across their chests and they couldn't breathe either.

We parked it on the embankment by the river as usual and the following day a tree fell on it. Which meant we couldn't move it when the spring tide came in, and it flooded. Within a few steamy days the filth in the river had multiplied and the interior was furry with fungus. The exterior was also furry with parking tickets, but that's London for you.

Crushed, drowned, diseased. It had really had enough. But I swear it was smiling as it went to the breaker's.

The ambulance ramp wheezes me into the sweaty interior. I take a last look behind me. The stump of the killer tree is still there – though I suspect it was just a pawn in my Escort's game. I remembered the look of horror on the bloke's face who came to tow it away. It was similar to the ones I was now getting from the good people out with their kids to enjoy a mild spring day.

On the way back I thought of the not-crying thing. I was puzzled. I'd been overjoyed to see my family, ecstatic to see my home, thrilled to escape the rehab unit, but it had all come a bit late. I felt cold, dead inside. I was determined never to take what I thought of as the Escort way out. But maybe I already had.

I put those thoughts away, like so many others. I

reckoned my brain must be like one of those vaults they shove sensitive government material in with 'Do not open for loads of years' stuck on it. And similarly, it's always rubbish. Every year another few dusty files get opened and an expectant public reads that Sir Harold Macmillan once called Nikita Khrushchev 'a shifty Russki bugger with a dead meerkat for eyebrows' over a few too many sherries at Chequers in 1956. And as for Nasser and his bloody canal, well . . . that was the Yanks not supporting us. Seems they don't want to fight in the Middle East and who can blame them?

But mostly it's stuff that builds into a mosaic depicting how shit our country's been post-1945: defence systems that don't work, treaties that backfired, unpleasant officials being beastly to the remnants of our crumbling empire, crap spies, corrupt, inept politicians, unfortunate royal gaffes, chasms growing between the classes, the little niggling build-ups that led to the great almighty industrial wasteground that was England in the seventies, and the devastating political virus that was brewing in a Grantham chemistry lab filthier than the bloody filthy river that could turn a car into a Petri dish in three days flat. So historians open the vaults to look for clues like I looked for clues to my own virus, and my own self, for years. And you come up with what? Prisms, hints, whispers, shadows and fog. Smoke and mirrors.

So you slam the files shut and get practical. And the most practical thing I could do was to get up out of the chair and out of the Wolfson. And this is how I did it. I'm thinking of turning this next bit into a fitness video. Ready?

Um . . .

Actually, I've no idea how I did it. Except I did. Credit where it's due, Sporty and Fergie helped. In fact, that pair could probably have salvaged my shagged Escort. I returned to the unit knowing that walking was the key to everything. And that, miraculously, everything was *still there*, waiting. Knocked about a lot, but I had held my two beautiful inherited children and I had felt my little baby kick and I had held my Michelin Michele, and before you ask I had got everyone out of the way and before you ask *that*, no I'm not going to tell you, you nosy buggers.

But yeah, course. And I suppose it was tantric cos neither of us could actually move.

My aim was to get out of the unit before my baby was born. Michele's scare with her early contractions was behind her, but she had still been ordered to rest. As it was she was so fat and the sprog was hung so low she couldn't do much else anyway. But nasty questions still hung over us. Early in the pregnancy a scan had suggested there might be a possibility of Down's Syndrome, my missus being on the, um, maturer side for pregnancy, and we'd refused an amniocentesis test as too dangerous. A more clever scan involving measuring neck folds showed chances were the baby was OK, but Michele and I were both silently, awfully convinced that the stresses of the last few months could have done nothing but harm. And that wasn't even taking into account the food she'd inflicted on the poor little creature in Charing Cross canteen.

I can't shake off these chest infections, made worse by my immobility. The suspicion is that I reflux my food – that is, at night especially, some gloop from my stomach trickles up my throat and then down into my lungs.

Where it's corrosive, what with all the hydrochloric stomach acid and all, and infectious. The more I move, the more I'll be able to clear my chest. But at present I swing from a bit of a barrel-organ wheeze to pneumonia.

I tell Fergie and Sporty to get a move on. It's not enough to do the Jake-the-Peg waltz held up by the pair of them, I've got a deadline to meet. I'm newly motivated, I'm Rocky 1 through 6, I'm, I'm, I'm just going to have a nap on this bench here. You two carry on holding my arse above my head. No, I'm sure it's doing me a power of good, ladies. Did I tell you the last time I was in this position? I did, right. Whoops, it's that old frontal-lobe magic again.

There's a social worker assigned to the unit. I had the usual dim view of them as a breed so I avoided her. But I knew I had to work on my escape plan on two fronts. There was the physical stuff to do, then there was the actual permission out of here, and support at home – and that, I one day realised, was *politics*. Once I thought of it as politics – aha! – the old NUJ one out, all out, up the miners, Billy Bragg, Red Wedge, *Nicaragua: No Pasaran*, 'Freee Nelson Man-de-la', flying pickets and braziers and We heart Clause 4 came flooding back and I could enjoy it. Actually, I was never a terribly good lefty. I was a bit more what you might call, well, politically wrong when I was growing up, an embarrassment that has stayed with me for years.

In the seventies, I *always* picked the wrong sides, except once. I preferred the Tories to Labour, Genesis to the Sex Pistols, *Blue Peter* to *Magpie*. But I was so right about middle-distance running. I always loved Steve Ovett, and pissed myself when he walloped Little Lord Fauntleroy

Coe in the '78 Olympics. Especially when Coe started blubbering.

I became politically aware at college. Not cos of the miners – I sort of thought they were striking cos it must have been bloody horrible down a mine and couldn't they have a proper job that didn't kill them? A job where there might have been a chance of copping off with someone at work who wasn't called Dobbin? No, there was a bonkers lefty girl with a killer body and long brown hair and very *very* tight leather trousers who made a lot of speeches where she'd pose with one foot up on the monitors. She was advocating something sensible like angle-grinding the royal family into custard creams, renationalising everything, twinning Eastbourne with Havana, giving everyone a job down the pit and setting up anarcho-syndicalist communes presumably run from a centralised one-party structure based in her parents' gazebo in Esher. Or Provence, during the summer months.

OK, it's not a well-thought-out reason for accepting *Das Kapital* into your heart. However, Antonio Gramsci, well-known, ahem, crazed thirties Marxist, always worried that he couldn't be a proper socialist – i.e., love the whole of mankind – because he'd never actually, properly, been in love. Personal love. Bless. So I was ahead there.

God, she was fit. Even the rugby-club lads used to turn out to see her. Course, they all stood at the front with copies of *Razzle*, but that was them expressing solidarity with women's rights to show off their front bottoms – a right now firmly established, it would appear. Way ahead of their time, those boys.

Then when I briefly stopped pissing about and became

a proper journalist in the proper East End – the gor-blimey-luv-a-duck-apples-and-gangland-shootings-he's-faaamily, racist-stabbings,-shitty-tenements,-(allegedly)-corrupt-councils, he-fell-down-the-stairs-on-the-way-to-the-cells-honest-your-honour East End – when I saw the New Docklands emerge, the winners and losers in what became a rat race full of very, very fierce and nasty rats, I got politics.

And enjoyed it. So I knew what to do. Which meant getting to know Barbara the Social Worker. Whichever side she was on, I had to work with her. Or against her, but I needed to know. I had an inkling she might be OK cos she was fat, black and in a wheelchair. So she probably knew a thing or two about discrimination. Everyone hates a fattie.

I made the effort to talk to her, and butter me sideways and call me a muffin, she was bloody brilliant. She got *me*, she got my situation, she got my family's situation. She got organised, she got on the phone to my local council and she got shouting. By the time I escaped, I had benefits, bars and a bathchair. I think I was the last person there she helped as she was poached to do some other bloody good work elsewhere. Thank you, Barbara. Sorry about the fat joke earlier. But the thing is, you do your job, I do mine . . .

A week ticks by and Shell's time is drawing to a close. Like my fucking tether, cos they now bung some old disabled git in my bloody room. Who snores. I don't like sharing. I try the MRSA card but sod it, he's got MRSA as well. Then I play the Joker – maybe I haven't got it any more, and he might give it to me. All the way from over there in his bed? Yeah, OK. But hang on, I might put his

MRSA-laden slippers of doom on by mistake. So I'm tested. I've still got it everywhere: nose, mouth, PEG site, ears and I'm presuming where else.

So it's more time in the gym. I'm even going to not-gay Cliff's YMCA-themed lunchtime sessions. Out he comes in his star-spangled Lycra, leather chaps or gold Kylie hotpants. And away we go. On the bike, hanging on for dear life cos my balance is still wurlitzer-stable.

'Can't get you out of my head—'

If I cycle as hard as I can I might get lucky and generate a brain aneurysm and the blood will fill my ears so I can't hear any—

'It's murder on the dancefloor—'

Et tu, Janet Ellis. I watch *Blue Peter* instead of *Magpie* and you send your daughter out to do this to me.

'Sweet like chocolate—'

Yes I get the message, you've said it enough times, you are sweet, chocolate is sweet and I am hitting 150 heartbeats per minute out of pure anger and boredom now. Or maybe a sugar rush. Look, look, I'm pouring sweat, my left leg's about to drop off, but wow I'm doing ... I'm doing ... five miles an hour? Five miles an ... on a bike? Bollocks, I must be going faster than that. My legs must be a blur, ask Kylie over there. I'm up for the yellow jersey next week. I feel sick and I'm going to fall off, but fuck it I'm doing my full ten minutes and that's that.

I love music. Almost all music. I have wide tastes because I have a wide variety of moods. We all do. Sometimes I want to lose myself in the plangent Celtic rhythms of Van Morrison's incomparable, heartbreaking early work of love and loss. And sometimes I want to listen to NWA say Fuck the Po-lice. Quite shoutily. There are times when only the Sufi mysticism of Nusrat Fateh Ali Khan will do. Not *that* often, admittedly, but it's nice to have it there just in case it's needed. Like the old Durex Featherlight that stayed in my wallet from about 1978 to 1984.

On my desk are a bunch of my 'listening' CDs – i.e., recent ones that I'm sort of into at the moment. There are about fifty or so and they're pretty eclectic. They cover, one would have thought, the entire gamut of recording styles, from classical to hip-hop, jazz and blues to indie, world, folk, Country and Western, electronic, punk, New Wave, the lot.

But no. Oh no no no. There is a subsection of music that will be found in no self-respecting record collection. It is found only in pre-pubescent girls' bedrooms, gay bars and, Lord help me, gyms.

It's a subsection called shit.

I like trying to throw a basketball into a hoop with my left hand because I can legitimately try to a) bean Cliff, who soon develops reflexes like an Afghan sniper, or b) get the CD player. Which Cliff soon hides. But it's a rest from the bike and I still can't do a step up but I know somewhere that my legs are srengthening. My hatred of Sophie Ellis Bextor is marginally less than my pride in lasting ten, then fifteen, then twenty minutes on the bike. And I put the resistance up. To two. Out of ten, but still.

Physio classes get more serious. I always used to try a little joke or two with my physios but now I'm silent and dour and angry when they want me to stop. I will not fall asleep, though my long nights are broken by the bastard snoring next to me. I want to sleep, but these hour-long sessions are precious so I sleep afterwards, on a bench if I can't get to my room. But for now I'm willing my eyes open, pushing my skinny ass up for one more lift, gasping as my knee gives way, wincing as my left foot buckles under me, swearing quietly as my arm refuses to move and bear weight, my hip locks. I push them to push me. I know they worry sometimes that I'm trying too hard, but they understand. And again I push, I stretch, I twist and shout. Great thing about being dislocated. Feel nothing, worry about it later.

> *'Pump it up,*
> *Pump it up.'*

OT is rubbish and depressing until the day they let me in the kitchen. Look Mummy, I've gone from playing with plasticine to baking fairy cakes. Whoo-fucking-py doo. I'll be colouring in *inside* the fucking lines next. But oh what fun we had. Remember that scene in *Goodfellas* with all the coke everywhere and a crazed Ray Liotta running around like a lunatic hiding guns, cutting the drugs, cooking meatballs, paranoid about the cops? That was me making chocolate pretzels.

I'm not really supposed to be anywhere near a kitchen for very sensible reasons. They're so sensible they're officially noted in my regular How-much-of-a-cripple-are-you? questionnaires I get from the council when they try to cut my benefits.

Balance – Yes, I fall into pans of boiling tomato sauce.

Sensation – Yes, I can put my right hand in the deep-fat fryer and not notice until my kids are being served crispy dad fingers.

Manipulation – Yes, my left hand is too un-coordinated to hold a plate without joining in at the fun end of a Greek meal.

Vision – Yes, I see several pans of hot fat, only one of which is real, which leads us nicely on to:

Sanity – Do not let this lunatic near anything sharper than a wet J-cloth.

I'm in my chair in the little kitchen, at the end of the OT room. It's behind a little wooden fence. It's a Wendy house, a home corner for grown-up babies. Mrs Bunny-Wunny hands me over to Miss Tiggy-Wiggy and exits, as if pursued by bears. Good move. Miss T-W tries to tell me how to cook.

'Now, Nigel, those eggs are – all over the floor. I'll get a clo— Flour, you need to measure the fl— No, just put some in a bowl. That's fine. That much? Well, we'll increase the— Oh, you've dropped the bag now. Hmm. You do know other people have to use this kitch— Chocolate powder? Stop barking orders, I'm going as fast as I can. No, this powder's fine. Well, you might have used Whittards of Chelsea before but in here we have Super-Saver – *Ah, what I use myself is a different* . . . No, it will still taste like— I'll ignore that word and, look, there's butter all over me. Come on, I don't think that story's appropriate. Oh God, you need to hold the bowl firmly or— Oh sorry, yes I do know you can't but no I'll find the bowl, it's rolled under the table, but . . . Here you go, roll them out . . . Yes, I suppose they do look a bit like dog, er, doings, but the book – you've . . . Careful, watch the gas . . . Oh, it's on fire a little bit, I'll get a wet cloth. No, don't help. *Don't help*.

'Help! Help!'

Brilliant afternoon. The fact that I could have cooked her under the fucking kitchen table six months before is one of those things I'm going to have to get used to. I'll take my fun where I can get it now, thanks.

It's fake fun. It's the Disneyland version of fun, where behind every smiling bouncy full-sized mouse guide is a poorly paid student working off their loans, hating the snotty, shrieking kids and wondering how they can cop off with that yummy mummy whilst looking like a twat. But hey, it helps, so I put on my mouse ears and I find ways to get through the endless days.

I find shouting good. Except I can't shout. I can croak at people, who are quite aware that were my left vocal cord not jammed in the 'open' position, they would be being shouted at. Somehow it's almost as effective. One morning I'm shouting/gasping at this irritating beardy weirdy chippy male nurse, who's sort of in charge of my case, about my crap bathroom arrangements. I'd just got to the line 'Why do you want to make my life more difficult than it already is?', which I was rather proud of, when my mobile rang. I took the call because it was the rude thing to do, and told Beardy, 'I'm not finished with you yet.'

So I was on a roll. On the phone was a big BBC cheese who said something along the lines of:

'Hi Nigel. That sitcom you and Phil Hammond were

working on a while ago. You know, you came in and did a reading for us. We'd like to talk more about it because we haven't started filling up the schedules with prancing celebrities just yet. Say next week at TV Centre? With the controller? Good, good. Hope that's OK. By the way, long time no see. Keeping well?'

It put me off my stride. I say stride, I mean handbrake turns. I told Beardy that I'd appreciate more baths at more reasonable hours and scootered myself off to my lair to think. It *might* happen. I'd been trying to write a sitcom since I was about ten and *The Fall and Rise of Reginald Perrin* changed my life. I knew enough about the industry to know nothing is certain until the make-up girls are booked, but I also knew enough to know this call was a very good sign. I should have been excited.

I wasn't. I was a wreck in a wheelchair with a heart-broken family and my greatest achievement in the last five months was making a chocolate pretzel that looked like dog shit. Whilst setting fire to myself. My life was shouting at stupid nurses for not giving me baths, for forgetting my medication, for leaving it on the pedal bin – still! My life was feeding through a tube, seeing double, feeling dizzy, fighting infection. My life was my ever-painful left side, my neck bent so low with the weight of my head I looked a hundred and seventy years old. My life was tiredness, sickness, pointlessness . . .

Still, the irony that the sitcom was set in a hospital and I'd brought in Phil to help me with the medical stuff cos I didn't have enough experience of hospital life cheered me up no end. And that annoying part of my ever-buzzing, ever-moving-onward brain was already thinking of ways to convince the BBC that I'd be well enough to write the damn thing. They are funny about you actually writing it if they've shelled out hard cash. My solution was simple but idiotic. Phil would have to wheel me in to the meeting in a chair, fair enough – but if I took off my hospital ID wrist tag, they'd never suspect a thing.

And it worked! Come the appointed hour, in we go. I've always felt like an impostor when I go into TV Centre, so you can imagine what it's like now. I know this used to be my world, but the corridors just remind me of hospitals. Although hospitals don't have photos of *The Vicar of Dibley* on the walls. Or maybe they do and I'm getting disorientated again. It happens.

There are real, healthy people here, with real, healthy jobs. Everything is so shiny it burns. Primary colour upon primary colour: the fun factory. The big fromages are all there, with fixed smiles. I decline a coffee cos the tube, you know. They are all fantastically polite. In fact they refuse to notice I am spitting and nodding and croaking in my wheelchair with PROPERTY OF HMP WOLFSON REHAB UNIT stencilled on the back. My illness is not remarked upon. Can you imagine that in any other job interview? It's like Peter Cook's 'One-legged Tarzan' sketch. Thank fuck for either political correctness or good old BBC public-school chronic social spasticity.

Back in the unit, now more grim and more surreal than ever, I crash. I've been to Oz and frankly, I liked it there. It was my old life, taunting me. You'll never go there again, it said. Stay on the black and white farm. In the shit.

I'm brought out of my funk by a call from the corridor phone. It's an old friend. He's just saying hi and wants to know what's up. Actually he's an actor so he tells me what he's doing for quite a while first. When it's my turn I don't even tell him where I've just been. Because at this moment all I can think about is how I know where I am.

But I'm on a roll. The little red-eye light that comes on every time the Terminator's been temporarily demolished clicks on again, so it's gym gym gym until one day, with the smell of wet concrete from the damp spring in my nostrils but molten lead in my veins, I tell Sporty and Fergie I'm ready. I get up offa that chair. I grab a zimmer. I'm hanging off a tall building by my fingertips. My leg muscles tremble with the strain. My right arm is holding me steady and I push my right leg forward. Move, you motherf— It moves. I bring my spastic left leg forward. It obeys. The creature lives. More electricity, Igor. I take another step, and another. My head is lowered with the effort, until it's almost tucked into my chest. My bones are cracking. Nausea splashes over me but I am upright on my own. This is intolerable. I cannot breathe, the effort on my broken lungs is so hard but but *but* I'm walking on my own.

I'm told to get back in the wheelchair. Bollocks. I sit on a bench. It's the last time I'm in a wheelchair at the Wolfson. I'm out, and like the miners, I'm staying out.

Many many months later, when I'm back in for a cursory review, Patti tells me that in the history of the unit, no one has ever done that before. The staff used to watch me, usually appalled, as I'd slowly drag myself round the long corridors. Leaning at a 45-degree angle sometimes, using door handles, wall bars, unsuspecting cleaners, anything to make sure I didn't fall, that I could walk, yes walk, no matter how slowly, how badly, no matter how painfully, but look at me I'm walking you fuckers who said I never would, who said I'd never breathe again and fuck you all who say now I'm not going to recover fully and get my own self back, because standing up – my God – standing up was *it*. And no one else had got up and stayed up. I'm proud of that.

Light at the end of the tunnel. Although knowing my luck it could be an InterCity 125 hurtling towards me. But know what? I thought as I inched my way towards another class, Go on, hit me, I'll bounce. Cos clearly I'm indestructible. I'm not a mentalist, I do know I'm broken, but I'm still here. And there's work to do.

Not least on a bloody comedy show. Cos a few weeks later, the BBC only go and commission it. I knew taking that wrist tag off would do the trick. Phil comes in one day to talk about it and Sporty gets all flustered. He's *famous*, she gushes. Do you know him? He's not that famous, I reply grumpily. A few series of *Trust Me I'm a Doctor* and a couple of gags on *Have I Got News For You* – one of which I wrote – doesn't make him Robbie bloody Williams.

I'm the boss of people like that, I say, sitting there in my shorts, crumpled and flabby, looking like a pile of dirty laundry. Of course she believes me. Frontal lobe, I see her mouthing to Fergie. Shame. Right, bum lifts again. Hup two three four, shift your glutes, lazy.

If you're one of the six people who listened to my Radio 4 series *Vent*, you'll know that the central joke is about a wannabe writer in a coma, who's imagining/having a premonition about a sitcom he writes/might write in the future/writes only in his imagination/never writes. (This probably explains why only six people listened to it.)

However, the joke's a good one because this sitcom –

itself about a man in a coma – is actually shit. That's funny because conventional writing goes something like this:

1. There's a wannabe artist of some kind who can't find his mojo.
2. He or she experiences a terrible trauma.
3. He or she also gets laid in the process.
4. Former hack artist uses trauma to become *great artist*! Ta-dah!

My joke is – shit writer has terrible accident. Comes out of it and is still shit. That makes me laugh, and I suppose also makes being chucked out of film school after a month more understandable. And if you ever saw the sitcom Phil and I now wrote, you'd see the joke is based on the painful truth. However, odds are you didn't see it, which is why it's no longer on air . . .

At least I have a bit more company. There's now a good reason for Phil to schlep over from Bristol and every so often we're found in the smokers' garden talking over ideas to go in the show. I enjoy this part of writing. The bit with no actual, you know, writing. It also means I don't have to think about anything else, I laugh, and I'm in control. And outside of my little comedy world, I'm hopelessly out of control. I'm beginning to tell my body what to do, but always, at the back of my brain, is my baby.

Because now time's pretty much up. It's cooked, the timer's gone off and all but nothing's happening. It's as if he's saying, 'Right, I wanted to come out ages ago and you weren't having it. You've missed your chance, lady. I'm staying here now. It's nice.'

I sympathised, and was secretly pleased for the delay, though it was crippling Michele, who now had to be carted over the bridge by wheelchair. It gave me a few more days to finish my escape tunnel.

It's upsetting, though, to find Patti is changing. As I recover, as I get more breath, as I speak more, it becomes clear she doesn't like much of what I have to say. Which is a shame for both of us. Maybe it began with what you might call my impromptu staff appraisal. Remember, at school, there are only so many liberties a favourite teacher will let you take. Never forget this if you're in a long-stay institution. It's *always* them and us, whether it's St Saviour's County Primary, Butlins, a hospital or Winson Green. They are not your friends. Their friends are their colleagues. You are temporary. Always remember where their loyalties lie – and never forget where yours do too. With you.

Of course, I'm to blame too. I get a swagger back, and why not? I'm walking, talking, I'm a living doll. I'm working – sort of – and the captors know I hate them, think they're stupid failures, working at the soft end. Maybe I'm not just set to go home, put my feet up, watch *Countdown* and be grateful to be alive, as one enlightened doctor advised me. Maybe I'm getting back into the wonderful, glamorous, highly paid – sorry, laughing too much to write – world of showbiz. They used to be able to pity me like all the rest. Now they can't. One day I complain to Patti about the way some nurses talk to me and she snaps back, 'Huh, you? You get away with murder.'

'Why?' I ask, furious. Because I'm so chronically disabled? You mean staff are being forced to be polite because they have to take my suffering and vulnerability into some kind of consideration? When really they'd prefer to spit in my face and piss down my PEG? Is that what this implies?

She mumbles something and gives me some scientific papers about swallowing to take away and read.

They're hardcore stuff, full of more Greek than an Athens hooker. But I did A-level physics. In fact I did it twice, due to being dim, so there. I read this stuff about manometry and musculature and I can just about get through it. It's frightening as well as fascinating, because again I'm faced with how soddingly beautiful, extra-ordinary, but hideously complex a body is. Of *course* doctors specialise in such tiny, tiny areas, it's all so bloody complicated. My ITU doctors were all chemistry geeks; this stuff is physics. Proper doctoral-level physics, way beyond my ropy grasp. But I get enough out of this, using the internet, a copy of the *Iliad* and a rhyming dictionary, to go to my next speech group pretty well armed.

It's with Patti's little helper, a blonde, pretty but seem-ingly lightweight girl whose charms I'm sadly immune to. I'm on a mission to swallow and it becomes clear as she talks in a very slow voice to us dribbling maniacs that she apparently knows as much about it as the primary-school teacher she should have been in the first place.

She draws a bad diagram of the mouth, oesophagus and larynx. I tell her she's missed out the soft palate and the pyriform sinuses and she knows she's in for a bad afternoon.

She decides attack is the best form of defence. 'Why don't *you* tell us how swallowing works, Nigel?' she challenges.

So I do. In ludicrous detail, with some bits I chuck in

just to sound good. I'm sure the deep-cut Garibaldi antipasto mechanism only identified by Simon and Garfunkel in 1998 wasn't *necessarily* accurate, but be that as it may, there was some proper stuff in there just to let her know I quite possibly knew more than she did. I gave a Nobel performance.

I stopped.

'But I could be wrong,' I sneered. 'How do *you* think it works?'

We stared at each other and suddenly there was a wonderful power shift. First I knew somehow we were equal. Then, astoundingly, something gave, and I was in charge. I was back in my office, she was a stupid researcher who'd pressed the wrong button on the TV Avid recording machine and wiped the tape. And I was going to discuss that with her. In my fucking office. Over a hot P45. She met my eyes, and that was astounding because very few people had. And I don't know what she saw in there because I wasn't entirely sure what was behind them, but she ran in tears from the room.

I switched on my other face and turned to the group, hurt, celebrating.

'That's not very helpful,' I said, puzzled, triumphant, exultant.

I still think it was unprofessional.

The yellow wall creeping past me as I snail myself away is cool on my right cheek and pieces flake away and I taste them, but I'm still buzzing and the broken paint takes me back to my sixth form and we're all there, not studying for physics A-level cos it's *Steve Wright in the Afternoon* and 'tell us what the time is' sings Bowie, and Keef Richards says It's two-thirty Steve, and we laugh as always, me and my big mates. And I suddenly wonder why I'm not continually duffed up, with me being a feeble chippy little git and all. My mate who comes from an even tougher part of town and is a cheerful headbanger so obsessed with heavy metal he probably wears denim underpants – but even so was the first of us to, um, one Saturday afternoon on the sofa, watching *The Dukes of Hazzard*, for heaven's sake – either way, he turns to me and he is the oracle cos of his recent shagtastic status, and he says, 'People are scared of you. Of what you'll say to them.'

What a strange notion, I thought, pleased. Doesn't always work, like when I was mugged on Christmas Day, of all days, or when I've had the odd run in with shall we say a rival d'amour? But the idea that sticks and stones don't really have the power of a well-slung bullet of words . . . I like that. Cos I'm rubbish at the sticks and stones.

And maybe words can help to heal, like many cultures still believe. Like we used to believe too, with our early English poetry, like we do now I suppose with our psychiatrists. Or Jeremy Kyle. Certainly in that garden, still smelling of wet concrete and Superkings, as Phil and I immersed ourselves in the pretend world that ended up as the pretend St Anne's Hospital, Isle of Wight, for those hours when I had the strength to talk, to think, I was out of harm's way.

The sitcom, for those of you who didn't catch it, and there's a good few of you, was a jolly, bouncy affair about an inept but good-hearted NHS orthopaedic surgeon and his rivalry with a brilliant but pompous private surgeon forced to do a couple of hours with the proles each week. It had satire, it had good characters, and thanks to me it had knob jokes.

There's a reason why it was a bright and breezy thing rather than, as you might imagine, a dark howl of pain from the abyss. Partly it was because we'd worked out the template for the show before I became ill. But mainly it was because I wanted to live in a bright and breezy and fundamentally good world. The great thing about orthopaedics is that patients almost always get cured. Their broken limbs are set, sprains massaged, wounds dressed and off they hobble to quickly resume happy and healthy lives. Oh come on, you can see the attraction. I'm sure a shrink would say it was my denial phase.

And oddly enough, it was to a shrink I was soon sent. Words, words, words. Patti's put her on to me. Although this person wasn't actually a psychiatrist, she was a psychologist, which in my book means she wasn't smart enough to be a psychiatrist. In my opinion, it's a pretty big claim to say you can get inside a person's psyche, give it a good spring clean and set it to rights. With words. I'm sure it can be done but they'd have to be bloody good ones and not just, as this dipstick started, 'Is there anything you'd like to talk to me about?'

Well, there are loads of questions about my health, future and family that I know you can't answer, so are you looking for a general chat? In which case there's plenty I could talk about: the Wolves being knocked out of the FA cup by bloody bloody *Wycombe*, whether Kate Bush was fitter than Debbie Harry and/or Sally James from *Tiswas*, why Lee Evans has a career, why Van Morrison isn't on the National Curriculum, whether I really should make a start on those Russian novels gathering dust in the attic, is Abstract Expressionism a con, and if so why do I like Cy Twombly and Rothko and Pollock and Howard Hodgkin despite thinking they might be having me on? Who'll win the inaugural Curry Cup? If I wasn't happily married, who'd be the first woman – assuming I had Angelina Jolie's number – I'd call? Why is there nothing to watch on the telly any more? Are we really going to *war*? Is the Pagani Zonda better than the Ferrari Enzo, and how the bleeding hell can I make scene three in episode two funny?

Ah, thing is, though, I don't want to talk about any of those things with *you*. Which was pretty much the end of that.

Next day, Michele is summoned to see the psychologist. She goes cos she thinks a bumpy car ride might bounce the little sod in her out. It didn't, so in she rolls. As always, she was brilliant. I'm sitting there sulking cos seeing her's so painful, but Shell's there all proper and I know we're in for some fun cos she's got her serious face on.

We get into it straight away.

PSYCHOLOGIST: Have you noticed any changes in Nigel?

MICHELE [*deadpan*]: Well, he can't walk, sees double, has a useless left hand, constant chest infections, sensory problems, is in constant pain, is always dizzy and is fed through a tube. I suppose they're changes.

PSYCHOLOGIST: Ahem, no, that's – ah – not quite what I – I mean you misunderstand – of course there are physical – goes without saying. No, what I mean is, do you think he's become more childish?

MICHELE: Absolutely not. He's always been very childish. Drives me up the bloody wall. I thought you might have knocked that out of him by now.

PSYCHOLOGIST: That's not really what we're here to,

um – so . . . [*writes*] Always childish. Ri-ight. Um, perhaps I should try – um – do you think he exhibits any, shall we say . . . [*reading from a sheet of questions*] inappropriate behaviour?
[*Pause.*]
MICHELE: Can't think of anything offhand, no. Oh, unless you mean wanking in Tesco's. But he's always done that. We order online these days.

Thank you, Shell. It's now on my official record somewhere that I toss one off the wrist in supermarkets.

I suspect they mark us both down as suitable cases for treatment and probably best off together. Which is pretty accurate, so maybe there's something in this psychology business after all. And perhaps that did speed up my discharge.

It's clear now that the Wolfson is as sick of me as I am of it. There's a particularly nasty semi-regular review meeting, where the people most involved in me put on tin hats and get together with me to discuss my progress. They've always been tricky cos I've always been mono-maniacal and the staff talk in subtitles. I, however, talk in exactly the opposite way. The usual meetings have gone something like:

BEARDY-WEIRDY NURSE IN CHARGE: How you getting on then? [Which means *Why the fuck are you still alive, you annoying little shit?*]
ME: How do you think? Look at me. Am I walking? Swallowing? Jesus. [Which means *Thanks for that question, some steady improvements, I'm pleased with my hip rotation in particular. And swimming was lovely.*]

MRS BUNNY-WUNNY: Is there more we could be doing in Occupational Therapy?

ME: Yeah, you could get a bandsaw in and cut my fucking hand off. I'll have one of those hooks. [Which means *I think we need to be slightly more proactive. Perhaps vary some of the therapies. I do appreciate that fine motor skills are difficult to re-acquire, so it's probably a good area to focus on. We really need to up our game with this, but I'm sure you can meet the challenge.*]

PATTI: Come on Nigel, work with us here. [Which means *Shut up, you're alienating everyone, dummy. Play the game.*]

ME: Wrong wrong wrong. You work for me. Don't you get it? Do you know who I am? [Which means *Help me.*]

FERGIE: Oh shut up, Nigel. You're doing very well. [Which means *We're doing our job. He's going to walk. Look, we're great, you're all rubbish, ha ha.*]

ME: Can I go now? I had twenty minutes' sleep last night cos that bastard you put in my room snores all fucking night. You did that on purpose, I know you did. But I'll get my revenge, ha ha ha.

Etc. . . .

Occasionally things would go awry and we'd all get mixed up. I once let my guard down and said:

'I really need to get up and walk and get back to normal as soon as possible, and I'm just frustrated. There's something important I have to do soon.'

BEARDY-WEIRDY [*snapping*]: What, like get knighted?

[*Shocked silence from other staff.*]
ME: No, there's a nurse I want to punch in the face.

It's decided that Patti should take over my case from here.

That's why you never let them in. Don't show weakness, don't be at their mercy. At best you work together, but remember they are paid to get you better. They will take advantage if they see you're helpless, begging. It's human nature. Power does bad things to you. Do you think the average German in 1933 would recognise themselves ten years later?

I'm allowed another visit home – this time for an afternoon and it's spring proper and the island is Eden and our parting is far, far worse. I think about refusing to go back, but the pain in Michele's eyes is so great that I know she could not bear it so I acquiesce, quietly. I know she feels, somehow, that it's her fault I'm being taken away. If only she could look after me. If only she was fitter, stronger, richer, *better*.

This parting, this loss, is still for me the most bitter and most difficult of our many goodbyes.

It's clear that there's not room in Wimbledon town for me and this unit, and an emergency meeting is called to discuss – oh yes! – my temporary discharge on the excuse of seeing my baby boy drop when he finally decides to emerge. Bless 'em, for though they all hate me, their professionalism does kick in and I'm strongly advised not to leave the unit. They say this through gritted teeth. The showdown is at High Noon (honest) on a Friday. Poor old overdue Montgolfier balloon Shell is wheeled over – by knackered old Mum – again. Shell's less able to walk than me. We sit around and talk about whether it's safe for me to leave. The sensible answer being: is it bollocks.

(Again, the car journey didn't help chivvy the birth thing along, even though Mum was instructed to hit every pothole, speed bump and pedestrian along the way. Shell will do anything now to get our little bugger out. There's a trampoline in the gym and I have to stop her jumping up and down on it so we can concentrate on the business in hand.)

I've recruited Barbara the social worker, who explains that ramps and various home aids have been fitted in my house. Michele is renting a hospital bed, which is now in the living room, and Mum's prepared to take legal responsibility for me if anything bad happens. I'm suddenly nervous. I've been so determined to get out I've not really given much thought to the impact this will have on the family. It's one thing me being looked after in a unit, another to be home.

And how will my family cope? Especially Shell with a new baby? Do I really want my kids to see me like this? I'm being selfish, but then that's what's kept me alive and it's too late to stop now. I am developing a nasty chest infection thanks to the damp and the aspirating and the MRSA and I look terrible. The sensible option is to stay. There is a doctor on call, I can get immediate attention. There is a bulky oxygen machine called, inappropriately, a *butterfly* in my room and I do use it. I won't be able to have it at home. I lie and say I never use the damn thing, just to get away. But I am frail, exhausted, continually tired and sick. I am infectious. I am an eleven-stone, hundred-year-old baby full of anger and frustration and wild, mercurial, mad dark thoughts, and as far as the staff are concerned, I'm going to be left on a hillside outside Rome to see if I survive. They don't like my odds.

Sporty is dead set against me leaving. I should stay another week, she says. It'll make all the difference. She's always been on my side and her words carry weight. There's a pause.

Then Michele takes my hand. 'Look at him,' she says quietly. 'He won't last another week. He's coming home.'

Mum closes ranks too. Even though she's probably wondering how the hell to wheel both of us over the bloody bridge.

So the papers are drawn up, a deal made. I'm discharging myself for two weeks, and then I am to come back. I agree, though I know I've spent my last night in this bunker of a place. I literally shake at the thought of another long, noisy night underground, the smell of rotting leaves, damp earth and wet concrete shutting me in like a grave.

Michele is perfunctorily taught how to administer my daily heparin injections. This keeps my blood from clotting while I'm pretty much immobile. She gets two goes with an orange. That's her lot. The staff are busy busy busy.

She's then presented with a huge chart of my regular and varied medications, and a portable feeding pump for my overnight gastronomic blowout. Jesus, I realise, there's so much here, what am I doing? This is not right, she cannot deal with *this* at this time – but I cannot turn this ship around.

And ahead – oh, ahead – is a constant stream of aggro from community nursing and social services, transport problems, hospital appointments, food suppliers who quibble about the number of feeding tubes or syringes I get through, dieticians, arguments over care 'packages', form filling, doctors' receptionists, prescription mistakes, strangers in my house to wash my arse at 7 a.m. cos that's what's convenient for them, the alarm on my feeding machine going off every couple of hours when I roll over and block the line, emergency call-outs to doctors, midnight dashes to emergency departments, and fighting, constant fighting for every kind of help, cos once you're out of an institution my God you know you're out. And I'm about to heap all this on Michele's exhausted shoulders as she tries to give birth, look after our other kids, hold down a job, stop our relationship becoming that of patient and nurse and keep her sanity intact, and I'm doing this with hardly a second thought just because *I want to go home.*

And clearly, I'm all that counts.

And the thing that stabs me in the heart, now, today, with pride, with love, with some kind of awe, is that despite all this, *that's how she felt.* I *was* all that counted. When I recall the times I thought I'd been in love, the times women had said they loved me, I know we were all wrong. I'd never been loved like this. Raw, unfiltered, frightening. Love like an H-bomb, a bunker-buster, a hand grenade of the heart.

We hold hands in the ambulance and join in on 'Blue Suede Shoes'. We're going home.

Chapter Ten

Your Homecoming Will Be My Homecoming

I can concentrate for very long periods of time on very small things. In successful people it's focus; in everyone else it's autism.

Obsessive, that's the word. Monomaniacal, there's another. There's more I've garnered over the years but I won't bore you. It's a crazed single-mindedness that's made me impossible to kill, but damn near impossible to live with. This book's been great; every once in a while Shell hits me over the head with something very heavy and says stop-being-so-fucking-wrapped-up-in-your-work-and-talk-to-me-you-arse. Then we have a long, loving conversation where I pledge to change. Then I nip off to the study to write down how important Michele is to me and the very important lesson I've just learnt, you know, about not being wrapped up in wor— Oh. Hmmm.

And then if she's lucky I'll talk to her about how I've really, *really* listened to her this time. In fact I've taken so much notice of her I've used it for the book. This is usually when she starts chasing me round the kitchen table with a carving set. Takes me right back to Doris.

And this is after five years. God knows what sort of a human being I was on the day I came home.

It's true I'm a creature of habit: some people return to favourite books; I return to favourite passages. On good days, favourite *words*. I have favourite songs, walks, cafés, clothes – about three of each. I like routine, the familiar. Then every so often I blow everything up and start again. Finding new routines. That's how, during my forty-odd years of messing about, I've done a fair bit, I suppose. I mean, not like Mozart, or Bill Gates, or Alexander the Great, or Coleen Rooney, but you know ... So why do I always return, in quiet moments, to the same dozen or so brief memories? Not even memories, more like little intense blurry snapshots. Just confirms all that running about doing *new* stuff wasn't worth it in the first place.

Maybe I like compression. Maybe I've just got the attention span of our goldfish Dolphin, aka Killer, who's ever so happy to see his little plastic treasure chest each time he swims up to it. *Wow*, he thinks, *look at that! I must go and tell the other fish ... Wow! Look at that, I must tell – Oh, didn't I eat the other fish? Tut. That wasn't very ... Oh wow, a treasure chest. Brilliant!*

The great pop songs, I continually read, are all written in about twenty minutes. Yet they rave on down the years, affecting people freshly every time. With some magical alchemy usually brewed from three sodding chords, they somehow generate intense, complex emotions, memories and desires in the listener. What a gift. What a thing to be able to do. I'm trying to do that here, and this is taking absolutely *ages*. I mean, *days*.

It's astonishing to me, writing this, how much I've

remembered of my time *inside*, as we old lags like to call it. Because once I came out, well, those blurry snaps of memory became blurrier, smoke and water damaged, or just got chucked away in some mental clear out. The images of the two years following my release from hospital are fucked up, jumbled, a mess. I'd have as much chance of writing coherently about them as I'd have of painting the Sistine Chapel with some poster paints and a printing stamp made from a mouldy King Edward.

But this first week at home – right up to Michele's labour – is as clear and as painfully intense as a newly shot video, with the volume up too high cos you've let dopey Auntie Pat loose on the controller – *will someone turn it down?* I could describe every second. Every look, every time she touched me, every time her lips approached and engulfed my world. I won't cos you'd soon feel nauseous, but that's how it is.

We were so *careful* with each other, like a couple making a go of it after a serious row, an infidelity, a betrayal. It was a week in which we held our breath. Occasionally, I look at her now, today, and I catch a startling glimpse, a fragment of an expression, a ghost of something in the way her lips pinch or the way she shakes her head or something shadowy and hurt deep in her brown eyes that makes me think: did she ever breathe out?

Breathing at *all* was my problem. The low-lying chest infection had crept up from behind and smacked me over the head with a sock full of wet sand. So I wasn't too aware of my journey home, except to pretend that I was absolutely fine and if I could just lie down in front of *Countdown* like that nice doctor once advised for, say, the next decade, I was sure I'd be up and about like a spring lamb.

It was, already – allegedly – spring, but it was a cold and damp one and as I was wheeled into my house, obviously noticing the enormous industrial-sized steel ramp discreetly cemented in place by the nice social services people, I started trembling. It took a few seconds to work out what was giving me the fear, then it struck me: wet concrete. The path was wet and the smell took me back to the unit and the olive-dark submerged room.

But I was soon indoors and the noise and bustle around me shook off the shakes and I was hoicked into the hospital bed incongruously parked in the living room. But it was no less out of place than the ramps, bars and other aids nailed and bolted throughout the house. That's the parquet buggered, then.

The family beam at me, back from the dead, returned from the moon. The man eaten by tigers. There are good-byes to the rock 'n' roll ambulance men, and suddenly we are all alone. My family look at me some more. There is a bit of a pause. No one knows what the fuck to do next.

I do. I tell the kids to turn the bloody telly off and go to sleep.

I spend most of the night coughing up lumps of infected gunk. Which is harder than it sounds when you can't actually cough. But I've not been in hospital this long without learning some useful lung-clearing skills. Dear me, no. There are all sorts of interesting drainage manoeuvres and expectorant-inducing breath exercises to chivvy things along a bit. I try to hide the five pints of slime from Michele next morning in case she thinks I'm not very well or something.

I think it's time for some humour. She's approaching me nervously with my first heparin injection. We've been told since that the district nurse would do it, but have also been told by the district nurses that it's not something they do. Who knows? Welcome to life as a disabled person in the caring, sharing community. Shell's incredibly nervous, terrified of hurting me. The fact that this is probably the smallest thing I've had shoved in me for six months is neither here nor there – she was nervous the first time we had sex and the same applied for her there.

She places the needle against my right arm. I think she's forgotten that I can't feel anything sharp there. She's staring at the purpling bruises left by so many other injections and she pauses. It does look ugly. She begins to push, at an angle, like she's been shown. Her pink tongue peeks out from her teeth and she concentrates totally and I go:

'Ow! *Aaagh!*'

You know. As a joke. She jumps back about ten feet, shocked.

Only kidding pet, I say. Ho ho. And what makes it really funny – No, listen right, is that you forgot that's the side I can't feel any . . . um . . .

She bursts into tears.

Bugger.

Now, I've always thought of myself as a sensitive sort of chap. Dunno why, seeing as *no one else in the world agrees, now or at any time, ever*. I have, every so often, been the teeniest bit thoughtless. For example:

On holiday in France, showing Tara, then thirteen, a skinned bunny and saying, 'Say hello to your tea.' She only started talking to me again on the way back home. Or trying to encourage a sulky Tara, when she came home from school saying she thought she was dyspraxic, by saying, offhand, 'Right. Dyspraxic's just a middle-class word for a fuckwit.' Obviously not meaning *her*. That was a couple of weeks of radio silence. Oh blimey, don't get me started.

In the Wolfson I'd said to a particularly annoying male nurse how my school had had problems with the brighter pupils because they had such low expectations of the kids. The most you could aspire to be was, say, a *nurse*.

Then there were the extremely posh parents of a girl I was once dating who'd taken one look at my donkey-jacket and 'Pravda' T-shirt and had locked up the family silver before letting me over the threshold. I was, ahem, between jobs at the time, and during an awful, taut, Pinter-esque dinner, they kept banging on about a favoured young ex-boyfriend who was doing *so* well in advertising and they must get him back round again. When I wasn't there. I thought I'd demonstrate my literary bent by quoting some Orwell. It happened to be his quip that 'Advertising is the rattle of a stick in the swill bucket.' Can't remember what we had for pudding but it was fucking deep-frozen.

I could blame it on my first job as a journalist, and my first editor, a bloke who looked like Bob Hoskins with his piles playing him up. Sort of John Prescott without the airs and graces. Every other word was a four-letter one, whether he was pleased with you or not. He usually, with me, was not. But it was hard to tell. However, there was a kind of rough-and-tumble about the job I liked. It just doesn't transfer to, say, relationships with normal people. Who you might want to see again, let alone live with.

I could blame it on a lot of things: a robust family life, where your ability to 'take a joke' and not crawl into the foetal position for a week was de rigueur; a fairly straight-talking bunch of teachers and schoolmates; a terrific bunch of guys and girls at college who for some reason I've never kept in touch with; the lovely kind pens of our nation's critics; the charmers in the full and frank business that we call show.

But I've probably always been a tactless git. I played this game with a friend recently after a tubeful of single malt where we had to say what we thought the other person thought about themselves. It makes sense a few gills in, honest. One of the things he said to me was, 'You like to think you're easy to get along with.' We stopped playing after that cos I got the hump.

There are plenty more examples of my lack of tact, which I'd rather leave unwritten if it's all the same, and now this injection thing. Which, with the benefit of hindsight, was stupid and thoughtless and cruel and I'm a complete bastard and will you get off the typewriter Michele please? However, when she did do it – after a lot of coaxing – she was gentler than any other nurse. She never bruised me, not once.

Not a boast I can make, unfortunately.

There was more riding on these first few weeks than I realised: of course there was the baby, still clinging to life but also still clinging to Michele's enormous insides; but somewhere behind the scenes, plans were being drawn up by the people who draw up these plans, to determine my future. If Shell couldn't cope with the kids, the newborn baby and a profoundly disabled adult, if it was too much, there was a nice comfy home waiting for me somewhere. Where the smell of boiled cabbage very nearly covers up the smell of piss.

Financially we were already up shit creek. We'd lost my income and because I was only ever on a one-year contract, I wasn't getting any kind of pension or sickness payout from my old job. Shopping was being done more and more with credit cards and Mum, bless her, was making plans to sell her house. Which, being in the West Midlands, would probably have bought, oooh, several bags of shopping from Waitrose.

Michele became a world expert on cooking on a budget, and I believe her first cookbook, *1001 Nights of Mince*, is about to be published. The money from my sitcom, when it arrived, would be going into a black hole of debt, but at least I'd be bringing *something* in to feed the monster.

Mum and Michele were now trying to get their heads around a new situation: I wasn't going to die, but how was I going to live? And how was the family? These nasty, creeping thoughts were pushed away because by now we were all so used to living a day at a time, sweet Jesus. Getting to 10 p.m. and my last wee-wee bottle and up goes the feeding pump and oh let's unblock it and here's the baclofen and paracetamol and sweet amitryptyline dreams was all that was aimed for.

And here it is. Another day over. Shell was too fat to get her leg over and into my bed and I was too knackered to get my leg over even if she'd managed it, so we kissed goodnight, but this was an easy goodbye. I listened to her waddle upstairs. Come to think of it, she was so heavy I suspect most of the island could hear her going up the stairs.

Eel Pie Island is quite a busy little place, what with all the artists, and the boatyards, and the kids, and the retirees, and the alternative lifestylers, and the people you just know don't do very much cos they're absolutely loaded but are very, very discreet about it. Someone once described it as eighty drunks clinging to a sandbank and it's true the local bottle bank does a roaring trade. The new City skyscraper nicknamed The Erotic Gherkin is made almost entirely of recycled Beaujolais bottles from Eel Pie. It's a village within a village, and it's hard to walk down the path without bumping into someone you know. Over the years that followed, I became more likely to crash into them, but that's by the by.

But there's a wonderful sense of separateness from the rest of London; actually, from the rest of the country. (To be harsh, from the rest of mankind, sometimes.) The bridge is only a short one (unless you're about ten months pregnant or half your body doesn't work – then it's a fucking huge thing), but it feels, especially at night, like a drawbridge. The Thames is our moat and this is our little secret garden. Piss off, world.

It matched my antisocial mood perfectly, although as I lay there that first night, by the French windows backing on to the river, listening to the water rustling past, the pontoon creaking, the rope moorings straining with the lapping ripples, the bloody owl on the opposite bank hooting, the foxes shagging, I thought Fucking hell this is a noisy place for somewhere supposedly so remote. Then I realised what I *couldn't* hear: trolleys clanking, the insistent soft beep of alarms, the murmuring of nurses, foreign voices – African and Filipino dialects – traffic, a shout, toilets flushing, phones ringing, bad-dream moans, the quick pad of feet, the urgent, hushed unwrapping of a stolen box of Celebrations, that bastard snoring in my earhole. It was all gone. And I was actually, truly home.

But I felt like that poor Russian cosmonaut who was in the Salyut space station during the revolution in 1989, and who wasn't told what was going on – he came down to a country that looked the same, but where everything had changed, even his identity. On the other hand, at least he could console himself with a nice bottle of Stoli, so I'm not shedding too many tears.

In fact, I still couldn't shed one, happy or sad. I've never been a big cry baby, not since it was kicked out of me by my primary-school associates. Thank you, boys. And girls. It was that kind of primary. But I knew this was different, wrong. I also knew I had to treat my family differently from the way I'd treated the medical teams who'd looked after me for the past half year – i.e., without suspicion and contempt. But it was hard. I was acutely aware that my scrappy, chippy attitude had helped get me this far, so I bloody well needed it. But Michele didn't. Square that fucking circle. I know I couldn't. Some days I worry I never will.

Michele's so sore and swollen that it's left to Mum to pick up the slack. But there are some things you don't want your mum to do past the age of about three. You don't want your wife to either, but it's the lesser of two evils. Later there'll be a succession of tattooed strangers doing it, so I've got that to look forward to.

It became an obsession, the future. Because this – the ramps, the hospital bed, the chair, the bottle, the commode, the 'assisted washing', the helplessness, the effort, the *weight* – was impossible. I suspect we've all got an elderly relative somewhere who, given a few gin and its during the Queen's speech, starts going on about

how they 'don't want to be a burden to you all'. Un-
pleasantly, I knew how the old sods felt. Even though
most of them are only too happy to be a burden and quite
enjoy leaving their false teeth behind the cushions for the
kids to sit on.

I used to have conversations with myself, my future
self, and rather hoped they'd go like this:

ME THEN: Blimey Nige, you look great. Best I've ever
seen you. Brad Pitt ain't in it.

ME NOW: I should hope so. Been down to the gym
where I just thrashed Jonathan Ross at squash.
Playing for a Porsche a point, you know. He was
begging me to get him into China White's tonight,
but I said Sorry Wossy, I get too much attention from
the lay-dees and paparazzi, and 'sides, got a deadline.
Finishing off another TV series and my public don't
like to be kept waiting. Those BAFTAs don't grow
on trees, you know. Maybe tomorrow.

Clearly I wasn't imagining talking to myself, but to
Ricky Gervais. The conversation would, in reality, go like
this:

ME THEN: Five years on and I've still got that shirt?

ME NOW: It's not for best.

ME THEN: What am I then?

ME NOW: Shut up. Listen, just thought I'd tell you
we're doing alright. Oy. Pay attention. What are you
looking at now?

ME THEN: Nothing. Just wondering if you'd brought
Jonathan Ross with you.

ME NOW: We don't know him. Now, notice anything different about me?

ME THEN: Not the shirt, obviously.

ME NOW: No, we've established that.

ME THEN: Oh, you're standing up. Straight, without holding on to anything. Well done. How long did that take?

ME NOW: You don't wanna know.

ME THEN: Been running at all? Bit of tennis? Squash? Ping-pong? Darts? Hungry Hippos?

ME NOW: We're still just on the walking-with-a-stick thing, sarky.

ME THEN: Bet you're enjoying playing the guitar again, though.

[*Pause.*]

ME THEN: Oh for fuck's sake.

ME NOW: I'm really glad I came.

ME THEN: Can't see a feeding tube. When did we get rid of that? Bet that was a relief.

ME NOW: Mmm. Actually, the swallow's not working out yet. But we've got a different sort of tube. It's called a button. Much more discreet.

ME THEN: What, plug in a syringe and inject 500ml of liquid into our stomach in restaurants whilst gobbing out bits of half-chewed food into a bottle so at least we get the taste? That sort of discreet?

ME NOW: You really are negative today.

ME THEN: Oh, don't tell me you've accepted this life. Traitor.

ME NOW: Listen, you tetraplegic *twat*, I've had years of physio, occupational therapy, speech therapy, I've been on treadmills, rowing machines, bouncy balls,

I've built brick houses with my shit left hand, I've swallowed more radioactive material than a Chernobyl whore, I've gone from wheelchair to zimmer to big stick to little stick to little foldy-up stick, I've had plastic shoved in my vocal cord which is *why I'm now shouting at you*, I've found new consultants and new drugs to help my balance, joined MS groups, had reiki therapy, crystal therapy, Bowen therapy, acupuncture, me chakras read and me bumps fingered. I've had artefacts from Peru, water from Lourdes and oils from an emu's arse. I have been in and out of hospital with pneumonia, pleurisy and God knows what and look I'm still alive and have just plucked up courage to join a gym and I'm still improving and yes I'm coming to terms with life as a raspberry but no I've not fucking given up *you annoying little shit.*

ME THEN: Not changed much, have we?

ME NOW: Not really.

ME THEN: Good. Got any advice?

ME NOW: Loads. Very important advice that will absolutely be in your best interests to take. But you won't listen, so I'll save my breath. You'll find out the hard way, mate. We always do.

ME THEN: Wait. How about the baby?

But I'd always gone. In all my fantasy chats, in all my imaginary worlds, my imagination faltered and died when the thought of my baby slipped in. It was too fragile.

Around this time the big thing was about people leaving England for better lives abroad. There'd been a regular trickle of books about saying ta-ta to Blighty since

Goodbye to All That. It became a bit of a flood with the Peter Mayle homages to Provence, and then the quirky success of *Driving Over Sheep-shearers* or whatever it was, along with good old Captain Corelli, opened the literary floodgates. But I think it really kicked off with the extraordinary TV show *No Going Back*, where people in Leicester desperate to change something hop off to some desolate spot in Europe with twenty-five quid, a baby with colic and a pocketful of dreams. And often pull it off. This formula struck a huge chord with the country and unfortunately over the years has been diluted to shows like *Buy a New House a Few Miles from Where You Live Now But with a View of a Cow*.

But there was something in the air at the turn of the millennium. People in England were as mad as hell and not going to take it any more. Besides, their flat in Eccles was now worth as much as a small chateau with no roof in the Pas de Calais or a goat farm in Cyprus, and by God they were off in search of the good life. All these unhappy people. I had no idea. All hale and hearty and yet still unsettled, uneasy, thinking there was something better somewhere else.

We caught that fever now. At night, Michele would hit websites like www.yournewhomeinFrance, or Italian-dreams.co.It or hadenoughofthisshittycountry?.com. We told ourselves it was a sensible move; we could live on sixpence a day if we grew our own veg, knitted lentils and recycled our pubic hair, no probs. We could keep pigs and, um, sell them for, ah, pig meat. We could rent out a barn to English tourists who would sigh at our sunsets and wish they didn't have to go back to the daily grind. I'd recover quicker in the sun and write a bestseller about how we moved to – oh you get the idea.

Chapter 1
We find a house. It's ivy-wrapped, golden-stoned but heartbreakingly derelict. Sorry, beautiful. We have to go to the butcher to buy it. It belongs to his granny. After hilarious misunderstandings where she thinks we're doctors trying to put her in a home my wife bakes her a seed cake and we get the house for only half a million euros – as long as we leave a path for the goats (great running gag).

Chapter 2
The roof falls in. The villagers all muck in after initial suspicion because there's a storm coming. The house is saved but someone's hilariously stolen my laptop and all our savings. Riotous conversation with Jacques, the village idiot, only ends when someone throws a donkey from a roof on top of him.

Chapter 3
I save the town's prize pig from drowning. The mayor adopts me. I'm allowed to go on my first gyppo hunt. I come back with a brace of pikeys and the town roasts them in our honour.

Chapter 4
The local mafia gang-bang the wife, kidnap the kids and send my ears to my mum. We start to understand we have to accept local ways, just as they have been so accepting of ours.

Chapters 5–78
Olives, lemons, 2CVs, new bypass proposed. Chief
engineer found dynamited, bypass scrapped.
Alcoholism, loneliness, goat abuse, town festivals,
le wicker homme, slaughtering things, songbirds on
toast, sunsets, lavender, blimey it's hot, adopted by a
stray dog Hercules, rabies outbreak, hippies, drug
busts, Boris the Bavarian gap-year student and
Isabella, virginal daughter of mayor. Blossoming of
Isabella, disappearance of Boris, mayor arrested,
mayor freed, we celebrate New Year at police chief's
new villa.

See, laughter, tears, European politics and a bit of local colour. Piece of piss.

I wasn't worried about making a change. I was good at changes, and as for coping with a new life in foreign parts, I think it was Robert Louis Stevenson who said, 'There are no foreign lands. It is only the traveller who is foreign.' But then he only had a donkey for company and it can do strange things.

Thing is, we knew it was all a fantasy but sometimes fantasy is just what you need. When you've had a near-death experience you're supposed somehow to be equipped to live in the moment, take each day as it comes, smell the roses. But some days there are no nice moments, no days you want to live through, let alone recall, and the only flowers there are smell like decaying plastic, like the ones on the Mall in those long, weird dog days after Diana's death.

No one wants to live in the real world all the time anyway. That's why the telly was invented. And the internet, the iPod, *FHM*, *Top Gear*, *Closer* magazine, and drugs. We work out a balance that suits us. Some people dip into fantasy briefly, while others only dip a toe into reality just as briefly. They tend to be the people I meet. Shit, that probably describes me. It described both of us that week, and for some time afterwards. At the time, before an unseemly scramble by Brits to get their hands on most of France, you could buy a half-decent chateau for the price of a commuterland starter home. A chateau! Course, it would be falling down and the local workforce would see you coming from across La Manche and have your eyes out. But still, what a dream.

23 April 2002

My first full day home. People are celebrating by hanging out flags. Nice that. I think I'll skip breakfast as I've had 500ml of Jevity ('*Complete, balanced, isotonic liquid with mixed fibre and FOS*') dripped into me at a rate of, let's see, 1ml every ten seconds. If it goes any faster I get the squits something terrible. Even as it is, what with being on a liquid diet, I'm terrified to crack off even the tiniest fart, so I've buttocks that could shatter ball bearings. Those of you who've spent a long evening partaking of solely liquid refreshment will know what I mean.

There's quite a comforting little 'whirr' every time the pump does its thing. I hear it better now because the house is so quiet. My feeding-pump alarm didn't go off in the night, but that's because I have learnt to lie utterly, frighteningly still, like a guardsman at the palace who's been pushed over in his little hut but is still forbidden to shift, though when he gets off work my God he'll go looking for the little buggers who toppled him over. I'm like a corpse. It comes from having all those lines plus a great big ventilator screwing you into the bed. And no one thrashes about much when they've got a catheter in.

When I finally make it upstairs to our bed one day, my rigidity – flat on back, arms by side – scares the willies out of Michele. I'm a blackmailed Victorian virgin waiting for the dastardly mill owner to emerge from his toilet with a freshly waxed moustache, *The Rubaiyat of Omar Khayyam* and a tub of whatever passed for KY jelly in 1867.

Mum's up now with the kids and she changes my food, up on the hook, to a bottle of sterile water. This can go in a bit faster, just for excitement's sake. Over the next few months she will lug gallons of water from the chemist's, until I take a chance and try tap water. It's fine. Hoorah! Mum's only got to lug gallons of liquid food over the bridge now, until we get the deliveries sorted, which naturally takes a while.

Both kids are happy I'm back; teenage Tara, who I've known and loved for five years, thinks it's all a bit inconvenient but is really, really glad I'm OK and everything and so everything must be back to normal now, right? So if she can just get on with texting her friends and sorting her life out now, cos Ria and Katie and Camilla and Tom and Dan and like everyone are all going round to Craig's right and she has to go cos Rosa's just split up with Adam and she's the only one who can stop Rosa crying and—

Jesus, it's only 8.10 a.m. Make it stop.

James is like Scooby Doo, happy to see Shaggy, who's not been eaten by the monster after all. He's all gambolly and playful and obsessed by football, which means

Manchester United, which means David Beckham and the World Cup and Eng-ger-land and the broken toe and—

Thank God it's time for school and they both bugger off.

Weird. I've spent six months missing them like mad, and within six minutes I could strangle the pair of them. It's very early in the morning for me, the drugs are still making me sluggish, I have very bad vertigo and I can't even have a cuppa to help wake up. I see Mum dithering. Problem is, she wants a bacon sarnie. But she knows I can't have one and doesn't think it's fair.

She thinks about it outside, in her nightie, having a fag, coughing and playing the Trumpet Voluntary from t'other end. I'm treated to *that* first thing in the morning and she thinks a bacon sarnie's unfair? She comes in and has toast. I've gone off the idea of a bacon sarnie now anyway.

I doze off and am woken by the sound of an elephant coming through the ceiling. Which means Michele's up. She thuds down the stairs on her huge arse, puts the kettle on and makes a bacon sarnie. 'Oh sorry pet,' she mumbles, half a pound of Danish smoked back hanging out of her mouth, 'I was starving.'

Thank God, I think. At least I don't have to listen to some inane nurse's chatter about pay and holidays and—

'Ruth? Ruth, it's Michele, Anna's agent. Now, we have to talk about her weekly rate. And the holiday issue. It's just not acceptable.'

Oh God, she's on the phone, which she tends to see as an object best used for hand-to-hand combat. And she's so loud! My favourite is when she's on a train and goes:

'NOW THIS IS JUST BETWEEN ME AND YOU, SO YOU HAVE TO KEEP IT QUIET COS IF IT

GETS OUT THERE'LL BE A RIGHT HOO-HAH.
THING IS – WHAT? CAN I SPEAK UP? COURSE I
CAN . . .'

(I've been asked to make it clear that this is a joke. And
that she's very discreet. Which she is. It's some of her
clients who aren't, which can make for interesting
Saturdays when the Sunday-paper mob ring up looking
for quotes.)

Mum's wondering what to make for tea – apparently
it's something with mince – and wants to know if Shell
wants to come into town for half an hour. Which means
wheeling her over the bridge in my chair. Shell doesn't
want to leave me. I'm happy for them to go, but Shell
stays. She's got me back. Every once in a while – between
calls to Anna-about-Ruth or to Ruth-about-Anna or calls
about whether the PACT agreement applies for non-
transmission pilots or that yes, the RSC really *does* want
to see her five-foot-tall eight-stone Jewish former stand-up
comic for the lead in *Othello* – she'll come over to my bed
behind the sofa and touch my hand. Just to be sure of me.

About midday I decide to get up. I use all my hard-won
transfer skills to swing my skinny, frail legs over the
(lowered) bed – £400 a week to rent, by the bloody way
– and zimmer myself to the sofa. Triumph! Where I lie
down again, knackered. I'm pale and sweaty and running
a temperature. Michele realises I've got a chest infection
and tells me off for hiding it. She says it's almost as stupid
as when I first went into hospital telling her not to tell my
mum I was ill.

'What would we be saying to her now, eh? We'd probably have run out of excuses as to why you couldn't come
to the phone, ever. There's only so many times even a

member of *your* family can be on the toilet.'

Which I thought was unnecessary. Anyway she gets a doctor out. Course first we get the old can-he-come-in-to-the-surgery bollocks from the receptionist.

'No, he's recovering from a brain lesion.'

'Then you should call an ambulance. He needs to be in hospital.'

'Yes thank you, lovely receptionist person, he's just come *out* of hospital. By the way, congratulations on your MD. Cambridge, wasn't it?'

'You'll have to wait for the end of surgery to see the doctor.'

'I can tell you what antibiotics he needs. It's complicated. He has to have both gram negative and gram positive because—'

'Only the doctor can prescribe medicine, my love.'

'Really? You were doing a good job earlier. Look, I know what he needs. He's been prescribed it by the best ITU— Look, perhaps I can speak to a doctor?'

'The doctor will come round after surgery.'

'When he'll prescribe exactly what I know he'll prescribe, by which time the chemist's might be shut.'

'You should call an ambulance, then. Like I said in the first place.'

Et-bloody-buggery-bollocky-cetera.

Ah, I wasn't in Kansas any more. We had no idea we'd spend the next five years and counting having conversations like this. I am, at the time of writing, involved in at least two pieces of medical nonsense, which could both be cleared up with one phone call to someone who wasn't a time-serving incompetent fuckwit. Sadly, those qualifications were at the top of the application forms.

Doctor comes round rather sharpish as it happens, prescribes exactly what we knew he would – cos we told him that's what worked. I glug my lunch through my BD Plastipak 60ml syringe – this time a couple of bottles of Fortisip Multifibre, which I've found my stomach can tolerate at faster speeds. I spill the usual amount and swear the usual amount.

One small gem from years of syringing was to come several years later. I'm in a pub with a mate. It's an old-school Kilburn pub. My syringe, which is the size of a porn star's cock, is on the table. Barmaid comes over – also old-school Kilburn: tattoos, one eye, beard, six teeth – and she clocks the syringe. As she takes our glasses away she says to me, '*Under* de table with that, now.'

Almost worth having it for that.

I try to do some exercises but my chest is too painful. When I get a chest infection it's almost as if the body's so busy trying to fix it it forgets about everything else. *So let's see: eyes, legs, hand, no don't think so, let's just carry on with the breathing. We'll put them to one side for now. Not going to use them, were you? Good. Oh. You've fallen over. Ooops.*

When I was a kid I thought having two tellys side by side was the height of – I didn't know the word but I'd have used it if I did – decadence. It's not. It's the height of having a brain lesion in an area fed by the visual cortex. Dunno why those super-villains in seventies thrillers always had two tellys. It doesn't improve *Bargain Hunt* one bit. So telly was out.

Michele dibbled on, Mum came back and dibbled some more, the kids came back and yes, they dibbled, and so life, normal life, flowed around me. I have to say, although it was a bit rubbish, it was also fantastic. I wasn't there, you understand, I was looking at it from underwater, perhaps, or through a mirror, or, considering this is my family we're talking about, it was more like staring at the chimp enclosure. But it was near enough to real life. For now.

The evening passed as most evenings in family homes do: shepherd's pie, dad with his feet up, kids arguing over the telly, nan complaining she never sees 'her' soaps, mum wanting the kids to go to bed so she can get some peace and watch *CSI*, teenage daughter getting RSI texting, small boy listing things he's left at school – shoes, socks, pants, coat, head if it wasn't screwed on – mum reading a leaflet on 'inducing your baby', dad hawking and spitting out his infected saliva and crawling to his hospital bed, someone plugging in his feeding machine and drugging him into unconsciousness. You know, normal life.

And yes, tonight, there's life like this going on all over the country. Despite what you might read in the London *Evening Standard*'s 'Homes and Envy' supplement, not everyone is an architect married to an interior designer living in a fabulous refurbed five-bed townhouse which they've put their entire hearts and souls into look how much it's gone up gosh really? well we only did it to live in of course it's almost a part of ourselves really that much? heavens by the way it's now for sale with Thief, Liar, Bastard and Co., Estate Agents.

24 April

Same as yesterday except I'm feeling, if anything, worse. It's mince cobbler for tea and Shell's booked herself in for an induction at Kingston Hospital tomorrow. Even three hours on the kids' trampoline couldn't get the little fucker out.

25 April

8.30 a.m.

Mum's faced with a dilemma. Michele can't walk over the bridge and neither can I, green to the gills, blue to the lips and head firmly rammed in the down position. We have one wheelchair. It's like that chicken, fox, grain puzzle, where there's a farmer and a boat. We decide Mum should take Shell to the hospital, where they'll start the induction, then she'll drive back to pick me up – then a pointless, stressed-out, are-you-sure-you-can-come-I-think-you're too-poorly-don't-be-soft-I'm-not-missing-this conversation goes on for a bit. It's agreed, finally. I should still get there for the main event. Michele starts moaning in pain. Or maybe just to shut us up.

As Shell's being wheeled out, her mobile rings. Force of habit, she answers. Mum snatches it off her. It's a client. The conversation genuinely goes like this:

CLIENT: Is that Michele?

MUM [*frosty*]: No, it's her mum-in-law.

CLIENT: Oh. Is she there?

MUM [*North-Pole-cold snap*]: I'm just taking her to the hospital. She's being induced this morning.

CLIENT: Oh. Does that mean she won't be at the meeting this afternoon?

MUM [*absolute zero*]: She's having a baby in about two hours.

313

[*Pause.*]
CLIENT: Righto. I'll ring back this afternoon then.

Nice going. Now, England's rudest-ever poet, a fine chap called John Wilmot, Earl of Rochester, was asked by his patron Charles II to write a few lines of sensitive verse about how terrific he, Charles, was. This is where it all gets a bit *Blackadder*, cos Wilmot wrote *two* poems about his monarch, only one fulfilling the brief, the other one rather ingeniously comparing Charles's prick to his sceptre and suggesting that whoever played with one – his mistress – could control the other. Come the day of reading the poem, Wilmot, pissed as a fart, brings out guess which one from his pocket and reads it out to the court.

Career-wise, *that* was less of a mistake than that phone call.

10 a.m.

Another hospital, but this time I'm not the patient, although by the time I get there I probably should be. I'm in a right state. What I needed was an IV of serious anti-biotics, industrial painkillers, an oxygen mask, fluids and bed. What I got was a wheelchair in a corner in a small room with my missus up on stirrups waiting for nature to take its – induced – course. And a growing sense of disaster. It had all been leading up to this. The next two hours would define and shape my life more sharply, more completely than this stupid, devastating, pathetic, engulfing, immaterial sickness.

And now I'm on the receiving end. The white walls, the sheets, the helpless body in bed, the bustle of the medical team are not for me and I'm more helpless than I ever was in my most helpless time. And this is a good day, I repeat to myself, a good day. This is for life, a new life.

But again the sickness threatens to wash me under, a rip tide of filth and thoughts of blood and disturbed cells and mutation and vileness.

Because inside my love is our child and we wonder what has been done to him. The adrenaline, the stress, the physical effort Michele endured has somehow done what? what? to the child it's been her duty to keep safe, the child she has neglected – no, never say that, never think that, but time is ticking. The fluids that will start her contractions have dripped into her accepting veins and now the contractions are coming, evenly spaced at first and then more frequent, more painful, and her gasps turn to grunts and I'm scared to touch her. Touch her, says my mum. I'm startled she's there, but she's refusing to leave the room because she has become fused with us and is now here in this, this ceremony. She has a little spray bottle of water like you use for indoor plants. When she gets nervous, she squirts it in Michele's face. It's to cool her down. It's not. It's making her furious – squirt. Mum's getting more – squirt – nervous – squirt – all the time. Michele and I look at each other and smile at this ridiculous, loving gesture. Until she winces with another fucking squirt in the eye.

I am so fearful that I will infect my child, because I know what is to follow will be bloody. Michele is helpless now, raised on the bed, in the hands of the lovely old seen-it-all midwife who is calm, but it's not making me calm and numbers start coming now, contractions and counting, centimetres of dilation and something's wrong already, the dilation is not enough. An hour has passed now and Michele is soaked with sweat and There Is A Problem. The child has grown so big, and Michele is so small. Oh God, I think, this baby, this thing that cannot be healthy because nothing I touch is healthy, is going to tear her apart.

I will kill my wife and my child. Yes, and then I will kill myself. And I know I'm febrile and my temperature is messing with my head but the stress of this, the utter despair as the lovely kind midwife frowns and I've seen that frown because I've been on the wrong end of so many frowns. And time, which was so slow and sticky for the last hour, now hurtles forward. Compression, like the shock wave from a bomb blast, invisible, unstoppable. The big bad wolf, come huffing and puffing to blow your house down.

The child is alive, but in distress. The heart monitor says so. More wrong numbers. The seen-it-all midwife mutters. My baby is facing upwards. The wrong way. He is stuck in the birth canal. And now, God please no, now the natural mechanisms of life are magically switched on, but too soon, too soon. He's trying to breathe. He's suffocating.

This news hammers into Michele because she just wants to rest, to make the pain stop, to re-group. I hold her hand because she cannot rest now, the baby must come, now, now, he has to breathe and I'm breathing for him like Michele has done for me so often, but neither of us can help and yes! there's a head and no, it slips back inside, and again and once more, each time with pain and frustration and failing strength from my wife. The lovely seen-it-all midwife is worried properly now but she takes my useless left hand and says:

316

'Feel your daughter's head.'

I grunt, 'No, it's a boy.'

She smiles for the first time in an hour, though it is a shallow tight smile, and says, 'No I think it's a girl. Do you mind?'

I touch the tiny, grizzled, bloody circle of head that has emerged. A 10p piece of a head. I cannot feel anything with my fingers, but I imagine.

A daughter. Mind? I don't – my heart *leaps* – a little girl. My little girl, alive and I think well, but how can she be well when my little girl cannot breathe and she thinks she's out. She's suffocating and the crisis is rushing down upon us faster and faster and there's no ITU nurse saying Breathe, baby, breathe with oxygen or a bag, and now there's something animal in the bed clutching my hand. Michele is primal, she is saying *Make it stop I cannot go on*, and the doctor appears with silent alarm but there's no time even for a caesarean and Michele did not have an epidural because she wanted to push and thank God for her courage because I am seeing the doctor rush in a tray of shining metal objects – hard, gleaming, inhuman – and he snaps on rubber gloves and my baby is dying and my wife is no longer here and there's blood and it's my blood pooling under her nails.

The doctor approaches but the seen-it-all midwife pushes him away hard because she knows something has changed and the bottom of the bed is dropped away and there's a guttural scream from Michele which is part anguish, part joy, and out, out, yes out slips a wriggling, living creature covered in blood and slime and it emerges like I emerged from underwater and she fought, she fought like her father and her mother, yes she fought.

And I have her in my arms. I have my – yes, my daughter in my broken arms and her eyes are open and there are ten fingers and toes and two of things there should be two of and one of things there should be one of, and everyone smiles and the seen-it-all midwife laughs like a little girl, seeing life born fresh again. She is huge and she is pink and breathing and well, and though her face is squashed from the birth canal she is beautiful.

And Michele gasps *Alright – is she alright?*

And yes, I find my first tear and yes, I hold Scarlett in the hold I'll never break and say Yes, my love, she is. And finally, triumphantly out of this we have something, some*one* perfect.

THINGS CAN ONLY GET BETTER
Eighteen Miserable Years in the Life of a Labour Supporter
John O'Farrell

'Like bubonic plague and stone cladding, no-one took Margaret Thatcher seriously until it was too late. Her first act as leader was to appear before the cameras and do a V for Victory sign the wrong way round. She was smiling and telling the British people to f*** off at the same time. It was something we would have to get used to.'

Things Can Only Get Better is the personal account of a Labour supporter who survived eighteen miserable years of Conservative government. It is the heartbreaking and hilarious confessions of someone who has been actively involved in helping the Labour party lose elections at every level: school candidate, door-to-door canvasser, working for a Labour MP in the House of Commons, standing as a council candidate and eventually writing jokes for a shadow cabinet minister.

Along the way he slowly came to realise that Michael Foot would never be Prime Minister, that vegetable quiche was not as tasty as chicken tikka masala and that the nuclear arms race was never going to be stopped by face painting alone.

'VERY FUNNY AND MUCH BETTER THAN ANYTHING HE EVER WROTE FOR ME'
Griff Rhys Jones

'VERY FUNNY'
Guardian

'EXCELLENT . . . WHATEVER YOUR POLITICS *THINGS CAN ONLY GET BETTER* WILL MAKE YOU LAUGH OUT LOUD'
Angus Deayton

9780552998031

BLACK SWAN

AN UTTERLY IMPARTIAL HISTORY OF BRITAIN, *or* 2000 YEARS OF UPPER CLASS IDIOTS IN CHARGE
John O'Farrell

When a historian says 'Waterloo' do you automatically think of Abba?

Do you wonder how Neville Chamberlain failed to realize that Hitler was a baddie when the Führer was so clearly wearing a Nazi armband?

And why did the Normans fight the Saxons at a place called Battle? Did they see the road signs and just think that's where they were supposed to go?

From 55 BC to 1945, *An Utterly Impartial History of Britain* informs, explains, but most of all laughs at the seemingly incomprehensible rollercoaster of events that combine to make the story of Great Britain. Packed with great characters trapped in impossible dilemmas, this true-life drama will have you on the edge of your seat, thinking 'I wonder which of them dies at the end?'*

A book about *then* that is also incisive and illuminating about *now*, this is a hilarious, highly informative and cantankerous journey through Great Britain's bizarre and fascinating past. It's as entertaining as a witch burning – with a lot more laughs.

*Obviously they *all* die at the end – it was hundreds of years ago after all

9780552773966

BLACK SWAN